Transforming
Teaching and Learning
Through
Data-Driven
Decision
Making

Classroom Insights from Educational Psychology Series

A Developmental Approach to
Educating Young Children
Denise H. Daniels and Patricia K. Clarkson

Transforming Learning and Teaching
Through Data-Driven Decision Making
Ellen B. Mandinach and Sharnell S. Jackson

An Interpersonal Approach to
Classroom Management: Strategies
for Improving Student Engagement
*Heather A. Davis, Jessica J. Summers,
and Lauren Miller*

Classroom Insights from Educational Psychology

Transforming
Teaching and Learning
Through
Data-Driven
Decision
Making

Ellen B. Mandinach ■ Sharnell S. Jackson

A Joint Publication

CORWIN
A SAGE Company

CORWIN
A SAGE Company

FOR INFORMATION:

Corwin
A SAGE Company
2455 Teller Road
Thousand Oaks, California 91320
(800) 233-9936
www.corwin.com

SAGE Publications Ltd.
1 Oliver's Yard
55 City Road
London EC1Y 1SP
United Kingdom

SAGE Publications India Pvt. Ltd.
B 1/I 1 Mohan Cooperative Industrial Area
Mathura Road, New Delhi 110 044
India

SAGE Publications Asia-Pacific Pte. Ltd.
3 Church Street
#10-04 Samsung Hub
Singapore 049483

Printed in the United States of America

Library of Congress Cataloging-in-Publication Data

Mandinach, Ellen Beth.

Transforming teaching and learning through data-driven decision making/Ellen B. Mandinach, Sharnell S. Jackson.

p. cm. — (Classroom Insights from educational psychology series)

A Joint Publication with APA Division 15: Educational Psychology

Includes bibliographical references and index.

ISBN 978-1-4129-8204-7 (pbk.)

1. Education—Data processing. 2. Education—Decision making. I3. Decision making—Data processing. I. Jackson, Sharnell S. II. Title.

LB1028.43.M362 2012+
371.33'4–dc23   2011045909

This book is printed on acid-free paper

Acquisitions Editor: Jessica Allan
Associate Editor: Allison Scott
Editorial Assistant: Lisa Whitney
Project Editor: Veronica Stapleton
Copy Editor: Terri Lee Paulsen
Typesetter: C&M Digitals (P) Ltd.
Proofreader: Jennifer Gritt
Cover Designer: Bryan Fishman
Permissions Editor: Karen Ehrmann

SUSTAINABLE FORESTRY INITIATIVE
Certified Chain of Custody
Promoting Sustainable Forestry
www.sfiprogram.org
SFI-01268
SFI label applies to text stock

12 13 14 15 16 10 9 8 7 6 5 4 3 2 1

Contents

Acknowledgments

Wе would like to thank a number of people and organizations for helping to make this book possible. First, we acknowledge the Educational Psychology Division (15) of the American Psychological Association and its Classroom Insights book series for recognizing that this topic, although not mainstream, is relevant to researchers and practitioners in educational psychology and beyond. Thank you to Division 15's editor Debra Meyer (who provided such outstanding feedback that she should be a third author!) and Corwin's Jessica Allan.

This work has benefitted from our interactions with Institute of Education Sciences (IES) Practice Guide co-panelists and co-authors, Laura Hamilton, Rich Halverson, Jon Supovitz, and Jeff Wayman. The work on the Practice Guide and subsequent Regional Education Laboratory (REL) bridge events were invaluable in helping us to consider both the research and the practical aspects that educators need to understand about data-driven decision making. We have gained helpful insights from bridge event participants who have challenged us and asked probing questions about the reality of the five recommendations and the interpretation of the levels of evidence for the research.

We acknowledge colleagues past and present who have helped to shape our thinking about data-driven decision making through research projects and actual practice.

A few colleagues need specific recognition. First, Ellen acknowledges Diana Nunnaley at TERC, who has provided major insights about creating data cultures, data coaches, and data teams; professional development; and the very nature of teachers as decision makers. We applaud her work as the director of the Using Data Project and as the intervention director on the IES efficacy study. Ellen acknowledges Andrea Lash for her collaboration also on the IES efficacy study and helping to understand just how hard it is to pull off a gold standard study to show the impact of training teachers to use data on classroom practice and student performance. Edith Gummer has collaborated on issues around teacher preparation for the Spencer Foundation and has pushed Ellen's thinking about what schools of education can do to improve educators' data literacy. Ellen also acknowledges Nancy Smith, whose work—first at the Data Quality Campaign, then the Statewide Longitudinal Data Systems Grants Program, and finally at DataSmith Solutions—has helped to concretize her thinking about many issues around state-level data use and data systems. Thank you to Ashley Lewis at the EDC Center for Children and Technology for contributing to the CHOPS concept.

Ellen would also like to acknowledge her many research projects and technical working groups that have provided an opportunity to interact with, observe, and learn from educators, policy makers, and other researchers across the country at the school, district, state, and federal levels. These interactions have provided invaluable insights into just how challenging it is to enculturate data-driven decision making into educational practice.

Ellen would like to acknowledge WestEd as an organization that respects and understands educators and educational research and has provided an intellectual home in which she can learn something new every day from excellent and caring colleagues.

Ellen would also like to acknowledge the input of her Stanford mentors, whose disciplinary expertise intersects in this work. Data-driven decision making reflects Lee Cronbach's impact on measurement, Lyn Corno's on instruction, Lee Shulman's on pedagogy, and Dick Snow's on aptitudes and individual differences. Even after all these years, their influence can be seen in my work.

On a personal note, Ellen would like to thank Kim Mooney for her friendship and being such a devoted second mom to Max, and now Houdi. Also to Susanne Lajoie and Susan Finkelstein, my real sisters. I am so fortunate to have had such dear friends through good and bad times. To my parents, Gloria and Irving Mandinach for their continued support and love. Unfortunately, my mother will not see this book in print, but she and my father have always known the immense impact they have had on my life. I will be forever grateful. To Sir Max, my ever-present, furry companion, who was a daily lesson in problem solving and decision-making feedback loops. You were a true educational psychologist who had me trained and even tried to write some of this book! You enriched my life beyond words with your dedication and affection, even if it was at 3 a.m. I will always love you dearly and will cherish the memories of you. And to our family's latest addition, Houdi, aka Henry Houdini. You brought brightness and laughter when we most needed it. You have become an adored member of the family.

Sharnell would also like to acknowledge the Chicago Public Schools district leadership, board members, administrators, e-Learning team, principals, classroom teachers, students, parents, and support staff. The Chicago Public Schools members provided the visionary leadership and collaborative planning opportunities that supported my professional learning in data-driven decision making to inform teachers' instructional planning, and by using multiple forms of data to improve student achievement of instructional outcomes in classrooms, schools, districts, states, and at the federal level.

Sharnell would also like to acknowledge IES Director John Q. Easton for inspiring me to pursue data-driven evidence and factors that affect student learning during graduate coursework and his research at the University of Chicago Consortium on School Research reports about scientific research designed to inform and assess policy and practice in Chicago Public Schools.

Sharnell would like to acknowledge the International Society for Technology in Education (ISTE), leadership, consultants, and support staff for their innovative leadership in transforming education through the use of data and technology. Everyone involved helped to facilitate the successful implementation of the Chicago Public Schools Principals Technology Leadership Institute (PTLI) over the course of many years, which provided invaluable professional leadership learning opportunities. PTLI focused on a vision of adopting a systemic process for using data to improve teachers' ability to improve students' learning and provide continuous school improvement in over 400 schools and thousands of classrooms.

Sharnell would like to acknowledge the Consortium for Schools Networking (CoSN), leadership, and CoSN board members for their visionary leadership in the Data-Driven Decision Making. CoSN's compendium publications were used to improve teaching and learning outcomes in CPS. Sharnell also would like to acknowledge the International Association for K–12 Online Learning (iNACOL), Susan Patrick, Matt Wicks, and Kemi Jona for supporting activities and policies that removed barriers and supported effective online education in CPS. iNACOL is continuing to help in leveling the playing field for students' through online learning opportunities worldwide.

Sharnell would like to acknowledge the Enlarged City School District of Middletown, New York, including superintendent Kenneth Eastwood, board members, administrators, principals, teachers, coordinators, coaches, students, and parents. The Middletown City School District continues to realize the vision of data use by involving all stakeholders in creating high expectations and rich opportunities that enable students to graduate, to reach their full potential, to become lifelong learners, and to be competitive, productive members of society.

Finally, Sharnell would like to acknowledge her parents, Evelyn and Alexander Martin; brothers Alexander Jr., Bruce, Henry, and Roderick; son-in-law, Derrick McFarland; sisters-in-law; nieces; nephews; cousin, retired CPS principal Beverly Slater who has been an invaluable mentor throughout my career; extended family members; friends for their humor, love, and support.

PUBLISHER'S ACKNOWLEDGMENTS

Corwin wishes to acknowledge the following peer reviewers for their editorial insight and guidance.

Jennifer Borgioli
Consultant
Learner-Center Initiatives, Ltd.
Floral Park, New York

David L. Brock
Science Department Chair
Roland Park Country School
Baltimore, Maryland

Charla Bunker
Middle School Academy Coordinator/Teacher
Great Falls Public Schools
Great Falls, Montana

Margarete Couture
Elementary Principal
South Seneca Central School District
Interlaken, New York

Jolene Dockstader
Seventh-Grade Language Arts Teacher
Jerome Middle School
Jerome, Idaho

Michael L. Fisher
Instructional Coach, Educational Consultant
The Digigogy Collaborative
Amherst, New York

Lauren Mittermann
Seventh- and Eighth-Grade Teacher
Gibraltar Area Schools
Fish Creek, Wisconsin

Cathy Patterson
Fifth-Grade Teacher/Former Assistant Principal,
   Elementary School
Walnut Valley Unified School District
Walnut, California

About the Authors

**Ellen B. Mandinach** is a senior research scientist at WestEd. Dr. Mandinach has been a leading expert in the area of data-driven decision making at the classroom, district, and state levels. Her work over the past several years has focused on understanding how educators are using data to inform practice. She has written and spoken widely on the topic, and has served on a number of technical working groups and advisory boards on data use. Dr. Mandinach served as an expert panelist on the IES Practice Guide for data-driven decision making and on the technical working group commissioned by NCES to understand how researchers can better use the statewide longitudinal data systems. She has led discussions, funded by the Spencer Foundation, about how schools of education can provide courses around data-driven decision making to build human capacity. She has been funded by the National Science Foundation, IES, and the Bill and Melinda Gates Foundation to study aspects of data-driven decision making.

Dr. Mandinach has served on the research staffs of Educational Testing Service, the Education Development Center's Center for Children and Technology, and CNA Education. Although trained in educational measurement, Dr. Mandinach's career has focused on aspects of educational technology.

Dr. Mandinach has authored a number of publications for academic journals, technical reports, and four books. She wrote *Data-Driven School Improvement: Linking Data and Learning*. She has regularly presented at international, national, and regional conferences on education and psychology. She has served as the president of the American Psychological Association's Division of Educational Psychology. She received an AB in psychology from Smith College and a PhD in educational psychology from Stanford University.

 **Sharnell S. Jackson** is a nationally recognized instructional leadership consultant, coach, and executive strategist for school districts, foundations, businesses, and corporations. She has more than 35 years of K–12 experience as a classroom teacher, teacher leader, assistant principal, state director, and chief officer of enterprise information and e-Learning. She has worked in rural, suburban, and urban school districts; state departments; and regional educational laboratories nationwide.

Sharnell is the founder/CEO of Data-Driven Innovations Consulting, with a mission of implementing consistent professional learning process and practices of formative assessment evidence to inform teachers' instructional planning, and by using multiple forms of data to improve student achievement of instructional outcomes.

Sharnell has served on a number of technical working groups, task forces, and advisory boards. She has served as a panelist for the IES Practice Guide for data-driven decision making, was a member of longitudinal data systems working groups commissioned by NCES, was a data model task force member for the National Forum on Education Statistics PK–12, served on Regional Advisory Committee member to advise the U.S. Department of Education on technical assistance needs of educators, served as a governance board member for the Schools Interoperability Framework, and is past president-elect of Illinois Computing Educators.

She received her Master's in Curriculum and Instruction from National Louis University, Illinois; a Master's in Science, Mathematics, and Instructional Technology from NASA Fellowship at Wheeling Jesuit University, West Virginia; a Master's in Educational Administration from Lewis Jesuit University, Illinois; and she completed advanced studies in high school astronomy, biology, chemistry, and environmental studies at The University of Chicago.

From Ellen:

To my "practically perfect in every way" husband, Eli Gruber, from whom I have learned so much about making decisions and pursuing one's passion. He has my enduring love and gratitude. He fulfills my life through his support and understanding. I owe him everything. And to the memory of our beloved Sir Maximilian.

From Sharnell:

To my loving, supportive, and devoted husband, Martin Jackson, the love of my life. To our wonderful children Jisun and Marty, and precious granddaughters Alexandria and Daja, whom I love with all my heart, helping me to live each day to the fullest with real purpose and meaning.

Introduction

This book is for classroom teachers, school and district administrators, pre-service teacher candidates, school psychologists, and other educators who are tasked with using data to inform their work and practice. It is for undergraduates, graduate students in teaching and administration programs, and for continuing education courses. We highlight educational psychology because the book series of which this volume is a part is sponsored by Division 15, Educational Psychology, of the American Psychological Association. The book series pairs a researcher and a practitioner to deliver a volume that is appropriate for practice, but grounded in theory and research. Thus, there is an emphasis on educational psychology, but the book is intended to be much broader than just the one discipline. It crosses many courses and topics covered in schools of education.

How Does Educational Psychology Fit Into the Mix?

Data-driven decision making is a broad and generic tool, which encompasses many topics that are incorporated into educational psychology. It has also been referred to as data informed and data based. We prefer data driven but the others work as well. It can be defined as the collection, examination, analysis, interpretation, and application of data to inform instruction, administration, policy, and other decisions and practice. Data-driven decision making is more than numbers.

It is about transforming the quantitative and qualitative data into actionable knowledge. It is generic in the sense that data-driven decision making crosses content areas and can be applied in many settings, from social studies teachers analyzing how students understand recurring theories in history to physical education teachers examining batting averages. It is comprised of a composite of skills and knowledge that typically would be accumulated through a variety of courses and educational experiences. These might include assessment, statistics, instructional psychology, pedagogy, differential psychology, and classroom management, among others. But no one research area, professional development workshop, or college course deals specifically with how educators transform data into actionable knowledge, whether in a classroom or in a school or central office.

Training or courses in assessment help educators to understand the general principles of measurement and how to construct classroom tests or interpret standardized results. Statistics courses for educators may help to analyze numbers at an elementary level, but they are usually quite abstract and fail to deal with the practical issues around data analysis. Instructional psychology deals with the theory of instruction while pedagogical principles focus on the actual practice of teaching. Differential psychology deals with the theory of how different individuals function cognitively and affectively, the foundation of differentiated instruction. However, teachers and administrators must ultimately plan and use feedback to meet students' varied readiness levels. Classroom management approaches may help educators translate some of the principles of differential psychology into practice through the concepts of whole class, small group, and individualized instruction. Each area from educational psychology has its own skills and knowledge to contribute. Data-driven decision making and data literacy skills are at the intersection of all of these areas and thus, its emergence is an important topic for educational psychology and shares the goal of improving student learning. We therefore hope that this book will fill a void not only in educational coursework but also in professional development and policy making.

WHY DO WE NEED ANOTHER BOOK ON THE TOPIC?

Books, journals, and online resources have begun to appear about data-driven decision making over the past decade. Among the books, some are for research audiences, while others are geared solely to policy makers or to practitioners. Many of the books for practitioners are written more for administrators than for teachers. Ironically, some are written as if they were elementary statistics texts, with little or no discussion of theory or practical implementation issues. Some of the books are how-to manuals for using data. Let us be clear, however, that this is not a how-to book. There are books that are quite excellent to which both of us turn often as resources. For example, for theory, we turn to Mandinach and Honey (2008), a compendium of chapters on how data are being used. We also turn to Herman and Haertel (2005) for information about data and assessment and Moss (2007) for excellent chapters about data use. We turn to Love, Stiles, Mundry, and DiRanna (2008) to help us understand how to teach educators to integrate data use into their practice through the development of data teams and data coaches. But few adopt the integrated perspective that we offer in this book. It is our goal here to integrate the research and theory with the realities of practice, recognizing that educational settings are not pristine laboratories and that educators need guidance with flexibility that can be adapted to their own circumstances.

Among the journals, most are geared toward research audiences. Wayman (2005b, 2006) edited two special issues focused on research on data-driven decision making. Few journals have been directed to practitioners. One notable exception was *Educational Leadership,* which published a special issue in 2008/2009 titled *Data: Now What?* (Association for

Supervision and Curriculum Development, 2008/2009). Online resources, however, are much more focused on helping practitioners to understand and use data. For example, the Doing What Works website (see http://dww.ed.gov/Data-Driven-Instructional-Decision-Making/topic/index.cfm?T_ID=30) provides resources, materials, references, examples of practice, and interviews with practitioners and data experts to assist educators in using data in their work.

An example of quality alternative sources for information on data-driven decision making is the IES Practice Guide on data-driven decision making (Hamilton, Halverson, Jackson, Mandinach, Supovitz, & Wayman, 2009). This document is not a book but a resource report in which researchers and practitioners examined existing evidence on the topic, rated the studies for their level of rigor, and from studies deemed acceptable, excerpted recommendations and action steps for educators to take when using achievement data to make instructional decisions. The guide can be a valuable resource for practitioners, but it has some limitations. First, its content is limited by the criteria used by the What Works Clearinghouse (WWC; see http://ies.ed.gov/ncee/wwc/reports/) in rating research for rigor and therefore credibility. Thus the Practice Guide contains only rigorous research and fails to report on many studies, particularly those that are formative, case studies, and implementation work from which much useful and relevant lessons can be drawn. This is not to say that the research reported is not informative. It is. But it simply does not go far enough in our opinion, and much work that has practical implications for educators may have been omitted.

Second, the Practice Guide was purposefully limited to data-driven decision making in the context of achievement data. The field is much broader, so this volume, although drawing some content necessarily from the report, is much more inclusive and comprehensive. It relies on vetted research as well as implementation and formative studies that do not rise to the level of the WWC criteria, as well as targeted scenarios from which educators can draw practical implications.

It describes the use of many types of data, not just standardized achievement test results.

Third, the Practice Guide focuses primarily on the classroom teacher and, to a lesser degree, the school. This volume is also more inclusive in that regard. Its objective is to reach teachers, instructional leaders, school administrators, and central administrators, all of whom use data and have different data needs. It also can be used by professional development providers. The volume therefore recognizes the need for institutionalization, the enculturation of data, and a holistic transformation to a systemic data culture.

WHY THESE AUTHORS?

Although our backgrounds are very different, they are completely complementary when it comes to the topic of data-driven decision making. Both of us have a passion for data-driven decision making and have a firm belief that, as a tool, the use of data can effectively impact educational practice if it is the right data for the appropriate purposes.

Ellen is an educational psychologist who approaches data-driven decision making as a researcher and from a systemic perspective. That is, the use of data forms a feedback loop that enables individuals and organizations to engage in an examination of practices through a process of continuous improvement. She has studied and collaborated with many districts and states across the country, examining how teachers and administrators use data, the opportunities educators see in data use, the challenges to data use, and the systemic nature of creating data cultures within schools, districts, and state education agencies (SEAs). She has been an observer of data use, trying to understand it theoretically, objectively, and practically.

Sharnell, in contrast, has lived data-driven decision making through her various roles in one of the largest school districts in the country. She has been a classroom teacher who used data to inform her instructional practices, well before data-driven decision making became a common term in educational circles. She helped to create a data culture in her classrooms and schools. She also has been a high-level central administrator, among whose responsibilities were to identify technological solutions to support data-driven decision making, to train teachers and administrators in data analysis, and to work directly with educators throughout the district to help them adopt, implement, and infuse data-driven practices in their daily work. She knows data from an insider's practical perspective.

Of course there are other researchers and practitioners who have worked in the area of data-driven decision making and who have much to say about the field. We know many of the researchers and have great respect for their work, which has informed our thinking. We see our research and practice as having taken parallel tracks that create a complementary, coherent, and realistic perspective of the field. Our paths have continued to cross at professional meetings, culminating as panelists on the IES Practice Guide on data-driven decision making (Hamilton et al., 2009). It was clear that the document as we mentioned above, although providing an evidence-based foundation and a guide for educators, did not go far enough to deal with the realities and practicalities of enculturating data into educational practice. Thus, helping educators to use data effectively by linking theory, research, and practice serves as the objective and foundation for this volume. We hope we have succeeded.

OUTLINE FOR THE BOOK

In the following chapters, we will address many of the key components that research has indicated are important for the effective use of data. Research only tells part of the story, because there are still aspects of data-driven decision making that have not yet been submitted to close examination. For example, we are making a logical assumption that the use of data will help students to learn and achieve better than if teachers simply used anecdotes or gut feelings, based on years of experience. The logic model that underlies this assumption is that training teachers and having them use data will somehow change their instructional practice, and those changes then will translate into improved student performance. This model, heretofore, has not been tested empirically. That said, the assumption is not baseless. Our experience leads us to believe that the logic model, indeed, is grounded in reality. But here and elsewhere, because of a lack of credible evidence in a rapidly growing field, we indeed are using anecdotes, observations, years of experience, and yes, gut feelings. Guilty as charged.

Thus, the following chapters will integrate empirical results with experiences and observations of data at work in real settings. How generalizable are these experiences? Sharnell's experience is grounded in her service as a teacher and administrator in the country's third largest school district. Her second career as a consultant on data-driven practices has taken her to many schools and districts, large and small, affluent and struggling, and urban, suburban, and rural. Ellen's experience has been through various research projects that have taken her to many states and districts across the country. She has conducted research in three of the largest districts in the country, but she has also studied data use in some of the most rural districts. She has examined data-driven decision making in the classroom and at the school, district, and state levels.

In Chapter 1 we present a context for this book. We describe why the time is ripe for data-driven decision making, providing an historical context into which we frame our remarks. We address why the topic of data use is important and why now.

Chapter 2 presents the research that informs the area of data-driven decision making. We share salient issues that inform the topic, setting the stage for the remainder of the chapters. First we describe the foundations of data-driven decision making, including data use, theoretical frameworks, and types of data. We then present the components of data-driven decision making, such as the vision for data use, data cultures, the technology to support data use, and the need to build human capacity through professional development to increase educators' skills and knowledge.

Chapters 3 and 4 focus on two of the most essential components of data-driven decision making: the technological infrastructure and human capacity. In Chapter 3, we discuss the kinds of technology-based tools that can be used to support data-driven decision making as well as technologies that may be on the horizon. The chapter also takes into consideration district size as it influences the kinds of tools that districts are able to acquire and use. Small or poorer districts are not likely to be able to afford or accommodate student information systems or data warehouses. Larger or more affluent districts may have these and other kinds of technologies that will support data. In the chapter we will discuss some of the alternative solutions and emerging technologies, recognizing the challenges of staying current and obsolescence.

Chapter 4 focuses on human capacity issues. We describe the kinds of skills and knowledge teachers and administrators are likely to need and discuss what we call pedagogical data literacy. The chapter emphasizes the need for continuous capacity building, rather than professional development delivered in a single, isolated workshop. It is grounded in the recommendations of the National Council for Accreditation of Teacher Education (NCATE) Blue Ribbon Panel (2010) about the future of teacher preparation using a clinical model. The chapter reflects two major policies: Race to the Top (U.S. Department of Education, 2009) and the four pillars of the American Recovery and Reinvestment Act (ARRA, 2009).

Chapters 5, 6, and 7 describe the fundamentals of data use. In Chapter 5, we focus on the continuous management that is needed for schoolwide or districtwide data use. For schools, this means the creation of data teams or professional learning communities around data. It also means appointing a data coach, facilitator, or champion who can lead the data inquiry process. This individual may be an experienced teacher, instructional leader, or building administrator. Schoolwide data use also entails the creation of cultures led by the data coaches and data teams but comprised of educators throughout the school. At the district level, there also is a need to create a data culture, but it is comprised of a different cohort of key, data-informed administrators, and it should be guided by an explicit vision for data use from senior administrators.

Chapter 6 focuses on how to use data. In this chapter we describe the kinds of data that are available to teachers, schools, and districts. It reinforces the need for data teams and a process of collaborative inquiry while addressing the fundamentals of how teachers use data and emphasizing the need for strategic planning. We then introduce scenarios of fictitious schools that play out the themes carried throughout the book. These schools provide examples of how data can be used or misused and the many components that are involved in data-driven decision making. We conclude with some challenges and opportunities.

Chapter 7 follows directly from the content of the previous chapter, describing class management issues that ensue from data-driven decision making. We focus on the principles of differentiated instruction. The chapter provides examples of small-group instruction as well as instruction for individual students.

The final chapter integrates lessons from the entire volume. The chapter provides numerous examples, both positive and negative, of how data are being used and the issues around data use. We call them the CHOPS[1]—the challenges to and the opportunities for data-driven decision making. The chapter briefly discusses the change management process with schools and districts depicted as learning organizations (Senge, 1990) and data facilitating that change process. We recognize and note that the process of using data effectively does not come without a price. It is not easy and is both labor-intensive and expensive. There are important opportunities to be gained from creating data cultures, but there are also challenges to creating such change. Change management requires a philosophical paradigm shift and a change in mindset. We recognize that old habits are not easily extinguished. We also recognize that implementing data-driven decision making is not a panacea or a one-size-fits-all solution. There must be flexible adaptations, contingent upon the specific circumstances of each classroom, school, and district. We conclude on a positive note reiterating the importance of the opportunities inherent in data-driven decision making, not just the challenges to its implementation.

1

The Context of Data-Driven Decision Making

W hy is data-driven decision making here to stay? Data-driven decision making has become an important topic linked to accountability, school improvement, and educational reforms. In fact, data have been pronounced to be "cool" by educational policy makers. Data use is no longer a passing fad, one to which educators can close their doors and assume it will go away until the next innovative idea appears. Data-driven decision making, in its latest incarnation, is innovative, but the use of data to inform educational practice is not new. Highly effective schools and classroom teachers have been using data for years and recognize the value to inform their work across all levels of the educational system. In the words of one educator, "data is no longer a four-letter word."

So why is there so much attention being devoted to data-driven decision making now? Why is data-driven decision making important? What is the historical context for data use?

What has changed and why is data-driven practice now expected? This chapter addresses these questions, contextualizing data-driven decision making in terms of historical and policy trends. In this chapter, we will describe how data-driven decision making is an essential process in education for classroom teachers, curriculum leaders, administrators, and policy makers. It provides a context for why we care about data-driven decision making and how our backgrounds enable us to write about the subject.

ANSWERING THE QUESTIONS

What Is the Historical Context for Data Use?

Data-driven decision making is not new nor is the quest for using evidence in education to make decisions. When IES was created in 2002 as the research branch of the U.S. Department of Education, a clear message was sent to the educational research community that it was time for the field to increase its rigor and become an evidence-based discipline. Legislation actually required the use of rigorous research methodologies and educational practice based on research findings. The WWC (see http://ies.ed.gov/ncee/wwc/) was created as a repository of studies in which educators could seek interventions or practices that were deemed methodologically rigorous. A by-product of this was, what many considered an unbending pursuit of rigor without sufficient consideration for realism, relevance, and the practicalities of education (Schneider, 2009). But as Easton[2] (2009) stated, rigor is important, but if we do not meet the needs of our stakeholders, we have not done our jobs.

The quest for rigor also impacted educational practice from SEAs to school districts and ultimately to classrooms in the name of accountability and compliance. The No Child Left Behind Act (NCLB, 2001) required increased attention to the provision of many kinds of data, much of which are measures of accountability. Districts have been required to collect a significant amount of these data that get transmitted to their state departments of education who then in turn, send the data to the U.S. Department of Education. Districts often see these compliance data as having little to do with helping directly to improve teaching and learning. Thus by the admission of many educators, there has been created an abyss between data for compliance and data to inform teaching and learning. Margaret Spellings (2005), who was the secretary of Education in the Bush Administration until January 2009, summarized the need for data:

> Information is the key to holding schools accountable for improved performance every year among every student group. Data is our best management tool. I often say that what gets measured, gets done. Once we know the contours of the problem, and who is affected, we can put forward a solution. Teachers can adjust lesson plans. Administrators can evaluate curricula. Data can inform decision making. Thanks to No Child Left Behind, we're no longer flying blind.

The data to which Spellings refers are to be used for compliance and accountability purposes.

More recently, however, a fundamental philosophical shift has occurred from data for compliance to the principles of data for continuous improvement. This perspective shifts the focus away from schools and districts achieving adequate yearly progress (AYP) to helping all students to learn. According to Arne Duncan (2009b), the Obama Administration's secretary of Education, "I am a believer in the power of data to drive our decisions. Data gives us the roadmap to reform. It tells us where we are, where we need to go, and who is most at risk." Duncan continues, "Our best teachers today are using real time data in ways that would have been unimaginable just five years ago. They need to know how well their students are performing. They want to know exactly what they need to do to teach and how to teach it."

Stating the case for teachers to acquire data literacy, Duncan commented, "part of what we need to do is figure out how we challenge schools of education to make sure teachers come into the profession not just with classroom management skills intact, and not just understand some of the philosophy of education, but being able to use data from day one to really drive instruction." Duncan (2010b) further noted that, "teachers were not generally being taught to use data to differentiate and improve instruction." Duncan's philosophy is one of continuous improvement in which data can be used to guide instruction to help all students learn.

The philosophy extends well beyond just data use to an impact on education more generally. The United States was called upon to engage in a new educational philosophy, according to President Obama (2009):

> I'm calling on our nation's governors and state education chiefs to develop standards and assessments that don't simply measure whether students can fill in a bubble on a test, but whether they possess 21st century skills like problem-solving and critical thinking and entrepreneurship and creativity.

This philosophy focuses on complex skills and requires new standards, new assessments, and new methods of understanding how students are performing (U.S. Department of Education, 2010b). The philosophy is reflected in the two state consortia that are developing new assessments: The Partnership for Assessment of Readiness for College and Careers (PARCC; see http://www.parcconline.org/) and the SMARTER Balanced Assessment Consortium, with its focus on teaching and learning (see http://www.k12.wa .us/SMARTER/). Data-driven decision making will be an important component in this evolution.

The paradigm shift is readily apparent and has direct implications for practice and the take-away message for educators. Data play a fundamental role in education. Data are no longer just to hold people and schools accountable. Instead, data are to be used to stimulate and inform continuous improvement. The new message is a positive one, and one that should resonate with educators, rather than the old message that caused some uneasiness among practitioners. The philosophical shift gives educators the license to use data to help all students by identifying the cognitive and affective strengths and weaknesses, thereby making individualized instruction possible.

Why Has Data-Driven Decision Making Emerged as an Important Topic?

As we have said, educators have been using data for many years, but only recently has there been a confluence of events that has made possible more effective ways to examine data. We highlight two particular phenomena that, in our opinion, we feel have facilitated data-driven decision making in educational settings. The first is the development of a variety of technology-based tools that can support data-driven decision making. The second is the increasing importance given to assessments other than summative measures. We now know that assessments for learning can inform instructional practice more directly than more standardized tests, which have only grown the pool of data from which we can draw information about learning and achievement.

As data have proliferated, so has the need to collect, analyze, and examine data in an efficient manner. Human capacity simply cannot handle the amount of data with which educators are being confronted. Thus, educators have turned to a variety of technology solutions to help them deal with this increasing data load. Technologies, for example, range from: (1) handheld devices on which teachers can assess students' literacy or mathematics skills and immediately provide results so that instructional steps can be prescribed; (2) school- and district-level data warehouses, either commercially available or home grown, that serve as a repository for data, including demographics, behavioral, achievement/ performance, attendance, financial, among others; and (3) state longitudinal data systems (SLDS) that are being used to track data trends over time to examine performance, policy, programmatic, and compliance data. These state systems have been the target of an unprecedented amount of educational funding, with over $514 million expended through the SLDS Grant Program (National Center for Education Statistics, 2010b) and ARRA (2009). This investment is recognition of the importance of collecting and using educational data. There are of course many other types of technologies that are being developed and used to support data use. We will discuss these tools in Chapter 3, and we will contextualize research around the tools in the literature review in Chapter 2.

The second evolving phenomenon that impacts data-driven decision making is the growing recognition that standardized achievement test data provide only summative and limited information about student performance and learning, and that other more instructionally sensitive data are needed. Summative data do not readily translate into actionable instructional next steps. Thus, there has been an emerging impetus for educators to collect and use formative, benchmark, and interim assessments that are better aligned to instruction (Bailey & Heritage, 2006: Black & Wiliam, 1998a, 1998b; Goertz, Nabors Olah, & Riggan, 2009b; Heritage, 2007, 2010a, 2010b).

Validity is at the heart of the transformation; that is, test scores being used for what purposes—accountability for a school or district to attain AYP or continuous instructional improvement. This is the difference that the literature has distinguished as assessment *of* learning or assessment *for* learning (Nichols & Berliner, 2007; Petrides, 2006; Stiggins, 2005). The closer and the more aligned data are to instruction, the more likely they will be integrated into practice (Mandinach & Snow, 1999). This is instructional validity. While collecting valid and reliable data is important, it is essential to remember that all forms of data are sensitive to validity issues. It is part of the data collection process. The ultimate goal here is to use data to improve student learning and build teacher capacity to enhance the teaching and learning process.

Why the Attention on Data-Driven Decision Making Now and Why Is It Important?

There are many uses for data in educational settings, ranging from compliance and accountability to data to inform instructional practice at the most diagnostic level. The push to use data has been emerging for several years as educators and policy makers recognize the need to rely on objective evidence, rather than on anecdotes. You often hear a teacher saying, "I know my kids; I know how each of them is doing." How do teachers know and on what do they base such knowledge? Certainly this occurs through the triangulation or the bringing together of many data sources, whether consciously or otherwise. This represents the important case knowledge teachers use to guide their practice. But how are these data sources analyzed and systematized? As one educator commented, "without data, you are just another opinion." Data do not lie. Data are hard evidence that can support or change practice.

At the same time, teachers and administrators are constantly being bombarded with increasing amounts of disparate data. Because of many forces, including pressure at the national level to increase rigor in the field of education, data use and data-driven decision making have risen to a level of national and international awareness. Policy makers and top educational officials are mandating the use of data. With increased demand comes the need for more resources. As we will discuss in this volume, certain parts of the infrastructure and support system are becoming readily available, such as technology tools, yet the human capacity has not caught up and must be addressed. There are few requirements for educators to acquire data literacy skills. Some states have certification and licensure requirements; many do not (Data Quality

Campaign, 2010a). Some courses are emerging in schools of education for pre-service teachers, but most courses are graduate-level ones for administrators. We may have a "build it and they will come" or "if they require it, they will do it" situation. Discussions have begun about integrating data practice into the accreditation process (Blue Ribbon Panel, 2010). The importance of demonstrating impact on student learning is fundamental to the National Board for Professional Teaching Standards (2002, 2007; Hakel, Koenig, & Elliott, 2008). The challenges and opportunities are abundant but uncoordinated. Monies are being devoted to technology to support data-driven decision making, while little has been spent on building the human capacity around data use, in part because data use falls between the cracks and funding tends to go to professional development around specific curricula and content areas. We see data-driven decision making as an essential tool that is embedded across content areas. It can be used in mathematics, language arts, and other high-stakes subjects, but also in low-stakes subjects such as art, music, and physical education. Data are pervasive. They are everywhere. And educators can no longer ignore them.

Mr. Rusty, a teacher at the Otis Elementary School in Montana, lamented that he wants to use data to inform his instructional practice, but his principal, Mr. Shiloh, does not believe in data and technology. Mr. Shiloh actually places impediments in Mr. Rusty's way to accomplishing his instructional goals. The school has no data system. All data are found on hard copies and housed in locked file cabinets. Mr. Rusty does an end-around by creating a data repository on his own computer to accumulate data from various sources on his students. He begins to share the data and the data structures so that other teachers will jump onto the bandwagon.

What is wrong with this picture?

Why would Mr. Shiloh actually impede the use of data rather than embrace the data's use?

What would you do if you were in Mr. Rusty's position?

Training on data-driven decision making is not just professional development; it is a lifelong commitment to a philosophical and holistic transformation toward continuous improvement. It is a systemic cultural shift. It requires a commitment across all levels of a school district—from the superintendent to the data entry clerk, from the district's vision for data to the assurance of data quality. It also moves beyond the boundaries of the school district to the state department of education, the U.S. Department of Education, to communities, parents, school boards, and other stakeholders. Data-driven decision making requires a systemic commitment to reform (Mandinach & Cline, 1994; Mandinach, Rivas, Light, & Heinze, 2006). Just as educators must be lifelong learners, acquiring new skills and knowledge such as data-driven decision making, schools and districts should be considered learning organizations (Senge, 1990) that also must acquire new knowledge and evolve over time through shared visions, collaboration, personal mastery, mental models, and systems thinking.

Educators do not work in isolation, and many influences create priorities and pressures, sometimes in competition with one another, that affect what they do and how they do it. A culture of data-driven decision making can help educators to work through the morass of information to find ways to create actionable knowledge from disparate data (Mandinach, Honey, Light, & Brunner, 2008). Easton (2009) sees data use as the vehicle for school improvement, through a four-step process toward continuous improvement and its ensuing feedback loop to: (1) use data to identify a problem, (2) identify possible solutions, (3) monitor continuous progress, and (4) use research to examine the impact (see Figure 1.1). The results of this process then get fed back to determine next steps. This inquiry cycle is what classroom teachers do with student data, and what building and central administrators do with a variety of data for administrative, programmatic, financial, and performance decisions.

Figure 1.1   Easton's Cycle of Inquiry

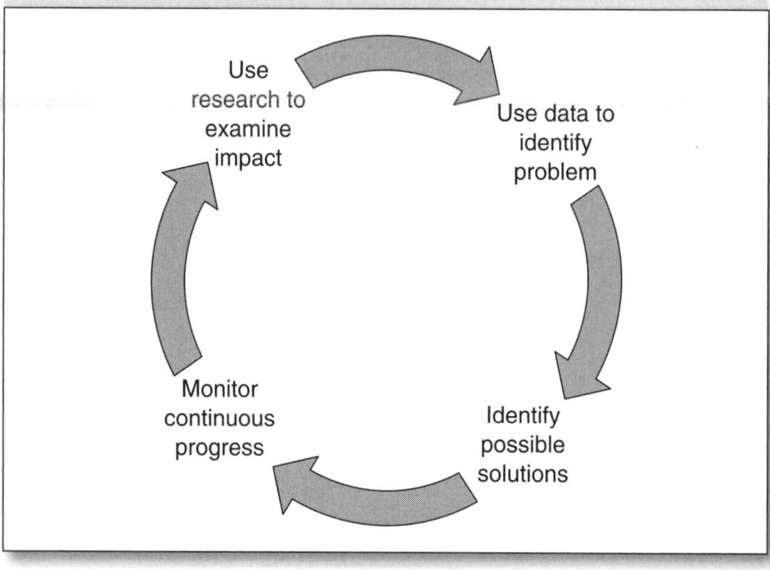

Based on Easton (2009).

Here Is an Example of the Inquiry Cycle

Wrigley School District in Arizona is losing students to neighboring charter schools. Each time the schools lose a student, the district loses substantial subsidies, thereby creating a financial issue. Wrigley decides to conduct a study to determine why students are leaving the district in favor of the charters. The study indicates that parents pull their children out after elementary school and place them in the charters to avoid attendance at large and often impersonal middle schools. The parents then re-enroll their children for high school because the charters do not have sufficiently broad course offerings. Because of the study's findings, the district decides to make changes to their middle schools by decreasing their size to make the schools more attractive to their stakeholders.

What the Wrigley School District did was apply Easton's (2009) inquiry cycle. It identified a problem, conducted research to understand the potential causes of the problem, and then instituted a course of action that could possibly remediate the problem. The next step would be for Wrigley to continue to monitor the inflow and outflow of students to determine if the changes indeed impacted the exodus of students to the charter schools.

So why are data important and why now? Educators need credible evidence to inform their practice. They need hard evidence to provide directions to help them solve pressing problems. Anecdotes no longer are sufficient. The time is ripe for sustained institutionalization and a transformation to data cultures. Public attention has turned toward education. Funding has become available in an unprecedented way. If not now, then when and why? The window of opportunity is here. We must seize this chance. *Carpe Diem!*

What is your current context for data-driven decision making?

Before you begin to apply data-driven decision making in your practice or improve upon current practices, we suggest that you stop and assess how you use the inquiry process.

Use data to identify a problem;

Identify possible solutions;

Monitor continuous progress; and

Use research to examine the impact.

Some Initial Questions

What is your current level of knowledge about data-driven decision making?

How do you use data?

Do you have technology to support your data use?

SOME HIGHLIGHTED REFERENCES

American Recovery and Reinvestment Act of 2009. (2009). Public Law 111-5. Retrieved from http://www.gpo.gov/fdsys/pkg/PLAW-111publ5/content-detail.html

Data Quality Campaign. (2010a). *DQC 2009–2010 annual survey results: Action 9*. Retrieved from http://www.dataquality campaign.org/survey/compare/actions

National Board for Professional Teaching Standards. (2002). *What teachers should know and be able to do.* Arlington, VA: Author.

U.S. Department of Education. (2010a). *Race to the Top Assessment Program.* Retrieved from http://www2.ed.gov/programs/racetothetop-assessment/index.htm

GLOSSARY

Adequate Yearly Progress (AYP)—Part of No Child Left Behind, AYP is a determination of how well schools are performing academically based on standardized tests.

Data-driven decision making—The collection, examination, analysis, interpretation, and application of data to inform instructional, administrative, policy, and other decisions and practice.

What Works Clearinghouse (WWC)—A repository of vetted studies used to inform practitioners about the efficacy of interventions. The WWC uses a strict set of evaluative criteria by which to assess studies based on the rigor of their research methodology.

2

What Research Tells Us About Data-Driven Decision Making[3]

An increasing amount of attention is being devoted to data-driven decision making in terms of research. Much of the research focuses on the implementation process and consists of intensive case studies. The literature review conducted for the IES Practice Guide (Hamilton et al., 2009) yielded close to 3,000 studies and reports, but only a small fraction of those reviewed attained the WWC's criteria for rigor. That said, much information can be learned from the vast body of literature that was omitted from the Practice Guide. Yet complications in the area remain.

A caveat worth mentioning here is that data-driven decision making is seen as an emerging field. Simply because the research evidence around the topic is deemed as "low" or "minimal" do not do the field justice. Research cannot measure what has not been implemented broadly or deeply. Research must mirror practice. Then the body or rigorous research will grow.

Despite the proliferation of research, one major study ironically continues to be missing from the literature, in our opinion. We all assume that using data makes a difference to teachers and students. But this has not yet been proven empirically. The logic model underlying data-driven decision making assumes that using data will impact what teachers do and their classroom practices, and that those changes ultimately will lead to improved student performance (Mandinach, 2009a, 2009b). Mandinach, Lash, and Nunnaley (2009) posed this model and proposed a randomized controlled trial to study the assumption. They received IES funding to conduct the study in 2010. At the time of writing this volume, the study is only in its earliest stages, and complications have arisen due to implementing a complex design in a district setting that requires participation of many schools and teachers over an extended period of time.

A further complication is the topic of data-driven decision making. As noted earlier, data-driven decision making is a generic tool that crosses content areas, grade levels, and all parts of the education system. Moreover, data-driven decision making is highly systemic (Mandinach, 2009b), comprised of many components that interact to influence data use. These components are the focus of this literature review. However, the complexity and the generic nature make research on data-driven decision making challenging and often fragmented, instead focusing on the subcomponents rather than the complete system. This review will do its best to try to describe as many of these interactions among the components as possible. For example, it is impossible to examine the vision for data use without studying the role of leadership, and it is difficult to examine the impact of data teams or data coaches without considering the school culture (see Figure 2.1).

FOUNDATIONS OF DATA-DRIVEN DECISION MAKING

As noted in the first chapter, top education officials in the United States have only recently begun to emphasize data-driven

Figure 2.1   Systems Map of a Data Culture

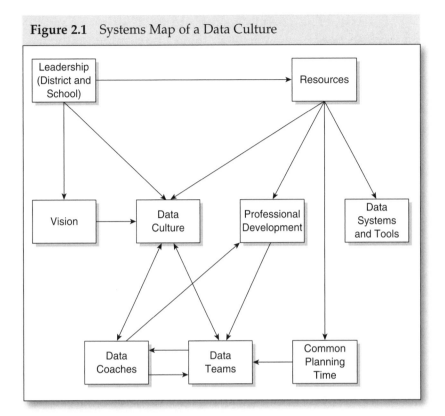

decision making for continuous improvement and to inform instruction. Before that, their rhetoric focused on using evidence from rigorous research to inform education in terms of accountability. And even before NCLB, researchers (Mitchell, Lee, & Herman, 2000) at the UCLA Center for Research on Evaluation, Standards, and Student Testing (CRESST) noted:

> Data-based decision-making and use of data for continuous improvement are the operating concepts of the day. These new expectations, that schools monitor their efforts to enable all students to achieve, assume that school leaders and teachers are ready and able to use data to understand where students are academically and why, and to establish improvement plans that are targeted, responsive, and flexible. (p. 22)

Because of the requirements of NCLB to use data to improve school performance, the educational community has become more interested than ever in data-driven instructional decision making (Hamilton, Stecher, & Klein, 2002), and this interest is continuing because of ARRA (2009) requirements. This trend toward data-driven decision making has also been further accelerated and augmented by the growing numbers of districts and states that have the capacity to process and disseminate data in an efficient and timely manner (Ackley, 2001; Thorn, 2002). Moreover, one noteworthy outcome of NCLB is that educators have been asked to think more systematically about decision making and to use data for their decisions on everything from resource allocation to instructional practice. However, despite encouragement at the policy level, there is growing consensus that many schools, districts, and states are not adequately prepared for this task (Herman & Gribbons, 2001; Mandinach & Honey, 2008; Moss, 2007; Olsen, 2003).

The publication of the IES Practice Guide on data-driven decision making signifies and recognizes the growing importance of the topic and the need for educators to begin to implement data-driven practices (Hamilton et al., 2009). The objective of this report is to help educators understand the research around using achievement data to inform decisions. A distinction should be made here between using achievement data and using data to assess student learning, progress, and growth. Achievement data can be seen as more summative; that is, determining how much has a student achieved at the end of a course or unit. Assessing student learning or progress is seen as more formative; that is, identifying what has been learned or not learned so further instruction can address the learning deficits. The report focuses on recommendations aimed at the classroom, school, and district levels, synthesizing and translating existing research deemed rigorous in terms that are readily understandable to a lay audience.

The Practice Guide poses five recommendations. First, data should be "part of an ongoing cycle of instructional improvement." This recommendation reflects U.S. Education Secretary Duncan's (2009a, 2009b) call for using data for continuous improvement, not just for compliance and accountability. It also reflects the recognition that the data inquiry process is cyclical and iterative (Abbott, 2008; Ikemoto & Marsh, 2007; Mandinach et al., 2008; Means, Padilla, & Gallagher, 2010). The second recommendation is that students should be taught to examine their own data and to set their own learning goals. Expectations should be made clear for student learning, and feedback to students should be given in an understandable and timely manner. The third recommendation is that there should be an explicit vision for how data can be used throughout a district. Moreover, the superintendent must make clear the expectations for and purposes of data use. This is also true for school-level data use. The fourth recommendation is that supports and resources must be provided to establish and sustain a data culture within a school. A school should have a data coach or data facilitator who takes the lead in assisting educators' work with data. This person is often the principal, an instructional leader, or an experienced teacher. Additionally, it is also important to structure and provide for collaborative planning time during which teachers can examine data and develop instructional strategies. The final recommendation is to develop and implement a districtwide data system. Because of the proliferation of data, every district now needs to have some sort of technology application to help it collect and analyze data, and report results. Acquiring such a system requires input from stakeholders about needs and how data should be used.

Data Use

Definition of Data-Driven Decision Making and Data

Recall from the Introduction that data-driven decision making was defined as the process by which an individual collects, examines, and interprets empirical evidence for the purpose of making a decision. The data-driven decision-making process is comprised of data or data elements. Data are pieces of information that, by themselves, are given meaning through the context in which they occur. They can be quantitative or qualitative. Context transforms data into information that is usable to a decision maker (Mandinach et al., 2008). Ultimately, the goal is to further transform this information into knowledge on which actions can be taken in a classroom, within a school, or elsewhere in the school system.

Why Is Data-Driven Decision Making Important?

Decision making in education for many years has lacked an evidential foundation. Decisions were made for many reasons. A superintendent looked to a trusted aide for advice or might have been subtly pushed into a decision for political reasons. A principal might adopt a particular curriculum or program because someone said that it was good or interesting. A teacher might assume students understand a concept because of a single classroom response, test result, or even a gut feeling. These are examples of ill-founded decision making, based on politics, anecdotes, and judgments. They are not based on evidence or data. As noted, by Coburn, Touré, and Yamishita (2009), district-level decision making sometimes still is based on such notions as political expediency.

Doctors make decisions based on data from multiple sources. Such results are sometimes from impressions, observations, and experience, but mostly are grounded in hard facts with some contextualizing based on the individual. So too must educators combine experience, impressions, and hard data to inform practice. It is no longer acceptable to base decisions simply on anecdotes; for without data, decisions are only based on opinions. And that is not good enough. Top education officials have made this abundantly clear (Duncan, 2009a, 2009b, 2009c; Easton, 2009).

Purposes for Data Use

The reasons for using data vary necessarily, depending on the role the individual plays in the education system (Wayman,

Cho, & Johnston, 2007). For example, chief state school officers or superintendents need to rationalize expenditures for programs, interventions, or new curricula. The collection of data can provide evidence about the return on investments for such activities. Program staff at SEAs use data to inform themselves about the effectiveness of specific programs. Research staff at larger school districts may ask similar questions. For example, the mission statement for the research department in the Jefferson County Public Schools in Louisville, Kentucky, is, "To provide valid, reliable, and useful data to decision makers in a timely manner" (Rodosky, 2009). The department provides data to administrators, teachers, policy makers, the school board, and other stakeholders for the purposes of making informed decisions.

In the not so distant past, educators were less than systematic about how decisions were made. For the most part, decisions were not necessarily based on data or evidence. Decisions instead were often made based on political expediency and pressure (Coburn et al., 2009; Coburn & Talbert, 2006). We asked a former superintendent who served several school districts, including one of the country's largest, what he did when he needed to make a decision. The response was surprising; he would ask someone whose opinion he trusted. He would not go to the literature or collect evidence. Times have changed, as have the pressures and realities of decision making. More superintendents are necessarily being armed with data.

The primary purpose for data use in most classrooms, schools, and districts centers around helping students to learn effectively by improving teaching and learning activities (Mandinach, 2010, 2012). Using data, as Secretary Duncan (2009a, 2009b) notes, is for continuous improvement. By this he means that data should and must be used to inform teachers about the instructional activities that are needed to help students learn. Continuous improvement also focuses on the steps that schools and districts need to take, more generally, to improve teaching and learning. Interestingly, the rhetoric was very different not that long ago. Data and evidence were to be used for accountability purposes. For example as noted in the first chapter, former Education Secretary Spellings (2005) made clear her objective for data-driven decision making within the scope of NCLB. Her view of data was to hold educators accountable.

Data for accountability have different characteristics and uses than data for learning and continuous improvement (Firestone & Gonzalez, 2007; Nichols & Berliner, 2007; Petrides, 2006). For instance, work done on the Quality School Portfolio (QSP) in Milwaukee indicates that educators are hesitant to base classroom decisions on data they do not necessarily believe are reliable and accurate (Choppin, 2002). Further, standardized test data are often not originally intended to inform instruction (Popham, 1999; Schmoker, 1999; Stecher & Hamilton, 2006) yet teachers are expected to use them. The literature distinguishes between assessments *of* and assessment *for* learning (Nichols & Berliner, 2007; Stiggins, 2005). Assessments *of* learning are seen as summative indicators of what students have learned and are typically used for accountability purposes, whereas assessments *for* learning provide indications of what students have learned or not learned so that the information can help to drive instruction. These assessments have different purposes, and therefore different kinds of interpretations can be made from them.

Means and colleagues (2010) found that districts use data for three reasons: accountability, instruction, and evaluation. The most frequent accountability-related activities include tracking school performance, analyzing student achievement, monitoring attendance, and examining achievement gaps. Instructional purposes include tracking measures of student progress, curricular development, and informing student placement. Evaluation activities include examining district or school climate and evaluating teacher and principal performance.

The literature focuses on various steps in data use to improve instruction and student performance. Long, Rivas, Light, and Mandinach (2008) examined how teachers and principals interpret test score reports and then modify instruction according to students' needs. Data can be used to identify students' strengths and weaknesses and prescribe appropriate instructional strategies (Brunner et al., 2005; Supovitz & Klein, 2003; Wayman & Stringfield, 2006) while also helping to prioritize instructional time (Brunner et al., 2005).

Data Use Strategies

The literature speaks to specific components or strategies that educators should use when examining data. The following are some of the strategies and associated references:

- differentiate instruction to meet the needs of all students (Long et al., 2008; Love et al., 2008);
- formulate hypotheses about students' learning needs and instructional strategies (Halverson, Prichett, & Watson, 2007; Herman & Gribbons, 2001; Love et al., 2008: Mandinach et al., 2008);
- collect and use multiple sources of data (Heritage & Yeagley, 2005; Kerr, Marsh, Ikemoto, Darilek, & Barney, 2006; Love et al., 2008);
- use formative, summative, interim, benchmark, and common assessments to make decisions, as well as student classroom work products (Love et al., 2008);
- modify instructional practice according to the data collected (Abbott, 2008; Mandinach et al., 2008);
- drill down to the item level to gain a deeper understanding of performance (Love et al., 2008);
- use student work, not just tests, and other sources of data (Halverson et al., 2007; Supovitz & Klein, 2003; Wayman & Stringfield, 2006);
- monitor outcomes (Easton, 2009; Love et al., 2008; Mandinach et al., 2008);
- focus on all children, not just the "bubble kids" (Booher-Jennings, 2005; Brunner et al., 2005; Love et al., 2008);
- look for causes of failure that can be remediated (Love et al., 2008); and
- work in data teams to examine data (Halverson et al., 2007; Long et al., 2008).

Some Questions

What have you already been able to do in terms of data use?

In which areas do you need more depth, attention, and skills?

Which of these skills do you have?

Which of these skills do you need to acquire?

Theories of Data Use

As data-driven practices have become part of the education landscape, researchers have been postulating theories or conceptual frameworks for data-driven decision making. There are at least six frameworks that have emerged since 2007. We will briefly describe those six. As you will see, the frameworks all have similar properties and components. Some have more detail than others. The first four focus on districts; one is generic; and one was conceptualized for state-level data use, but can be generalized to the district level. As a note of clarification, these frameworks were selected for discussion here because they are based on research. Other frameworks exist, based on practice and practical experience, such as Data Wise, Using Data, and Bernhardt. These are discussed in Chapter 4 under professional development.

Mandinach, Honey, Light, and Brunner's Conceptual Framework

Mandinach and colleagues (2008) published what may have been the first conceptual framework for data-driven decision making, with earlier drafts on which other researchers elaborated. This framework was based on data collected in six case studies of school districts, including three of the five largest districts in the country. The framework was developed, in part, to stimulate discussion among colleagues about the components for data-driven practice, rather than presenting a definitive model. Underlying the framework is a continuum of data in which data are transformed into information and ultimately to actionable knowledge (see Figure 2.2). For each step along the continuum, the authors posit two cognitive skills that data users employ: collect and organize for data; analyze and summarize for information; and synthesize and prioritize for knowledge. Once the data user has moved along the continuum, a decision is made and actions implemented, and then the outcome or results of the decision determined. The user may need to return to collect more data, reanalyze the results, or invoke one of the other processes. Thus, there is a continuous feedback loop that moves the user across the data continuum. It forms an iterative process.

Ikemoto and Marsh's Framework

Ikemoto and Marsh (2007), although having published their model before Mandinach and colleagues (2008), used an earlier draft (Mandinach, Honey, & Light, 2006) to critique and elaborate. The point they make is that the draft model failed to account for variations and real-world contexts, such as time constraints that might cause a nonlinear progression along the data continuum. Ikemoto and Marsh (2007) characterize different kinds of data use in their model. It includes two dimensions, one for the complexity of data from simple to complex, and the other for analysis and decision making from simple to complex (see Figure 2.3). Thus, there are four quadrants. The authors term the quadrant with simple data and analysis, "Basic." The simple data, but complex analysis quadrant is titled, "Analysis-focused." The complex data and complex analysis quadrant is called "Inquiry-focused." And the complex data, but simple analysis quadrant is "Data-focused." This model does not address the skills needed for data use.

Figure 2.2 Conceptual Framework for Data-Driven Decision Making

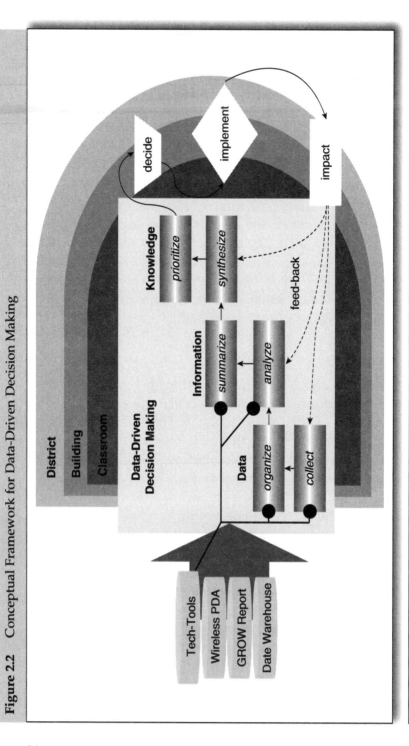

Figure 2.3   Adaptation of the Ikemoto and Marsh Framework

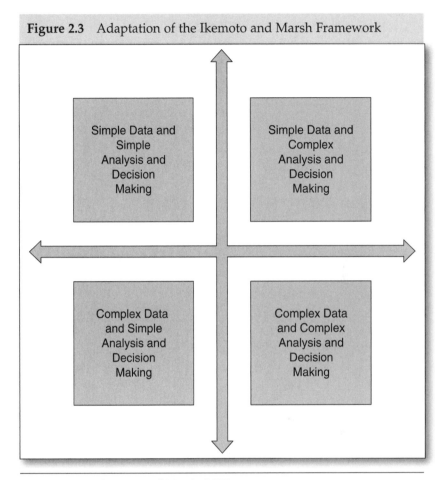

Simple Data and Simple Analysis and Decision Making

Simple Data and Complex Analysis and Decision Making

Complex Data and Simple Analysis and Decision Making

Complex Data and Complex Analysis and Decision Making

Adapted From Ikemoto and Marsh (2007).

Means, Padilla, and Gallagher's Conceptual Framework

As part of a large-scale study that included a nationally representative survey of district-level data use and case studies of exemplary districts, Means and colleagues (2010) posited another conceptual framework for data-driven decision making. It consists of a cycle of data-driven continuous improvement with planning, implementing, assessing, analyzing data, and reflecting as the key elements

Figure 2.4   The Data Cycle[4]

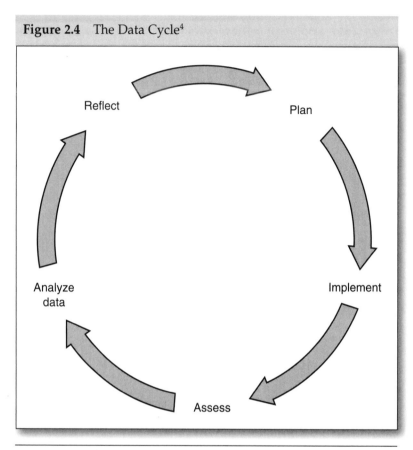

Adapted from Means, Padilla, and Gallagher, 2010.

(see Figure 2.4). The authors state that there is no specific starting or ending point in this process and that users jump into the cycle. The authors also note six supporting conditions for data-driven decision making on which the cycle is grounded: (1) data systems, (2) leadership, (3) tools for generating data, (4) social structures and time for reflecting on data, (5) professional development and technical support, and (6) tools for acting on data.

The Cycle of Instructional Improvement
From the Practice Guide

The model presented in the IES Practice Guide (Hamilton et al., 2009) is geared specifically to school-based educators and is referred to as the data inquiry cycle. It is a cyclical model without a specific beginning point (see Figure 2.5). The authors posit three steps that can be used for a variety of purposes, such as the examination of student performance data or the evaluation of instructional effectiveness. Depending on the objective or question, the steps, in no specific order are: (1) collect and prepare multiple sources of data about student learning; (2) interpret the data, developing hypotheses; and (3) modify the instruction to test the hypotheses so that learning is enhanced. The data use cycle represents an iterative process of data collection, hypothesizing about instructional improvement steps, and testing out those hypotheses.

Figure 2.5   The IES Practice Guide's Cycle[5]

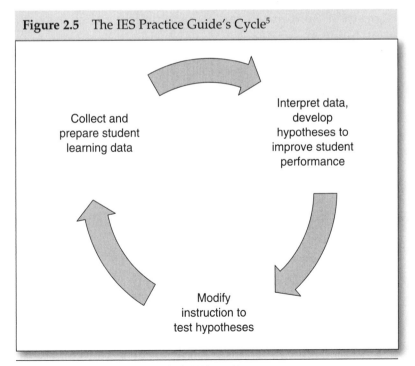

Adapted from Hamilton, et. al. (2009), p. 10.

Easton's Cycle of Data Use for Continuous Improvement

Easton (2009), the director of IES and formerly the director of the Consortium on Chicago School Research (Bryk, Sebring, Allensworth, Luppescu, & Easton, 2010), led efforts to collect and analyze data that would inform practice in the CPS. The model is one that uses data that can be fed back to CPS in ways that impact the decisions that teachers and administrators must make.

Easton's model contains four components, beginning with the identification of an educational problem (see Figure 1.1). A teacher or an administrator first identifies the problem and defines the context in which the problem resides. Second, educators suggest possible solutions that might address the problem. These solutions might be short term or long term, depending on the problem. The possible solutions then are enacted. Third, the educators or researchers monitor progress as the solution is implemented. Finally, the process is grounded in research and seeks to understand it and how the solution is working. This process should be formative so that results can form a feedback loop to determine if more data need to be collected and the data inquiry process continued. Thus like the other frameworks, Easton's model is iterative.

Abbott's Functionality Framework

Abbott (2008) posits a functionality framework of state-level, data-driven decision making, but it can be generalized to district and school-level decision making. Abbott's framework is founded on the concepts of assessing, planning, implementing, evaluating for improvement, followed by internalization and collaboration as part of readiness (see Figure 2.6). The skills from *assess* to *evaluate* are part of improvement. The *internalization* and *collaboration* are part of readiness. Both are informed by data. These concepts are grounded within the context of distributed leadership that includes the provision of supports for data-driven decision making and program content. This model also is cyclical.

Figure 2.6   Abbott's Framework of Improvement and Readiness[6]

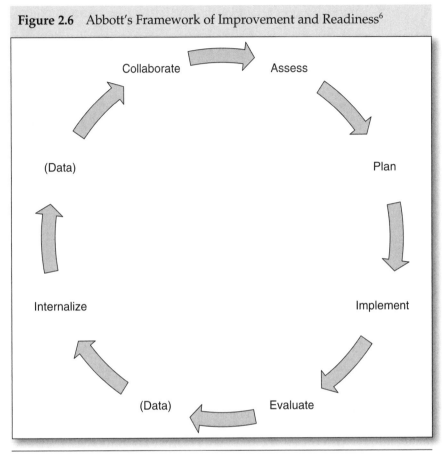

Adapted from Abbott (2008), p. 269.

Types of Data

The types of data that educators use are as varied as the purposes for which they are being collected and used. Data also vary according to the level and one's role within the education system (Long et al., 2008). Even the same data element may have different uses, meanings, and interpretations depending on the role of the individual users. A test score may mean one thing to a teacher, something different to an instructional specialist or principal, and something different again for a central administrator. Classrooms, schools, and districts all use different data and some of the same data at different levels of aggregation. Teachers across grade levels, content, and types of students (e.g., general, special education, gifted and talented), instructional leaders, guidance counselors, school psychologists, principals, central administrators, and superintendents all use different forms of data to different extents.

Assessment Data

As noted above, there are different kinds of assessments from which data result: for achievement or for learning. But even this distinction does not have an easy fit. Typically, assessment for achievement is aligned to standards. The assumption is that those are then aligned with the curricula. But this is not always the case, thereby causing a disconnect between test results and what is being taught and measured in the classroom.

A primary form of data that educators use is from various kinds of assessments. State assessments are required for all students at various times throughout an educational career. The grades at which these tests are required differ across states, as do the passing cut scores. These tests are summative, in that they are intended to provide a snapshot of how well students have gained proficiency in specific content areas. The tests are supposed to be aligned with content standards and curricula. However, there are many concerns about their ability to inform instruction because of the alignment and timing between testing and instruction. As Heritage and Yeagley (2005) note, assessment data must be aligned to expectations, be valid and reliable, and be sensitive to differences among students and student groups.

Many critics believe that these tests are not sufficiently instructionally sensitive (e.g., Heritage & Yeagley, 2005; Nichols & Berliner, 2007; Petrides, 2006; Stiggins, 2002), and that there must be improved alignment between the measures and the standards (Porter, 2002). There is a belief that formative assessments (Heritage, 2007, 2010a, 2010b; Heritage & Niemi, 2006; Stiggins, 2002, 2005) and interim assessments (Goertz, Nabors Olah, & Riggan, 2009a) can provide the kind of instructional sensitivity that is needed. As Black, Harrison, Lee, Marshall, and Wiliam (2003) note, an assessment is considered formative "when the evidence is used to adapt the teaching work to meet learning needs" (p. 2). The distinction, as mentioned above, is assessment *of* and *for* learning.

State summative tests are assessments *of* learning in that they provide information about what or how much a student has learned. They are snapshots. As Stecher and Hamilton (2006) note, the features of the state assessments limit their utility for data-driven decision making, particularly for use by teachers to inform instruction.

Assessments *for* learning are those tests that can inform the instructional process. They are sufficiently sensitive to what students have learned or failed to learn so that instruction can be modified in ways to address learning needs. Formative, benchmark, interim, diagnostic, and common assessments all are able to provide more instructionally relevant data than are summative assessments (Love et al., 2008; Mandinach, 2009a).

Formative, diagnostic, benchmark, or interim assessments (see Goertz et al., 2009a; Heritage, 2007, 2010a, 2010b; Heritage & Niemi, 2006; Perie, Marion, & Gong, 2007; Stiggins, 2005) provide data that educators can use to directly inform instruction. They provide feedback to teachers and students at regular intervals for the purpose of identifying or diagnosing learning strengths and weaknesses. The results of such assessments provide information that enable teachers to modify their instruction. Yet, recent research indicates that using interim assessments does not substantially change teachers' instructional practice (Goertz et al., 2009a). Instead, they are used to reteach content and determine which students need additional instruction. Additionally, formative assessments have been distinguished from other assessments as a process, not simply the measure itself (Heritage, 2010a, 2010b).

At even a more local level are common assessments. Many content areas lack standardized assessments, causing educators to collaborate to develop tests that can be shared across classes and schools within districts. Such common assessments can be used for comparison purposes so that, for example, a principal can observe how all third-grade classes or life science classes are performing at a specific time.

There is a recognition that no single type of assessment can provide all the data needed from which to make decisions (Koretz, 2003). This is why the literature recommends using multiple sources of data (e.g., Love et al., 2008). For example, state assessments may not be instructionally sensitive and because of the time delay between when the tests are given and the results delivered, the data are not as useful as they could be (Long et al., 2008). Such data are often referred to as autopsy or dead on arrival (DOA) data. However, these data still serve an important function and, in conjunction with other forms of data, indeed can be valuable sources of information.

Other Forms of Student Data

There also are other types of assessment data that educators use. These include standardized tests such as the ACT, ACT Plan, ACT Explore, SAT, PSAT/NMSQT, and Advanced Placement tests. Some states are requiring these tests to help determine levels of college readiness of their students. Kentucky is one such state that requires the ACTs.

Teachers regularly collect all sorts of data in their classrooms. These range from assignments, unit tests, classroom activities, projects, papers, portfolios, and observations (see Love at al., 2008). Grades also fall into this category. These data provide a foundation for teachers to understand how their students are performing. These are data that teachers have used for a long time.

Other data sources also can inform practice. These include demographics, behavioral, disciplinary, medical, transportation, special status (e.g., English Language Learners, special education, gifted and talented), course, teacher, among other data sources. Bernhardt (1998, 2008) has categorized the data into school process data, perception data, and demographic data. Such data can provide contextual information about children. For example, it would be helpful for a teacher to know that a student is the bread winner in the house and is holding a full-time job, in addition to school work. The fact that a student has a two-hour bus commute may impact a teacher's understanding of the student. Or that the parents of a student have aspirations for the student to attend a highly competitive university, yet the student is struggling in fundamental skills. Such information can help to inform decisions about the students and the actions that might be taken to help them.

Data Characteristics

As can be seen in the above description of the different types of data, data differ. Discussions of the psychometric properties of tests, such as *reliability* and *validity*, are measurement concepts and can be more comprehensively addressed elsewhere, such as in assessment courses. That said, both reliability and validity can also be seen as properties of data. For the purposes here, let us say that data need to be valid for the purposes for which they are being used. There is a story in New Jersey that real estate agents come armed with local SAT scores because they are used as a proxy for the level of effectiveness of the school systems. One cannot imagine that the test developers at the Educational Testing Service constructed the SAT for the purpose of the results being used to assess schools and therefore property value. Validity resides in the interpretation of the results as much as the properties of the assessments (Cronbach, 1970). It is really about how the performance data are being used that is of interest, and this goes to the heart of data-driven decision making. Validity also speaks to the *alignment* issue. Ideally, the data are well aligned. This means that a test, although psychometrically valid, must be aligned with content, curricula, and instruction to maximize its instructional utility.

There are other properties about data that can be drawn from the literature. Foremost may be that no score or data point should be used in isolation. It is highly recommended that *multiple sources* of data be used whenever possible (Choppin, 2002; Love et al., 2008; Mason, 2002; Supovitz & Klein, 2003). This is called "triangulating." Data must be *accessible* and must be *timely* (Ikemoto & Marsh, 2007; Mandinach, Honey, Light, Heinze, & Rivas, 2005). Autopsy data that arrive months after testing typically are of limited use, particularly to inform instruction. Data must linked to instruction and relevant to the classroom (Mandinach, Honey, Light, Heinze, & Rivas, 2005). The presentation of the data should be *flexible*, in that data can be manipulated in such a way so that different educators can examine them with different forms of presentation and levels of aggregation (Mandinach, Honey, Light, Heinze, & Rivas, 2005).

COMPONENTS OF DATA-DRIVEN DECISION MAKING

The Practice Guide on data-driven decision making on which we both were panelists and authors presents five recommendations (Hamilton et al., 2009). As noted earlier in this chapter, the recommendations focus on the inquiry cycle, helping students to use data, creating a vision for data use, establishing a data culture, and implementing technology to support data-driven decision making. The implementation of these components in schools and districts creates the need for systemic change. Schools and districts can be seen as learning organizations (Mandinach & Cline, 1994; Mandinach, Rivas, Light, & Heinze, 2006; Senge, 1990; Senge et al., 2000) in which data-driven practices are fundamental.

This section describes the research on some of the key components that make possible data-driven decision making. These include those identified in the Practice Guide and in the organizational learning literature. These components, taken separately, are necessary but not sufficient to make data-driven decision making happen in classrooms, schools, and districts. However, taken as a system of interrelated parts, these components combine to facilitate the use of data in educational settings.

We begin by discussing the importance of having a vision for how data are to be used. We next describe research around the creation of data cultures. Vision and culture are intimately related as the culture is an outgrowth of the vision, along with leadership, support for data-driven practice, data mentors, data teams, and resources to support data-driven decision making. We then describe some of the research about technology to support data use. We leave much of the practical aspects of the technological tools to the next chapter. We conclude by exploring issues around human capacity; that is, educators' knowledge and skills around data use. We term this *data literacy* or *pedagogical data literacy*. The discussion of human capacity goes hand in hand with issues of professional development and training to improve data literacy.

Vision

A first essential component is for a district and its schools to have a vision for how it wants its educators to use data (Datnow, Park, & Wohlstetter, 2007; Hamilton et al., 2009) and the vision should come from senior administrators (Knapp, Copland, & Swinnerton, 2007; Knapp, Swinnerton, Copland, & Monpas-Huber, 2006; Long et al., 2008). The more explicit, sustained, and consistent the vision is, the better. Also, the more aligned across levels within the district, the more advantageous. This means that ideally, the visions that building and central leadership have should be consistent, giving educators the same message. Conflicting messages only serve to create confusion. Principals and their superintendent should be on the same page. So too should their teachers and instructional leaders. Of course there are circumstances in which teachers may want to use data and their principal is less inclined. Or the principal is data-driven, but it is not a priority for the superintendent. Thus, it is clear that the same message should begin with the senior leadership and flow to the schools and classrooms. Studies have documented that the absence of a clear vision can be a barrier or challenge to effective data use (Mandinach, Rivas, Light, & Heinze, 2006; Means et al., 2010).

Vision can be communicated in several ways. A vision for data use is communicated by district and school leadership both through explicit verbal messages, but also by the actions taken, and the resources provided by the leadership to support data-driven activities (Bettesworth, 2006). Principals and superintendents model data-driven decision making by giving speeches that are armed with data (Long et al., 2008). When a superintendent or principal makes a speech that is grounded in data or meets with stakeholders and uses data to support talking points, such use of data provides a strong statement about the importance of data. They provide resources and support for data-driven inquiry in their districts and schools, such as the provision for a data coach, a data team, and common planning time.

The vision for data-driven decision making can be seen in the creation of data cultures, in which planning, leadership, implementation, and attitudes influence data use (Hamilton et al., 2009). Primarily, a vision is communicated through the establishment of strong data cultures (Datnow et al., 2007; Williams Rose, 2006) within schools and districts, collaborative data teams (Datnow et al., 2007; Feldman & Tung, 2001; Knapp et al., 2006; Wayman et al., 2007), and of the development of a data plan (Armstrong & Anthes, 2001; Datnow et al., 2007; Mason, 2002) that may be integrated into the school improvement plan. Strong leadership around data is essential (Long et al., 2008; Wayman et al., 2007; Wayman & Stringfield, 2006), paving the way for data use throughout a district or school. Administrators should set examples and communicate clear expectations for data use (Means et al., 2010).

Districts can provide a variety of supports that reflect the vision for data use. Such supports include the provision for technical experts, data coaches, data dashboards, and the development of more instructionally sensitive assessments such as interim and common assessments (Means et al., 2010). Yet, the national survey found that only 50% of the districts provide data coaches for some of their schools and less than 33% provide coaches for all their schools. The survey also indicates that 80% of the districts provide technical expertise. The biggest barriers to data use include time, the lack of professional development, teacher preparation, the lack of technical skills for the data systems, the preparation of principals, the lack of a clear vision, system usability, data not considered useful, and the timeliness of the data, all of which can be incorporated into districts' planning and vision.

Other studies also have noted that time is a key element (Ikemoto & Marsh, 2007). Time is the educators' four-letter word. One way a district can show commitment to its vision for data use is through the provision of common planning time in the academic calendar so that teachers and instructional leaders can come together to discuss data in teams. Take, for example, the Tucson Unified School District in which Wednesday afternoons have been set aside for common planning time during which teachers collectively examine data (Long et al., 2008). Eventually data will become part of everyday practice as data use becomes enculturated in the school and district.

A roadblock concerning the vision for data use is if there are conflicting or ambiguous messages given to educators from different administrators. A superintendent may say one thing and a principal says something different. There needs to be a consistent message from leadership about how data are to be used. Another roadblock is that a vision is articulated but actions don't match the words. For example, a principal tells staff that he expects them to use data in their classrooms, yet he fails to provide any resources or support for such activity.

Examples of Visions for Data Use

Use data to improve the teaching and learning process

Use data to achieve accountability mandates

Use data to decrease the achievement gap

Use data to better serve our students with disabilities

Use data to provide better services to high-risk students

Use data to provide enrichment opportunities for the gifted and talented students

Use data to determine if particular programs, curricula, or interventions are making a difference

Use data to determine the effectiveness of staffing decisions

Use data to help students better prepare for college

Establishing a Data Culture

Vision is exhibited through the creation of a culture for data use (Datnow et al., 2007). There are several key components to the enculturation of data use. First, clear expectations for data-driven practice must be established through the creation of a plan for data use (Armstrong & Anthes, 2001; Mason, 2002; Wayman et al., 2007). The plan should specify responsibilities and roles within a school. The plan should include attainable, measurable, and realistic goals.

Roles and Responsibilities

Principal

Appoint a data coach

Appoint a data team

Provide common planning time, resources to support data work

Create a culture of data-driven decision making throughout the school

Make explicit expectations for data use

Model data use through speeches, meetings, and actions

Motivate staff to use data

Data Coach

Lead the data team

Model data use throughout the school

Help other educators to use data

Work with the technology staff to integrate data tools

Help to train other educators to use data

Motivate colleagues

Data Team

Model data use with colleagues

Examine data to inform instruction, administration, and other forms of decisions

Work with other educators to help them use data

Motivate colleagues

Technology Staff

Maintain data systems and tools to support data-driven decision making

Help to ensure that staff know how to use the data systems and tools

Building a data culture requires strong leadership (Choppin, 2002; Feldman & Tung, 2001; Herman & Gribbons, 2001; Ikemoto & Marsh, 2007; Lachat & Smith, 2005; Long et al., 2008). Administrators show their vision for data use by facilitating the creation of data teams and by appointing data coaches (Feldman & Tung, 2001). A data leader, coach, mentor, or facilitator should be identified and a data team created (Halverson & Thomas, 2007; Love et al., 2008; Wayman et al., 2007). A data team may be comprised of the principal, an instructional leader, a senior teacher, and a group of teachers. Their role is to collectively examine data within the school, at a grade level, or within a content area. With the data coach, whose role it is to help facilitate data use throughout a school, the individuals can help colleagues to use data, with a turnkey model of internal training.

Administrators also show their vision for data use by providing resources and incentives for these data teams to function. For example, a key to data teaming is the provision for common planning and meeting time (Ingram, Louis, & Schroeder, 2004; Supovitz & Klein, 2003; Wayman & Stringfield, 2006). A typical school calendar does not always provide such a luxury, but there are models that have been established to allow for such collaboration (Choppin, 2002; Feldman & Tung, 2001; Ingram et al., 2004; Long et al., 2008), for example the aforementioned Wednesday afternoon meeting time in Tucson. In other districts, time is built into the school calendar, such as an hour one day per week where teachers meet after school to examine data (Knapp et al., 2006). Time is a valued commodity for educators because of the constraints of the calendar and union restrictions.

The data culture is also supported through the provision of a technological infrastructure and professional development activities that build human capacity around data-driven practices. We next turn to the technology.

Technology to Support Data-Driven Decision Making

Having local technology solutions to support data-driven decision making is one of the recommendations in the Practice Guide (Hamilton et al., 2009). The report recommends that a district "develop and maintain a high-quality data system" (p. 39). This is not new. The work from Johns Hopkins University (Stringfield, Wayman, & Yakimowski-Srebnick, 2005; Wayman & Stringfield, 2006; Wayman, Stringfield, & Yakimowski, 2004) provided the first comprehensive reviews of the tools available, identifying some of the technical and usability issues that districts face when selecting an accordant data application that supports instructional planning at the district level.

Often there are different systems for different purposes: systems for student information, finance, student performance data, and the like. Wayman (2005a, 2007) identified four different kinds of data systems that are used in schools and districts: data warehouses, student information systems, instructional management systems, and assessment systems, although hybrid systems and other technologies are now emerging. No one model is right for every district, and often the types of applications are quite similar in function. Many commercial vendors now are providing suites of applications, combining functionality.

In a national survey, Means and colleagues (2010) found that nearly 100 percent of the districts reported having student information systems, but fewer had data warehouses (77 percent), assessment systems (79 percent), and instructional management systems (64 percent). This survey found no significant relationship between district size and economic status of the district, although the districts without any systems indeed were small but equivalent in economic status to other districts. The survey indicated that districts with multiple systems continue to experience interoperability problems. The survey also found that the acquisition of the systems was primarily driven by accountability requirements, rather than for purposes of continuous improvement.

Some districts indeed have a wealth of technology solutions. Wayman and colleagues (2007) conducted a case study in which seventy-three different applications were used in one district to support data practices. Mandinach (2012) also found that some districts have multiple applications, whereas some districts may rely on large and comprehensive suites of applications, and other districts have very limited resources, therefore relying almost exclusively on the SLDSs (National Center for Education Statistics, 2010b).

Where there are multiple systems, there are challenges to make the systems talk to one another. Some districts may have their attendance data in one system and their student performance data in another system. The term that is used is *data silos,* and these silos create the need for interoperability among the systems. Districts also face technical challenges that include data storage, data entry, analysis, and presentation.

A district's investment in technological solutions is not trivial, not only because of the substantial cost, but also because it is critical to make sure that any system is aligned with the district's vision and its educational objectives (Breiter & Light, 2006; Long et al., 2008). Regardless of the sophistication of the technology tools, it is important for the district to consult with possible end users about their needs in relation to system capabilities (Breiter & Light, 2006; Hamilton et al., 2009).

Human Capacity and Professional Development

A district can have a vision for data use and the technology infrastructure to support data-driven decision making, but if the staff lacks the capacity to use data effectively, the whole enterprise will collapse. Building staff capacity around data is essential (Baker, 2003; Choppin, 2002; Feldman & Tung, 2001; Ikemoto & Marsh, 2007; Mandinach, 2009a, 2010; Mandinach & Honey, 2008; Mason, 2002; Miller, 2009), as teachers and administrators lack the skills and knowledge to effectively use data. Educators must understand how to use data, not in the abstract like Statistics 101, but in terms of how to apply data skills to instruction and practice; that is pedagogical data literacy (Heritage & Yeagley, 2005; Mandinach, 2009a, 2012). Although having a data coach is essential, as mentioned above, it also is important for all educators to gain skills and knowledge about data. Data use should become part of every teacher's regular repertoire of tools.

Pedagogical data literacy is quite unique. It is not just the numbers of data-driven decision making, nor is it simply knowledge of assessment or instruction. It is a unique intersection of different skills and knowledge. While teachers and administrators need not be experts in psychometrics, they should achieve some degree of assessment literacy (Webb, 2002). However, because most educators are not trained in testing and measurement, they are not proficient in assessment literacy (Heritage & Yeagley, 2005; Popham, 1999). With that said, data literacy and assessment literacy do differ. Data literacy, or pedagogical data literacy, involves transforming data into instructional strategies to meet the needs of the students (Knapp et al., 2006; Long et al., 2008; Mandinach et al., 2008).

Additionally, many teachers and administrators do not know how to make even basic queries to obtain the kind of data they need to answer their questions. In fact, research shows that teachers do not think consistently about the relationships between instructional practice and student outcomes (Confrey & Makar, 2005; Hammerman & Rubin, 2002). Teachers also tend to examine data on a case-by-case basis rather than look for trends and patterns class-wise or grade-wise (Confrey & Makar, 2002; Hammerman & Rubin, 2002, 2003; Kearns & Harvey, 2000). Additionally, educators need to go beyond descriptive data and bivariate relationships to include multivariate analyses (Heritage & Yeagley, 2005).

It is important for teachers to understand principles of assessment and statistics. It also is important for educators to understand the technology that can support the use of data, assessment, and statistics. Teachers and administrators find problems in the interface with the technology, the quality and utility of the data, or the lack of time, resources, vision, and support needed to make use of the data.

Means, Chen, DeBarger, and Padilla (2011) identified five components of data use and examined teachers' ability to use these skills. They identified data location, data comprehension, data interpretation, instructional decision making, and question posing. The study found that teachers were able to locate data and knew how to differentiate instruction but had difficulty with data comprehension skills, data interpretation, and posing questions. Teachers struggled to manipulate numbers in data displays and tended to focus on the extremes of student performance. They also had limited knowledge of validity, reliability, and measurement error—all concepts within assessment literacy.

Thus, there is a pressing need for courses to help educators build capacity to use data (Mandinach & Gummer, 2011) and for professional development resources to help educators interpret and translate data into instructional or administrative practice if educators are to attain the goal that Secretary Duncan (2009b) has set. Currently, no states have implemented comprehensive plans for professional development and credentialing of educators around data practices (Data Quality Campaign, 2010a). Few states have a provision for credentialing and licensure for superintendents (11), principals (12), and teachers (13), yet over half the states have such plans for 2012 and beyond. In a more recent survey (Data Quality Campaign, 2011b), the numbers are slightly improved with 14, 15, and 14 states having a provision for credentialing and licensure for superintendents, principals, and teachers, respectively.

If schools, districts, and states are going to rise to the challenge of helping all students meet academic standards, there must be high-quality training for teachers and administrators in the use of data to improve student performance (Baker, 2003; Mandinach, Rivas, Light, & Heinze, 2006; Schafer & Lissitz, 1987; Wise, Lukin, & Roos, 1991). As Wayman and Stringfield (2006) note, few educators are prepared to use data effectively and demonstrate data literacy. Not only must practitioners be trained to use data, but also they must understand how to translate data into actionable instructional practices (Baker, 2003; Herman & Gribbons, 2001; Mandinach & Gummer, 2011; Mandinach & Honey, 2008; Mandinach, Honey, & Light, 2006; Mason, 2002). Means and colleagues (2010) found that over 90% of the districts in their national survey have provided professional development for at least some of their administrators and teachers, but generally, not systemwide. Principals receive more training than do teachers. Yet, the survey also notes that districts report that ongoing support is more important than formal professional development. For example, districts seek examples of good data practices.

As Marsh, Pane, and Hamilton (2006) also note, having data is only part of the solution; the other part, which is more labor intensive, is providing for the appropriate infrastructure, including professional development, technology-based tools, and the organizational culture and leadership. These are all part of the recommendations from the Practice Guide (Hamilton et al., 2009) and show the systemic nature of using data. Most important, in the chain of causality, data use changes teacher practice (Chen, Heritage, & Lee, 2005; Kerr et al., 2006) and data-driven decision making leads to improvement in achievement or student performance (Feldman & Tung, 2001; Schmoker

& Wilson, 1995), which is one of the reasons educators are trying to use data to inform their practice.

Professional development on data use within a district is role dependent. From data entry clerks to teachers, and to administrators, data skills may vary based on the demands of the position (Wayman & Cho, 2009). Training needs to be in data skills as well as the technology that supports data use (Knapp et al., 2006; Lachat & Smith, 2005; Wayman et al., 2007). Professional development on a continuing basis is seen as more beneficial than formal, one-time training (Means et al., 2010).

Hamilton and colleagues (2009) lay out an array of professional development opportunities that are appropriate for principals, teachers, information technology staff, and other district staff. Training opportunities range from system use, to instructional and administrative data use, and how to establish a data culture. However, there are still disparities between the professional development opportunities that districts currently have versus those that they report needing. Districts vary tremendously in their capacity, willingness, and interest in providing such training. In an apparent philosophical shift, districts are now seeking training opportunities to help their staff effectively use formative assessments.

Two other issues surround the training of educators to use data. The first is the lack of formal courses in schools of education that directly deal with data-driven decision making (Mandinach & Gummer, 2010, 2011). Duncan (2010b) notes that teachers are generally not "taught to use data to differentiate and improve instruction." Some graduate-level courses have begun to emerge, particularly for administrators. Courses exist at the University of Texas, Virginia Tech, Brigham Young University, Wilkes University, the George Washington University, Western Oregon University, among others. Fewer courses exist for teachers. If human capacity around data-driven decision making is going to improve, data-driven concepts must be integrated with existing courses and formal pre-service courses, along with in-service professional development and continuing education opportunities, will become essential.

A second and related issue is whether data-driven decision-making skills are required for licensure and certification. As mentioned above, the Data Quality Campaign (2010a, 2011b) conducted a survey and found that only a small but slowly increasing number of states have such requirements and only half of the states have plans for licensure and certification by 2012. Without such requirements, it will be difficult to realize widespread and comprehensive training in data use. The NCATE Blue Ribbon Panel (2010) recommendations for teacher preparation and accreditation may begin to stimulate the inclusion of data use in future requirements.

Concluding Comments

As can be seen, the implementation of data-driven decision making in educational settings is a complex and highly systemic enterprise. It is comprised of many interrelated components that provide support for data-driven practices to occur. Although educators have been using different kinds of information from which to make decisions for a very long time, now the emphasis is to base those decisions on evidence and hard data, in addition to other forms of information. Yet, despite long-standing use, many educators continue to feel uncomfortable with data use and express skepticism toward such use. The literature has begun to emerge to answer some, but not all, of the questions about the domain. Technologies are evolving and research needs to keep pace. The two essential components going forward must be to improve human capacity, beginning at the pre-service level and progressing into in-service and continuing education, and to establish visions for data use and data cultures, making them key and fully integrated parts of schools and districts. The recognition is there that data-driven decision making is here to stay. Now educators must do the hard part—making it happen within the context and constraints of educational systems.

Some Questions

If educators have been using data for a long time, why is there skepticism and why do so many feel uncomfortable with the notion of data-driven decision making?

How are data different from anecdotes, experience, and gut feelings?

Which of the components of data-driven decision making do you have?

Do you have any technologies?

Does your school have a vision for data use?

Do you have a data team or a data coach?

Are there people in your school who have the skills and knowledge to be a data coach or serve on a data team?

SOME HIGHLIGHTED REFERENCES

Abbott, D. V. (2008). A functionality framework for educational organizations: Achieving accountability at scale. In E. B. Mandinach & M. Honey (Eds.), *Data-driven school improvement: Linking data and learning* (pp. 257–276). New York, NY: Teachers College Press.

Hamilton, L., Halverson, R., Jackson, S., Mandinach, E., Supovitz, J., & Wayman, J. (2009). *Using student achievement data to support instructional decision making* (NCEE 2009-4067). Washington, DC: National Center for Education Evaluation and Regional Assistance, Institute of Education Sciences, U.S. Department of Education. Retrieved from http://ies.ed.gov/ncee/wwc/publications/practice guides/

Ikemoto, G. S., & Marsh, J. A. (2007). Cutting through the "data-driven" mantra: Different conceptions of data-driven decision making. In P. A. Moss (Ed.), *Evidence and decision making: 106th yearbook of the National Society for the Study of Education: Part I* (pp. 104–131). Malden, MA: Blackwell Publishing.

Mandinach, E. B., Honey, M., Light, D., & Brunner, C. (2008). *A conceptual framework for data-driven decision making*. In E. B. Mandinach & M. Honey (Eds.), *Data-driven school improvement:*

Linking data and learning (pp. 13–31). New York, NY: Teachers College Press.

Means, B., Padilla, C., & Gallagher, L. (2010). *Use of education data at the local level: From accountability to instructional improvement.* Washington, DC: U.S. Department of Education, Office of Planning, Evaluation, and Policy Development.

GLOSSARY

Assessments for learning—Assessments that provide indications of what students have learned or not learned so that the information can help to drive instruction.

Assessments of learning—Assessments that provide summative indicators of what students have learned and are typically used for accountability purposes.

Interoperability—The capacity of data systems to communicate with one another.

Pedagogical data literacy—The ability to transform data skills and knowledge into instructional actions. Pedagogical data literacy combines the understanding of data-driven decision making and pedagogical content knowledge, thus enabling the transformation of data into instructional steps.

Vision—Typically an explicit set of statements, actions, and provisions of resources and support made by district or school leadership to express why and how data are to be used and why data-driven decision making is important. The vision is typically linked to a district or school improvement plan.

3

Technology to Support Data-Driven Decision Making[7]

Some Questions

What kinds of technology do you have available to help you use data?

Does your district or school have a data warehouse? An assessment system? Other tools?

Have you had any training on using these technologies?

How accessible are the technology tools?

Do you have easy access?

A CAVEAT

Technology is an essential factor in helping districts, schools, and educators to become more data-informed schools. Yet it is important to note here that the field of technology is constantly evolving. What is cutting edge today will be outdated tomorrow—and obsolete the next month. This is a constant issue in terms of any technology, whether it is your cell phone, your computer, or technology applications to support data-driven decision making. It is hard to keep up. Even though as technologies evolve, new applications emerge, power increases, and costs decrease, it is hard to continuously purchase or upgrade to the latest and greatest releases. It may be simpler for individuals to upgrade their iPhones every two years when their contracts expire and there are promotions for the new technology. For schools and districts, this issue is even more difficult. It has been an issue since districts began purchasing personal computers and having to deal with obsolescence. Budgets are stretched to the limits, so typically districts maintain the status quo.

Savvy vendors will create business strategies for upgrades and incorporate new components to existing systems. Savvy consumers will figure out ways to make older technologies work for them for as long as possible. Smaller and less expensive tools are emerging. Not every tool to support data-driven decision making is a huge and expensive data system, as can be seen in the following pages. However, for these large systems, the associated costs are not just for the hardware and software, but also for the updating of constantly evolving data needs. One SEA estimated that the annual cost of simply entering state data into their data warehouse and maintaining the system was over $1 million. This is not a trivial issue. It is one worth serious consideration.

The Importance of Technology

Having a technology system to support data-driven decision making is one of the five recommendations in the IES Practice Guide (Hamilton et al., 2009). An increasing number of student information systems, assessment systems, instructional management systems, data warehouses, and other emerging technologies are being used as efficient means by which educators can access and use student data for continuous improvement. Technologies that support data-driven decision making have the capacity and affordances to transform the teaching and student learning process. These technologies provide schools an unparalleled opportunity for using multiple measures of assessment and other data for analysis by helping educators to focus on specific questions about learning needs and ancillary information, to guide what data they can use to improve curriculum, instruction, and student learning decisions.

The reality is that standardized tests alone can measure only a few of the important skills and knowledge students will learn. Teachers in classrooms need access to a variety of assessment data for analysis that can improve instructional practices. These data offer pathways with a focus on accelerating student learning toward mastery that is central to college and career readiness preparedness, a primary focus of the U.S. Department of Education (Duncan, 2010a, 2010b). To be effective, all levels of educational organizations in large, medium, and small school districts must use data systems, computing devices, and emerging technologies to support data-driven decision making to increase efficiency, instructional effectiveness, and academic excellence. The one-size-fits-all education model of the past no longer works for today's knowledge-based economy. Students must be prepared to be competitive, collaborative, and college and career ready for tomorrow's rapidly evolving workforce (U.S. Department of Education, 2010b).

TECHNOLOGIES APPLICABLE ACROSS DISTRICTS

Data systems are proliferating and being implemented across school districts with increasingly sophisticated functionality, and analysis and reporting tools to help educators use student data to individualize learning in efficient and effective ways (Means et al., 2010). All data systems are not created equal and each provides different functionality. Data systems created for small school districts are not generally scalable to meet the needs of medium or large school districts, and vice versa. As reported earlier, Means and colleagues (2010) found in a nationally representative sample of 529 districts (427 responded) that the only districts without any technologies to support data-driven decision making were the smallest ones. A school district with 50 total students will have very different needs than a district that serves 50,000 students or even 5,000 students. Ultimately, there is no single data system that can solve all the education problems of a district or state or include all the needed data. This is why there are different technological tools and why schools and districts select a variety of data systems for different purposes.

There are four main types of data systems used by school districts to provide access to student data for classroom teachers to use for instruction: (1) student information systems, (2) assessment systems, (3) instructional management systems, and (4) data warehouses (Wayman, 2005a, 2007). Wayman notes that these systems typically do not perform all of the needed functions individually. Thus, commercial vendors are seeking applications that combine features and provide diverse solutions. Vendors now are providing suites of separate applications under one tool. Wayman and colleagues (2004) provided an early summary of some of the technologies that had been developed, including detailed descriptions and critiques of their capacities. This is a helpful document that provides information about different types of applications and their functionalities.

Student Information Systems

A student information system (SIS) is a software application used by schools and districts to access and manage data. SISs provide a unique identifier for each student record. They typically have multiple capabilities: enrolling new students; creating class schedules; course and class management; entering and tracking attendance; accessing assessment scores; monitoring test data through an online grade book; health record management; discipline and incident reporting; tracking team participation; recording service hours and club participation; bus route management; school and state reporting; offering parents a communication portal with information about their children; and providing information to manage data needs in schools, districts, and state departments for federal reporting purposes. SISs host information to manage day-to-day functions in districts and SEAs throughout the school year. They are not designed, however, to store, analyze, or compare assessment data over time for classroom teachers to answer questions about student learning needs.

Assessment Systems

Assessment systems provide dynamic use of assessments. They are grounded in the belief that the applications and their assessments must provide data to inform ongoing improvement in instructional practices and student learning. Assessment systems help to support data-driven decisions that can be used to determine the effectiveness of teaching, instruction, program, and initiative effectiveness. They provide information about what students should know and be able to do as a result of their learning experiences.

Assessment systems should be user-friendly and accessible. They should have the capabilities to share data with other systems (interoperability), maintain quality data, and provide access to analysis and reporting tools. The systems should be managed as part of an integrated system of teacher development to guide instructional decisions, classroom-based assessments, and external assessments. Many assessment systems are organized around a clearly defined set of state learning standards to include item banks, lesson planning tools, curriculum mapping, pacing charts, and digital content resources to help teachers differentiate instruction based on identified student learning needs. Assessment system requirements should be based on what classroom teachers need to evaluate student learning, including feedback loops between instruction and curricula to improve teaching and learning. Assessment systems are not designed to access or store large amounts of historical data from year to year due to their dynamic processes and the volume of data used to improve daily teaching and assessment practices.

Instructional Management Systems

The primary focus of instructional management systems is to improve the instructional process. These systems provide connections between student data and instructional supports such as curriculum resources, learning standards, staff communication, and home and school linkages (Wayman, 2005a).

Instructional management systems offer a range of services for developing and assessing curricula, instruction, and assessments. They include web-based interfaces for customizing, monitoring, and managing the instructional process more efficiently to improve student achievement. Instructional management systems provide tools to align curricula and instruction with specific state standards through customizable resource libraries. They also align the instructional progress of students to assessment data and create learning plans. These systems can also deliver multiple professional development resources as well as tracking and monitoring both teachers' instructional effectiveness and students' performance. Instructional management systems provide professional learning opportunities, communication, and collaboration tools to assist teachers in reflecting on their instructional strengths and weaknesses. They provide a range of reporting tools that deliver customizable, longitudinal, and multidimensional reports for increasing their capacity to improve student learning.

Data Warehouses

Data warehouses are designed to be repositories of information for analysis and reporting. They enable users to store, integrate, and consolidate large volumes of historical data from a variety of sources within a district or state department of education. Many district and state data warehouses contain diverse data, including data for compliance and accountability, and high-stakes assessment data used to monitor AYP and schools that are underperforming with regard to the federal reporting regulations of NCLB. In addition, data warehouses store locally administered assessment data, demographic information, historical student assessment data, and teacher information for state certification and credentialing requirements.

Data warehouses also serve an informational purpose for various stakeholders. Districts and SEAs have been encountering growing requests from legislators, policy makers, the public, and other stakeholders for information about their school systems and their performance. Today, most of the information is stored in disparate data systems, making it difficult to access and comprehensively analyze data to inform the teaching and learning process. Data warehouses will alleviate a district's and SEA's need to aggregate data from different systems repeatedly once the data are stored in a single location. The intent is for these technologies to increase efficiency, consistency, timeliness, and accuracy of data-driven decision making (Mandinach, Honey, Light, Heinze, & Rivas, 2005). The key benefits of a data warehouse include:

- promoting data quality with regular consistency checks;
- enabling data-driven decision making;
- enabling a shift from collecting to analyzing data;
- increasing organizational efficiency and effectiveness;
- providing a consistent reporting environment; and
- enabling the district or state to answer complex questions.

The key features of a data warehouse, when used to inform classroom practice, should be based on instructional and student learning needs first and foremost. Administrative use should secondarily determine other features, including, web-based graphical analysis and data dashboard displays with drill-down capabilities, filters and comparison features to identify and solve education problems, advanced security determined by user roles; robust data validation to maintain quality, an exception reporting processes to eliminate redundancies, comprehensive reporting features, and automatic data loading to ensure organizational efficiency.

It is important for districts to have central repositories of data and data warehouses serve this function. Militello (2005) found that districts experience difficulty when data are stored in disparate locations or data silos. Further, districts encounter problems when data are stored in ways that make them inaccessible (Mandinach, Honey, Light, Heinze, & Rivas, 2005; Stringfield et al., 2005). Having data in different locations and in hard to access applications makes data analysis a difficult task.

The IES Practice Guide's fifth recommendation is for districts to determine whether to build or purchase a data warehouse (Hamilton et al., 2009). Many studies reviewed in the report outline aspects salient to the need for such technologies. For example, it outlines the need for data warehouses to meet the needs of its users and stakeholders (Breiter & Light, 2006; Brunner et al., 2005; Choppin, 2002; Datnow et al., 2007; Kerr et al., 2006; Long et al., 2008; Mieles & Foley, 2005; Thorn, 2001; Wayman et al., 2007). The report notes that access, data security, bandwidth, consistent identifiers cost, data quality, and storage are all important features of a desirable data system.

The development of data warehouses continues to evolve. The functionalities of the data systems are becoming increasingly more sophisticated in terms of linking various forms of data, consolidating sytems, query tools, graphic displays, and remote access to support the instructional needs of teachers. Educators need to have timely and easy access to all sorts of data, including common, interim, and benchmark assessment data, to drive continuous instructional improvements. A data warehouse can be an important tool to address these needs.

EMERGING TECHNOLOGIES

Powerful and innovative technologies are emerging and being implemented in schools and districts. These emerging technologies are providing actionable academic and operational data that enable educators to access learning information on their students' performance and many other forms of data.

Diagnostics and Progress Monitoring Tools

One trend in tools to support data-driven decision making are handheld applications (Dede & Dieterle, 2004; Hupert, Heinze, Gunn, & Stewart, 2008; Sharp, 2004; Sharp & Risko, 2003). The trend began several years ago when federal requirements around the Reading First program mandated that teachers use diagnostic assessments to monitor the progress of students in kindergarten through grade 3 (Hupert et al., 2008; Hupert, Martin, Heinze, Kanaya, & Perez, 2004). To meet the requirements of Reading First, Wireless Generation (see http://www.wgen.net), a then rather new technology company, developed a technology application that runs on handheld devices to deliver the DIBELS early childhood literacy assessment. The application is called the mCLASS. Wireless Generation has since developed an application that delivers an assessment for early mathematics, also delivered on the handhelds. Teachers administer the assessments using the handheld device, record the answers, and get immediate feedback about a student's performance. The results are then uploaded to a website, which enables further analysis and reporting. A teacher can see the trajectory of a student's learning and reading ability over time as assessed by the DIBELS, noting if the student is performing above or below expectations. The teacher also can see how the entire class is performing, and a curriculum supervisor or principal can compare performance across classes. The strength of the device is the capability to immediately deliver diagnostic results to the teachers so they can make real-time instructional modifications.

Existing studies on the handhelds have focused on the DIBELS application because it was developed first (Hupert, 2005; Hupert et al., 2008; Hupert et al., 2004; Sharp, 2004). These studies have found that the mClass saves teachers administration time, and allows teachers to identify the skills and knowledge students know and don't know. Teachers then can customize their instruction according to the results almost immediately (Mandinach, Honey, Light, Heinze, & Nudell, 2005).

Other studies on handhelds have been conducted that indicate that teachers can easily monitor their students' progress and link student performance to instructional steps in effective ways (Penuel & Yarnell, 2005; Sharp & Risko, 2003). The handhelds help teachers to be reflective about their students' performance. The power of these devices can be found in their capability to help teachers obtain real-time performance information about their students that can then influence their instructional strategies, customized to the needs of individual students (Hupert et. al., 2004; Sharp & Risko, 2003). Such a strategy places assessment squarely in the middle of classroom, where its potential can count the most.

Interactive Whiteboards

Interactive whiteboards have become pervasive in classrooms in recent years and are replacing blackboards and chalk. Teachers use the whiteboards to deliver instruction, allowing them to engage students with web-based resources, images, video, and audio delivered on a computer and projected by the whiteboard. Classroom teachers use whiteboards to deliver dynamic lessons, and write notes in digital ink, that can be saved electronically with the simple touch of a finger. Teachers use the resulting data to drive instruction. They use the interactive whiteboards to deliver targeted instruction to students based on identified learning problems. The instruction can address students' learning styles by capturing notes to send to students, along with interactive activities that are aligned to the standards-based, curriculum-embedded interactive assessments.

Data Dashboards

Data dashboards or performance management dashboards can provide an overall view of a school for administrators. Districts place great importance on whether schools meet state and national standards. Consequently, principals focus on "power standards" that are critical metrics by which schools are measured on the state report card. The dashboard interface allows administrators to identify and focus on standards that are highly valued, but where a school has experienced low success. Dashboards assist administrators in communicating a clear vision because they have been able to identify areas of low success. The communication of the vision and targeted objectives assists teachers in adopting a data-driven process for identifying standards that need to be incorporated into instructional plans based on the highlighted dashboard data. Thus the dashboard facilitates continuous progress monitoring.

Dashboards are interactive collections of charts, gauges, reports, and other visual indicators that educators have selected to monitor. Unlike a "scorecard" that offers a snapshot of data at a particular moment in time, dashboards are more effective at viewing data in a specific period of time and over time. They are used to monitor daily operations and performance progress because the data and information are delivered in real time.

In the classroom, dashboards give teachers access to historical, real-time, and predictive assessment data on all students to help manage academic performance and anticipate issues that could arise throughout the year. The process of data collection is automated, so teachers don't have to spend hours sifting through reports and combine multiple measures of assessment data to compare and identify students' learning problems. Teachers have access to the data when it is convenient. The technology allows them to eliminate the labor-intensive process of poring over grid paper, spreadsheets, and pivot tables which heretofore have required enormous amounts of instructional and personal time. Teachers can access summarized, useful information via a single dashboard on their computers. Perhaps most important, they can spend less time accessing and analyzing data, and more time focused on meeting the needs of each student. By receiving information on a regular basis, teachers can reflect on their instructional practices, adjust their instruction, and address the actual identified needs of their students.

Classroom Response Systems

Classroom response systems are intended to help teachers facilitate activities by tracking student responses to questions (see Bruff, 2007, 2009, 2010; Cheesman & Winograd, 2008). For example, the systems present multiple-choice questions and log student responses so that a teacher can immediately see how the class is doing. Each student's responses are submitted to answer the questions using a handheld transmitter, called a "clicker." Their responses are collected by the teacher's computing device with aggregated results to produce graphs or charts showing how many students chose each of the answer choices. The teacher can then make immediate instructional adjustments in response to students' answers. Classroom response systems can assess students' higher-order thinking skills by engaging them in effective clicker questions that go beyond recall. The systems can assess students' understanding of important concepts such as conceptual understanding, knowledge application, and critical thinking. They can require students to analyze relationships, share opinions, assess their confidence, and conduct experiments, while monitoring performance to determine where students are in the learning process.

Teachers can use classroom response systems to rapidly collect and analyze data to adjust instruction according to the individual learning needs of their students. Teachers can increase the levels of student engagement to include homework, determine what students do or do not understand, promote peer instruction, implement question-driven instruction, use formative or summative assessments, and implement problem-based learning instruction. Teachers also use classroom response systems to maintain students' attention, promote active engagement, promote collaboration among students during classroom discussion or webinars, check for understanding and instructional effectiveness, adapt classroom instruction to the immediate learning needs of students, and display visual representations of how students are answering questions by using graphs to create active learning environments.

Virtual Learning Environments and Assessments

Virtual learning environments are being used for a variety of purposes to include online and blended learning. Online learning is typically a structured learning environment used to enhance educational opportunities facilitated by teachers. The teachers use data from the interactions with the virtual learning environment to drive instruction and monitor student learning progression. Blended or hybrid learning includes a combination online learning with face-to-face and other methods of instructional delivery.

Online learning includes a wide variety of purposes and choices. Such learning can provide an expanded range of course options to students when they are not readily available in their schools. It can provide highly qualified teachers in subject areas that are not available and afford students flexibility in dealing with scheduling conflicts. There are opportunities for accelerated students to seek advanced courses that are not readily available at their own schools. Homebound and hospitalized students have an opportunity to continue courses while they are not able to attend school. Online learning provides dropouts, migrant youth, pregnant, or incarcerated individuals an opportunity to continue their courses toward high school graduation. It provides at-risk students options for remedial instruction. Online learning also provides professional learning opportunities for teachers, including mentoring and professional learning communities, to increase instructional effectiveness.

A teacher's roles and responsibilities are slightly different in an online course than in a face-to-face course. Online teachers must assess the understanding of learning objectives with embedded assessments, create and facilitate group discussions, develop group projects, make regular adjustments to course resources based on student learning data, and respond to students' learning needs and questions—through the virtual environment. They do not have the benefit of visually observing their students and making decisions from those observations. They must resort to the online interactions from which to make decisions.

Online teachers can enhance their online instructional skills by participating in professional learning opportunities that help them develop advanced communication skills. They must be able to recognize learning needs and adapt their lessons to meet all students' needs; refine time management skills, which are critical to online learning; and include multimedia components to make online content more interactive and engaging.

Online learning systems record all teacher and student interactions. These electronic records provide feedback loops in which data can be used to drive instruction and meet the individual learning needs. These electronic records are not possible in a traditional classroom environment.

Web-Based Tutoring Tools

Web-based tutoring has the potential to improve the access, quality, and speed of information in the instructional process. It provides anytime, anywhere learning. Web-based tutoring provides students with assistance from experts all over the world, with access to educational support outside the traditional classroom. Such tutoring may provide assistance to students who are failing in school and do not need more of the same type of instruction in the same modality.

Web-based tutoring systems provide a student-centered approach to instruction that is personalized to meet their individual needs, using experienced online instructors and assessment tools to guide the learning process. These tutoring systems provide online diagnostics to identify weaknesses, tools for monitoring progress, and curricular activities with intelligent embedded assessments that can inform educators' instructional planning. Web-based tutoring systems can provide detailed reports about skill deficiencies and assign interactive activities with formative assessments to develop student mastery of skills.

Some web-based tutoring systems alter the traditional teacher as a dispenser of knowledge paradigm. The role of the teacher becomes a facilitator of student inquiry-based learning.

The tutoring environment can generate activities based on student responses and makes adjustments to learning content based on assessment results. Thus, it uses data to make instructional decisions.

Computerized Adaptive Testing

Computerized adaptive testing (CAT) is becoming an attractive assessment option. In CAT, the test is tailored to each student with test items being selected by the system to individually match the ability level of students. The tests have the capability of determining which items are delivered next to the test taker, based on their pattern of responses. The CAT system begins by selecting an initial item to administer; if the student answers the item correctly, a more complex item is selected for administration. CAT adapts the difficulty level of items selected, and the system is able to more accurately measure student ability level.

CAT has a number of advantages. It has immediate score reporting, decreased administrative burdens, increased security of testing materials, and adds flexibility to the testing scheduling. Major testing companies, such as the Educational Testing Service, have administered some of its standardized tests using CAT technologies for a number of years. Now the U.S. Department of Education (2010a) is promoting that the next generation of state assessments will be delivered using CAT.

Universal Design for Learning and Assessment

The current education system does not work effectively for all students, especially those with learning disabilities. The concept of universal design for learning and assessment increases accommodations for special-needs students through the accessible design of educational materials, more accurate assessments, and the use of technology (Rose & Meyer, 2002).

New digital media facilitate working across different media. The media allow for multiple representations that can facilitate enhanced meaning to enrich the communication and comprehension of information to improve learning and mastery of material. Such media include audio text, images, video, and networked environments. As teachers learn to use data to identify students' strengths and weaknesses, they can better choose when and how to use what medium and how to select material and methods to meet a range of learners' instructional needs and make appropriate accommodations for learners' disabilities.

Technology-Based Assessment Systems

Technology-based assessment systems provide teachers with relevant and timely data to analyze students' progress. These data can be used to improve instruction and teacher quality. The systems can inform the data inquiry process but require technical support to effectively plan instruction. Technology-based assessments can help teachers to identify deficiencies and assist in solving learning problems. The systems also provide opportunities for continuous growth and the use of feedback loops to modify teaching and learning activities based on data-driven evidence. Many states, districts, and schools are implementing technology-based assessment systems with curriculum-embedded assessments to test competency in skills. The systems include online assessments, portfolio assessments, blended assessments, and performance assessments. Technology-based assessments are being used to improve student achievement, remediate student learning, track individual student growth and progress, and achieve continuous school improvement. When combined with assessment and instructional management systems, technology-based assessment systems can be used formatively to diagnose and modify the conditions of learning and instructional practices, while at the same time determine what students have learned for grading and accountability purposes.

Vodcasting and Assessment for Learning

Vodcasting or "video-on-demand casting" is online video content made available through the Internet. It uses a subscription system in which users set their computers to automatically download new content as it becomes available and played directly on the computer using free software such as Windows Media Player or iTunes. Vodcasts can be transferred and played on any MP3 video player.

Vodcasting allows teachers to reach students using a social networking medium, something with which students are comfortable and familiar. Vodcasting is an inexpensive way of creating digital content for classroom instructional purposes and at the same time tap into a way of more effectively engaging and motivating students to learn at their own pace.

Vodcasting is being used as a way to allow students to listen to teacher-created lectures of curricular content with discussion questions in wikis and blogs for homework. The technology helps to structure classroom instructional time in a way that uses assessment data to focus classroom instruction on facilitating individual learning student needs and project-based learning group discussions. These discussions may lead to the generation of students who have acquired higher-order thinking skills and advanced communication skills.

Teachers can also use vodcasting for data-driven instruction by creating testing review sessions or tutoring on skills or concepts with which students are struggling. Vodcasting can provide benefits for students who have individualized education plans (IEPs) by giving them the opportunity to watch classroom content as many times as needed to attain understanding. Students who are homebound or absent from school can benefit by downloading content and keeping up with classroom instruction and discussions to expand learning opportunities. Vodcasting can be used to facilitate teaching, instruction, and student learning in a number of ways. It can record classroom lectures and discussions, and it can provide supplemental instruction, obtain information from experts in the field, and access vodcasts from colleges and universities. Students can share projects and content. They can create digital storybooks and conduct interviews for a variety of instructional purposes.

Mobile Learning and Assessment

There is a growing disconnect between the way students use social networking to communicate and collaborate inside and outside of school. Mobile computing devices such as modern smartphones, electronic tablets, and netbooks have become pervasive throughout society, including schools. Mobile devices connect teachers and students alike to the Internet with substantial computing power. The connection is anytime and anywhere. These technologies can be used in schools to provide easy access to the technology solutions that students constantly use and to promote learning and enhance engagement (Blackboard K–12, 2010; Prensky, 2005). Ironically, some school districts have prohibited the use of phones and other communication devices while on the school premises (Blanche, 2008; Delisio, 2002). The mobile devices, however, do have the potential to equalize the digital divide because many students, regardless of economic status, have access to smartphones (Blackboard K–12, 2010).

A major problem facing K–12 education throughout the country is student disengagement. There are a growing number of students dropping out of school before graduation due to lack of rigor, relevance, engagement, and individualized instruction (National Center for Education Statistics, 2010a). Schools must find ways to use data to drive instruction by delivering content and assessing student learning in more systematic ways to capitalize on the affordances and strengths of mobile computing devices to address the engagement problems. These devices can help students to work at their own pace using a medium that is familiar and comfortable.

Mobile technologies are being promoted as a new way to deliver course content. They are even being promoted by Secretary Duncan as important and viable instructional media (Carter, 2009). Mobile learning and assessment systems enable teachers to do what they do best, which is working with students individually to overcome challenges that inhibit learning. Teachers can no longer teach to the middle. They must use data to drive continuous improvement of instructional effectiveness to meet the individual learning needs of students by using the data inquiry process. They must find ways to be more efficient. Mobile learning and assessment technologies can provide a solution. The increased engagement that results from mobile learning and assessment used by teachers to individualize learning means that students may be more likely to spend more time working on homework, writing assignments, and researching curriculum topics outside of school (Laurillard, 2007).

Social-Based Learning and Assessment

Students are using technology to learn every day. They develop sophisticated strategies, solve problems, and participate in collaborative partnerships. They join virtual communities and teach each other. Social-based learning allows students to take advantage of the affordances of the technology, communication, and collaboration tools. They create personal networks that transcend the classroom.

Teachers must use data from curriculum-embedded assessments to inform instruction and better understand how students are building their own learning networks. Teachers must work through the social networks "where the real learning is taking place." It may be possible for teachers to use relevant social-based learning along with project and problem-based learning modules that are aligned to formative assessments to facilitate the monitoring of the mastery of learning objectives and to help students discover learning paths that meet their unique needs.

Visual Data Analysis Tools

Much has been written about the visual display of data and how important such displays are in facilitating understanding and interpretation (Tufte, 1990, 2001, 2006). Visual data analysis is a promising tool to help educators understand the social process of learning. Data collection, analysis, and reporting no longer require the cumbersome technology used even a decade ago. New technologies allow for enhanced and more flexible graphical displays, with options for illustrating patterns, trends, and relationships. Visual data analysis tools facilitate the work of teams so they can make meaning from multiple complex sets of information.

Take, for example, TinkerPlots (see http://www.keypress .com/x5715.xml), a software package developed for students to help them visually explore data. TinkerPlots can be used effectively by teachers as a visual analytic tool for data-driven decision making (Rubin & Hammerman, 2006). Such tools need to be in the hands of teacher data teams to engage in rich visual interpretations of the teaching and student learning processes. Visual data analysis can help teachers to understand the teaching and learning process (Love et al., 2008). The technology can deal with multiple data points interacting in ways that are not well understood. This is an essential component in helping teachers to use data to inform their practice.

Teacher Professional Development Tools

Tools to help teachers with their own professional learning also are emerging as new technologies. Such tools may be data dashboards that include personalized growth plans. They also may include evaluation tools. For example, Schoolnet (see http://www.schoolnet.com) contains a tool for classroom observations, using mobile devices. Data from classroom observations can be collected and examined in relation to pre-defined standards or templates laid out by districts or by SEAs. The applications can help administrators and teachers examine and manage the observations so that they can be used as learning tools for the educators. Results from such tools can help measure teacher effectiveness and add to professional growth.

THE ROLE OF STATEWIDE
LONGITUDINAL DATA SYSTEMS

A program was authorized in 2002 in the National Center for Education Statistics (2010b) to support the development of

SLDSs (Whitehurst, 2006). Four rounds of funding, beginning in 2005 and continuing in 2007, and two in 2009, have helped states develop, enhance, and expand their data repositories and capabilities. After the fourth round of funding, forty-one states and the District of Columbia have received funding, totaling $514 million. The program:

> is designed to aid state education agencies in developing and implementing longitudinal data systems. These systems are intended to enhance the ability of States to efficiently and accurately manage, analyze, and use education data, including individual student records. The data systems developed with funds from these grants should help States, districts, schools, and teachers make data-driven decisions to improve student learning, as well as facilitate research to increase student achievement and close achievement gaps. (National Center for Education Statistics, 2010b)

The Data Quality Campaign (see www.dataqualitycampaign .org) monitors the progress of the SLDSs. The organization has developed ten essential elements that the SLDSs should contain to address the needs of the stakeholders and its users. These elements include: (1) unique student identifier; (2) student-level enrollment, demographic, and program participation information; (3) matching individual student test records across years; (4) information on untested students; (5) teacher identifier system that can match teachers to students; (6) student-level transcript data; (7) student-level college readiness test scores; (8) student-level graduation and dropout data; (9) matching student P–12 records with postsecondary systems; and (10) state data audit system. The Data Quality Campaign (2010b, 2011a) found that twenty-four states have all of the elements, an increase from twelve states in 2010 and eight states in 2008. In 2005, no states had attained all of the elements. In 2010, only two states had fewer than five elements and thirty-four had eight or more elements. In 2011, five states had seven elements and the remainder had eight or more elements. Thus, it is clear that almost all states are making substantial progress in developing their technological capacity around data.

More recently, the Data Quality Campaign (2011a) adopted another rubric by which to measure the developmental progress of the SLDSs. In addition to the essential elements, they added ten key actions. The actions include: (1) link data systems; (2) create stable, sustained support; (3) develop governance structures; (4) build state data repositories; (5) implement systems to provide timely access to information; (6) create progress reports using individual student data to improve student performance; (7) create reports using longitudinal statistics to guide system-wide improvement efforts; (8) develop a P–20/Workforce research agenda; (9) promote educator professional development and credentialing; and (10) promote strategies to raise awareness of available data. Only thirteen states have achieved six or more of the actions and nineteen states have three or fewer.

A longitudinal data system identifies which schools and districts perform well. To better understand what it costs to improve student performance, states are also collecting financial information at the state, district, school, and program levels and link the data to student achievement over time. A variety of other data also are being collected and reside in the SLDSs.

The SLDSs provide invaluable data to states and districts. However, there is a contention that the data are more meaningful for the states. The districts feel that they collect and send a tremendous amount of data to their states without little return on their time and effort (Smith, 2009). According to Smith, the former director of the SLDS program, there needs to be a two-way data highway in which data are sent to the state and federal levels for use and data returned to the district with utility. Data from these systems must be meaningful and have utility, beyond providing compliance and accountability to the U.S. Department of Education. This is often referred to as the disconnect. That is, the data that reside in these systems fail to inform in meaningful ways at the district and school level.

The most recent trend for the SLDSs is to move beyond the K–12 arena to increase the scope of data that reside in the systems. Through ARRA funding, 20 states received monies to expand their systems, beginning with early childhood data through to institutions of higher education and the workforce

(National Center for Education Statistics, 2010c). These data will enable the longitudinal analysis of individuals from their earliest years beyond education and into the workforce. However, two concerns emerge from this expanded capacity. One is the fear that "big brother is watching" and that too much data may not be a good thing. That said, the second concern is about privacy and compliance with the Family Educational Rights and Privacy Act (FERPA; see http://www2.ed.gov/policy/gen/guid/fpco/ferpa/index.html).

The Data Quality Campaign (2007) outlines some of the important uses of the SLDSs. They have the capability to:

- follow students' academic progress as they move from grade to grade;
- determine the value-added and effectiveness of specific schools and programs;
- identify consistently higher-performing schools so that educators and public can learn from best practices;
- evaluate the effect of teacher preparation and training programs on student achievement; and
- focus school systems on preparing a higher percentage of students to success in rigorous high school courses, college and challenging jobs. (pp. 4–5)

To take full advantage of the power of the SLDSs, states must provide useful data to the districts and institutions of higher education, and must be able to exchange data across state lines, due to high mobility rates. Educators must know how to mine and use these data. Additionally, the information that results from these systems also must be interpretable by policymakers, the public, and other stakeholders.

Using data to inform decisions has long been a strategy of high-performing and learning organizations (Senge, 1990). The growth of the SLDSs and other available technology provides educators more timely and user-friendly access to data, especially longitudinal data. With an increasingly mobile student population, sharing those data across districts, states, and even higher education systems has never been more important.

Many educational data systems are not able to share information due to incompatibilities in technology. A lack of human capacity is a major impediment. Taken together, these issues inhibit the quantity and quality of longitudinal data use. Fortunately, interoperable systems are becoming more prevalent due to the leadership of several organizations such as the Schools Interoperability Framework Association (SIFA; see http://www.sifassociation.org/us/index.asp) and the Postsecondary Electronic Standards Council (PESC; see http://www.pesc.org). With these systems, policy makers will be able to answer timely questions such as:

- How well do high school exit requirements align with postsecondary entrance requirements?
- What characteristics of high school graduates, including courses taken, predict postsecondary success?
- Which students require remediation in core subjects upon entering college?
- What are the career paths of college graduates upon departing from community colleges and universities?
- How does programmatic spending relate to students achievement? What is the return on investment?

Answering these and other policy questions requires not only having longitudinal data but also connecting and exchanging information among disparate data silos. These data silos frequently are designed and maintained in isolation from each other, not just across departments (e.g., child welfare, health), but even within departments of education. For example, to determine which high school programs provide the greatest return on investment as measured by graduation from a two- or four-year higher education institution, policymakers must be able to assess longitudinal data from across P–12, postsecondary, and financial data systems.

In addition to interoperable data systems, portability improves data quality, access, and use. Portability is the ability to exchange student records and transcript data electronically from system to system, across districts, and between

P–12 and postsecondary institutions within a state and across states. Portability has at least three advantages:

- academic records of students can be moved across districts and states;
- there will be time and cost savings from the electronic transfer of students' records and transcripts; and
- there will be increased tracking ability of students as they move, such as to identify dropouts among students who transfer out of state or to other districts.

Many states have made great progress in developing their SLDSs. Much more progress is necessary both in terms of the technology and human capacity. The systems have been built and enhancements are being made. Now the users must come, have ready access, and know how to use them. Educators at all levels of the education system must understand how to use these data and make decisions from them. The data have many important uses and are an essential component for educational decision making going forward.

SUMMING UP

Technologies to support data-driven decision making hold great promise for increasing the efficiency of education agencies at all levels by enhancing the effectiveness of teaching and learning activities, accelerating student achievement, and improving administrative, programmatic, and organizational performance. They have the potential to engage students and capitalize on learning styles (Dieterle, Dede, & Schier, 2007). Educators need professional learning opportunities to build their capacity to use data and access to the technology systems that support data-driven decision making. These systems are vital to the successful implementation of data-driven practices.

Data systems and emerging technologies to support teaching and learning in education are no longer nonessential items. They cannot be designed and implemented solely by technical experts with no knowledge of education. The use of data systems is still an emerging field of practice. Research indicates that a wide variety of stakeholders need to be involved in identifying the specifications and functionalities to meet users' needs (Hamilton et al., 2009). Schools, districts, and state departments should be building or buying systems that are focused on providing data for improving classroom instruction and on making programmatic and administrative decisions. Educational agencies must support the professional learning of teachers and administrators to ensure the effective use of the data systems and other technologies.

Enhancing teachers' and administrators' knowledge and skills requires continuous professional learning opportunities, with easy access to data systems and technological tools. These technologies can be used to inform instruction, access online assessment systems with progress monitoring tools, and use emerging mobile technologies to personalize students' learning needs. Instead of teaching to the "average" student, teachers need to be able to use data systems aligned to standards and emerging technologies to develop personalized learning for all students.

Anderson (2006) coined the term *the long tail* as a means of expressing new business models that succeed because they sell to niche markets rather than mass markets. What do new business models have to do with education? Applied to education, the long-tail business model means that learning must be personalized to motivate and meet the needs of each individual student. We need to provide every student with an opportunity to tap into a niche and discover the pleasures of learning by using mobile computing technologies. These technologies contain competency-based learning pathways and online social networking environments that can involve others who share common interests and can facilitate peer-to-peer instruction.

We have discussed many types of technologies that can support data-driven decision making. It is not an expansive list. They include: 21st century innovative data systems, assessment systems, emerging technologies to include progress monitoring tools, dashboards, virtual learning environments, online learning, web-based tutoring tools, computerized adaptive testing, digital learning tools, vodcasting, podcasting, wikis, blogs, mobile learning devices, social-based learning, e-portfolios, and visual analysis tools that enable educators to personalize learning. Many of these technologies provide varied curricula, assessment, and instruction that circumvent the one-size-fits-all model of education. And new technologies are constantly evolving.

Assessments of all kinds loom large in the data-driven decision-making process. Technologies can and must be used to support the creation, administration, scoring, and reporting of the assessments. Assessments can be used formatively to improve students' learning in addition to measuring what they have learned. Educators should be provided with professional learning opportunities that teach them to use assessments formatively to improve instructional practices.

Building the capacity to use technology and the data to measure what matters takes time. States, districts, and colleges of education should connect data, assessment, and technology experts with education policy makers and practitioners to support the need for capacity building. This should include creating forums and resources that enable experts to advise states and districts about using technology to improve the quality of their assessment materials, competency-based approaches, and processes focused on learning. Such expertise should be continuous, rather than one-time events. An exemplar can be found in the Arkansas Department of Education (2007). The department has hired Margaret Heritage, an expert on formative assessments, to work with the SEA to implement these assessments throughout the state. Dr. Heritage's collaboration is an ongoing enterprise, evolving over several years. The assessment results are stored in the state's technology system.

Interactive assessment technologies and systems have the capacity to support the measurement of complex performances that cannot be assessed with conventional testing formats. Technological innovations, such as mobile technologies, social networking, and virtual learning environments, are desirable because they are highly engaging. They provide immediate performance feedback so that students always know how they are doing.

States and districts should consider adopting the different kinds of data systems and the emerging technologies as they become available. They provide invaluable resources and tools for educators at all levels of the educational system. Their power is unprecedented. It is now contingent upon educators to harness that power to inform their daily practice.

To what kind of technologies do you have access?

Data warehouses

Student information systems

Instructional management systems

Assessment systems

Handheld diagnostic tools

Data dashboards

Other tools

CHOPS

What challenges and opportunities currently exist around your technology to support data use? How do these challenges and opportunities relate to key ideas expressed in this chapter? For example:

Do your schools have any technology to support data-driven decision making?

Do you have access to it, or do only a few people have access to it?

Is it user-friendly?

Have you received training on the technology?

Was your training so long ago that you have forgotten what to do?

Do you have experts to which you can turn for help?

How frequently do you use the technology?

Is the technology aligned to your needs?

Is your technology too obsolete to use? If so, what strategies are being used to remediate the problem?

Some Highlighted References

Hupert, N., Heinze, J., Gunn, G., & Stewart, J. (2008). Using technology-assisted progress monitoring to drive improved student outcomes. In E. B. Mandinach & M. Honey (Eds.), *Data-driven school improvement: Linking data and learning* (pp. 130–150). New York, NY: Teachers College Press.

Long, L., Rivas, L., Light, D., & Mandinach, E. B. (2008). The evolution of a homegrown data warehouse: TUSDStats. In E. B. Mandinach & M. Honey (Eds.), *Data-driven school improvement: Linking data and learning* (pp. 209–232). New York, NY: Teachers College Press.

Means, B., Padilla, C., & Gallagher, L. (2010). *Use of education data at the local level: From accountability to instructional improvement.* Washington, DC: U.S. Department of Education, Office of Planning, Evaluation, and Policy Development.

Wayman, J. C. (2005a). Involving teachers in data-driven decision-making: Using computer data systems to support teacher inquiry and reflection. *Journal of Education for Student Placed at Risk, 112*(4), 521–548.

Wayman, J. C. (2007). Student data systems for school improvement: The state of the field. *TCEA* In *Educational Technology Research Symposium: Vol. 1* (pp. 156–162). Lancaster, PA: ProActive Publications.

Wayman, J. C., Cho, V., & Johnston, M. T. (2007). *The data-informed district: A district-wide evaluation of data use in the Natrona County School District.* Austin, TX: The University of Texas.

Wayman, J. C., Stringfield, S., & Yakimowski, M. (2004). *Software enabling school improvement through analysis of student data* (CRESPAR Tech. Rep. No. 67). Baltimore, MD: Johns Hopkins University, Center for Research on the Education of Students Placed at Risk. Retrieved from www.csos.jhu.edu/crespar/techReports/Report67.pdf

Glossary[8]

Assessment system—A technology application that enables educators to create tests, score and analyze them, and then report results.

Classroom response system—A technology tool in which students are given clickers that enables them to respond to teachers' questions by clicking a response and then classroom responses are aggregated and displayed for analysis.

Data dashboard—A technology tool that organizes important data elements in one place, typically on a desktop, presenting these data through immediate, easily accessible, and understandable graphical representations.

Data warehouse—A technology-based repository of data that collects and manages data from a variety of sources within a school district or SEA. Some data warehouses also include the capacity to analyze and report data.

Governance—Corporative agreements among agencies that enable the sharing of data. For example, among early childhood agencies, SEAs, institutions of higher education, health departments, etc.

Instructional management system—A technology-based tool that assists educators to design and structure their instruction, using data to inform their instruction.

Statewide longitudinal data system (SLDS)—A repository of data, located in a state department of education, with data collected from schools and school districts, as well as state data. The system communicates accountability data to the U.S. Department of Education. All states must have such data systems. The purpose of the SLDS is to manage, analyze, and use education data, including data at the student, school, and district levels.

Student information system—A technology application that helps districts and schools collect and manage student data.

Whiteboard—An interactive tool that provides interaction between the electronic whiteboard and a computer. What is written on the board can be communicated to the computer, recorded, and reviewed later.

4

Continuous Capacity Building

Data-Driven Decision-Making Skills and Pedagogical Data Literacy

This chapter describes the need for educators and educational institutions to build their capacity for data-driven decision making. As we have said earlier, building human capacity for data use is an essential component of effective teaching and learning. But building the necessary capacity is not done through a one-time workshop or one-stop shopping (i.e., simply by purchasing data systems and expecting people to know how to use them). It is attained through continuous capacity building that must begin in teacher preparation programs and continue throughout educational careers. Data-driven decision making is a human resource that must be continuously developed.

THE CONTINUUM FROM PRE-SERVICE
TO PROFESSIONAL DEVELOPMENT

Educators never stop learning. From the time they take their first college course to the moment they retire, educators are continuously learning, gaining new perspectives on teaching, learning, curricula, and classroom management through their interactions with students and colleagues. Educators must be lifelong learners in the truest sense of the term.

The field of education is constantly evolving despite critics who believe that it rarely changes, that educators have been doing the same thing for decades or even centuries, and that there is a one-size-fits-all approach to education. The notion that teachers teach and students passively receive information is a passé scenario. Education is interactive, changing moment to moment as teachers and students participate in the instructional process. Effective teachers constantly monitor their students through every interaction, question, response, comment, and work product. These outcomes enable teachers to diagnose and determine what particular students know or don't know, what the students' learning strengths and weaknesses are, and what might be the appropriate next instructional steps to capitalize on the strengths and remediate the weaknesses.

Good teachers have been doing this for years. So what is different now? The proliferation of data and sources of information that teachers need to take in and use is increasing and may be overwhelming for many. As has been described in the previous chapter, emerging technological solutions are making possible the ready access to data anytime and anywhere. What has not caught up yet are education courses on data-driven decision making, either at the undergraduate or graduate level, and professional development for in-service teachers to help prospective or current educators acquire the knowledge and skills to use data effectively, the pedagogical data literacy. What the field does not know yet is how best to introduce the concepts of data-driven decision making to educators along the developmental continuum from undergraduate education majors to experienced teachers and administrators (Mandinach & Gummer, 2011). The field is questioning whether the data literacy skills differ at different stages of experience and how best the skills can be taught to meet the varied needs, whether through stand-alone courses, integrated into existing courses, or integrated suites of courses.

What implications do these trends have for training teachers? As we noted earlier, data-driven decision making is a generic tool that lies at the intersection of several different courses. This will become clearer when we describe some of the skills involved in data use. We describe a new movement in teacher preparation that may influence how educators gain data literacy. We discuss the role schools of education can play in building capacity among educators. We also mention the paucity of professional development opportunities on data use.

Improving Clinical Preparation

A Blue Ribbon Panel convened by the NCATE in 2010 released a comprehensive set of recommendations about what teacher preparation should look like in the future. The recommendations are far-reaching and should have a direct impact on training educators to use data. The approach is called "clinical preparation," modeled after medical training. As Duncan (2010b) notes, the medical model of training will stimulate the clinical preparation of educators with "evidence-based knowledge interwoven with academic content and professional courses." The Panel states that teacher candidates, "need to have opportunities to reflect upon and think about what they do, how they make decisions, and how they 'theorize' their work, and how they integrate their content knowledge and pedagogical knowledge into what they do" (p. 9). The report further espouses the notion that teacher preparation must provide "the opportunity to make decisions and to develop skills to analyze student needs and adjust practices using student performance data while receiving continuous monitoring and feedback from mentors" (p. 10). These are the principles of data-driven decision making and continuous improvement applied to teacher preparation and to practice.

Two of the Panel's ten design principles relate directly to data-driven practice. The first principle speaks to skills and knowledge teachers need to obtain.

> Candidates must develop a base of knowledge, a broad range of effective teaching practices, and the ability to integrate the two to support professional decision making. To be successful teachers in challenging and changing environments, candidates must learn to use multiple assessment processes to advance learning and inform their practice with data to differentiate their teaching to match their students' progress. Further, effective teachers are innovators and problem solvers, working with colleagues constantly seeking new and different ways of teaching students who are struggling. (Duncan, 2010b, p. 5)

The second principle espouses the role of schools of education.

> Those who lead the next generation of teachers throughout their preparation and induction must themselves be effective practitioners, skilled in differentiating instruction, proficient in using assessment to monitor learning and provide feedback, persistent searchers for data to guide and adjust practice, and exhibitors of the skills of clinical education. (Duncan, 2010b, p. 6)

Clinical preparation has the potential to improve capacity, but it may be dependent on the models that students see among current educators. A problem might be that pre-service candidates do not see good or effective data use either in the field or among their professors, and therefore their clinical experiences may not be fruitful. The second recommendation is critical. Schools of education must show evidence of their own data-driven decision making and model it for their students. They must build their own capacity.

A Successful Example

Here is an example that schools of education can indeed build internal capacity and that of their students.[9] Western Oregon University has integrated data-driven decision making throughout their course offerings. Students get data training in their courses. They get data use in their practica. Further, faculty members must be versed in data-driven decision making. They are expected to model data-driven practices to their students in all of their courses. It can be done!

Standards

Reviews of standards for teachers and administrators produced by the Council of Chief State School Officers (CCSSO; 2008, 2011) indicated that there is limited coverage of data-driven decision making among the standards. For teachers (CCSSO, 2011), the Interstate Teacher Assessment and Support Consortium (InTASC) notes nine knowledge standards, nine disposition standards, and twenty performance standards that discuss the use of data to support teaching and learning.[10] For example, Standard 5, Innovative Applications of Content, refers to information gathering skills and knowledge. Standard 6, Assessment, focuses on the need to use multiple sources of assessments, with data being used to monitor student progress and plan for subsequent instruction. At least four other standards, including Planning for Instruction, Instructional Strategies, Reflection and Continuous Growth, and Collaboration, all have data components.

For administrators (CCSSO, 2008), the Educational Leadership Policy Standards: Interstate School Leaders Licensure Consortium (ISLLC) contains at least three standards relevant to data-driven decision making. One standard discusses the need to "collect and use data to identify goals, assess organization effectiveness and promoted organization learning (CCSSO, 2008, p. 14). Another standard refers to the analysis of data to identify and examine trends.

Teacher Education in Data-Driven Decision Making

To date, few courses on data-driven decision making are offered as stand-alone classes in the teacher preparation process. Stand-alone courses may not be the appropriate model. Data-driven instruction is more likely to occur in other courses. Students may get snippets of data use in their measurement courses as they learn about the development of and the kinds of assessments that can be used to measure student learning and progress. They may get different perspectives in courses on instruction and curriculum when they learn how the instructional process is replete with sources of information about how students understand course content. They may get yet another perspective from methods and classroom management courses in which they learn how to translate student work into instructional steps and organize class structures. Cognition courses add another dimension concerning how students think and learn. Data-driven decision making also involves knowledge of statistics, yet data are more than the numbers that can be plugged into equations. Data need to be transformed into information that teachers can use to determine instruction. Statistics courses are necessary, but not sufficient for data-driven decision making, although several books exist that treat data use as an introduction to statistics.

Graduate courses are seemingly emerging more quickly than undergraduate courses (Mandinach & Gummer, 2011). The trend is for administrative programs to undergo redesigns to address current gaps in education, data-driven decision making being one of them. The graduate-level courses are typically for administrators whose use of data differs from teachers and goes beyond instructional decisions. Use may involve helping teachers with instructional issues. However, administrators need to learn how to use diverse sources of data for resource allocation, personnel evaluation, curricular decisions, and other administrative functions. Just as with instruction, it is no longer sufficient or acceptable for administrative decisions to be based on anecdotes, gut feelings, or even political, parental, or stakeholder pressure. Thus, it is imperative for administration candidates to learn how to use data and translate them into practice.

Unfortunately, we are confronted with a chicken and egg problem. Because certification requirements for data-driven decision making for teachers, principals, and superintendents are not pervasive (Data Quality Campaign, 2010a, 2011b), courses are not as widespread as one would expect based on the emphases from the U.S. Department of Education (Duncan, 2009b, 2009c, 2010a, 2010b). Even the Data Quality Campaign's (2010a) projections are less than optimistic, with only half the states slated to require data-driven decision-making preparation by 2012 and beyond for licensure and certification. A recent Data Quality Campaign's (2011b) survey of state data directors indicates that fourteen states require data literacy skills for superintendents as part of certification, fifteen for principals, and fourteen for teachers. Given that the secretary of Education is stressing the need for data and evidence for decision making, it is somewhat surprising to see that SEAs are slow to respond through the evolution of their requirements.

A Self-Evaluation of Your Training and Course Work

Have you had a course in data-driven decision making?

Has data use been integrated into any of your courses?

Do you consider yourself data literate? If no, where might you get the needed training?

Have you had a course in how to transform data into instructional action? For administrative action?

Have you had a course in formative assessment? Summative assessment? Do you know the difference?

Did your pedagogy course help you to understand how to use data to inform your instructional practices?

Have you learned how to differentiate instruction based on student learning data?

Have you had a basic statistics course and understand the concepts of central tendency and distribution?

What Can Schools of Education Do to Build Capacity?

Little is known about what schools of education are actually doing to develop and implement courses on data-driven decision making (Mandinach & Gummer, 2010). Nor does the field know the extent to which existing courses integrate the principles of data-driven inquiry. Efforts to fund a comprehensive survey have not yet come to fruition. A limited survey was conducted that indicated that courses are being implemented but it is unclear just how broadly (Mann & Simon, 2010). The reason we say that the survey was "limited" is because of the small and select sample that was used in the study and the limited nature of the questions.

To try to understand the issues around implementation, Mandinach and Gummer (2011) organized a brainstorming conference to which schools of education, researchers in the field, professional developers, professional accreditation agencies, and the U.S. Department of Education were invited. Several key findings and recommendations resulted from this conference.

A first issue is that there are multiple meanings or interpretations of what data-driven decision making is. To different people, it means different things. The field needs a common understanding in order to move forward toward the implementation of courses that integrate or teach data-driven inquiry. Similarly, and as noted previously in this chapter, there are multiple skills sets and perspectives about what knowledge and skills comprise data literacy. Third, the field needs to understand how different sets of standards impact and support the preparation of educators to use data. Fourth is the conceptualization of a developmental continuum of where educators are in terms of their preparation, career, and attitudes toward data use. And these factors will affect the delivery of training. For example, pre-service candidates may need different types of course presentations and different content than might a master's candidate who has been teaching for several years. An administrator may need even more different topical coverage. Fifth, there is a need to explore and address the potential for different venues of course delivery for different phases along the developmental continuum. These venues or modalities include face-to-face courses, virtual courses, and hybrid (combinations of face-to-face and virtual) delivery. Additionally, the use of web-based courses might be an ideal modality for continuing education courses for the broadest possible dissemination. The sixth issue relates to the Blue Ribbon Panel's (2010) recommendation to address the capacity of schools of education to deliver data-driven courses. This issue explores whether institutions of higher education have the faculty to provide data-driven courses and if not, how they might obtain such expertise (i.e., adjunct faculty, training existing faculty, hiring professional developers all as possibilities). The final theme is the recognition that integrating data-driven courses into schools of education is a highly systemic issue. Schools of education are seen as learning organizations (Senge, 1990) that must function within a complex system comprised of other agencies and organizations that interact with and impact how such courses might be implemented. For example, professional organizations, SEAs, accreditation agencies, school districts, and testing organizations all might impact the decision to implement courses.

Four recommendations for further exploration resulted from the conference. First, there is a need for specific research. First and foremost, there needs to be a rigorous and comprehensive survey of schools of education to ascertain what courses, integrated courses, or suites of courses exist, including plans for future courses. There also needs to be an inventory of SEAs and their accreditation agencies to determine what regulations exist around licensure and certification. Second, there are issues that involve practice. Schools of education do not function in isolation. Their graduates go to work in school districts. Thus, there must be an alignment between districts and schools of education in terms of the relevance of courses and the responsiveness to districts' needs. Third, there is still ambiguity about how best to serve all educators along the developmental continuum. More discussion and parsing out of the issues need to happen. Finally, because of the complexity and systemic nature of the issue, there needs to be more professional discourse to address how different agencies can come together to affect change in this arena.

Professional Development on Data Use

Professional development around data-driven decision making is the next step in continuous capacity building. It targets the current teacher corps. Professional development may be conducted by knowledgeable staff within a district or schools or by organizations that deliver professional workshops. Regardless of the provider, professional development should be ongoing, not a one-time event (Hawley & Valli, 1999; Means et al., 2010). Continuous professional development, interspersed with technical assistance, is a model that is being implemented and makes good sense (Love et al., 2008). This model is being tested using an experimental design in a large, urban school district (Mandinach et al., 2009). Further, Garet, Porter, Desimone, Birman, and Yoon (2001) note key characteristics of professional development that include content focus, opportunities for active learning, and coherence or alignment with other teacher learning activities. We examine two forms of professional development: that provided by school districts and by external professional development providers.

District-Provided Professional Development

Districts may not be able to afford professionally delivered workshops, so they must make sure that the individuals responsible for providing the professional development are sufficiently knowledgeable about data-driven decision making and how to train educators in data use. Hamilton and colleagues (2009) report the need for schools to designate a data facilitator who may or may not be the provider of training, but who can help staff use data appropriately. Ideally, each school would have a data facilitator or data coach who can work with staff. Larger districts may have this capacity. They may also have expertise at the central office to assist the schools.

However, in smaller districts, there may not be sufficient expertise so there may be fewer internal potential data facilitators. Part of the role of the data facilitator is to meet on a regular basis with teams of teachers (e.g., grade-level or subject-related) to help them examine data and interpret them in ways that can be translated into instructional actions. The data facilitators model data use and may even help with the training of colleagues.

Hamilton and colleagues (2009) identify fourteen different kinds of professional development that are deemed appropriate and relevant for teachers, principals, technology staff, and other staff. Topics include how to interpret educational data, using data for instructional improvement, school leadership, data safety, data system use, and how to collectively use data. What we are saying here is that professional development around data-driven decision making is not one-stop shopping or a one-size-fits-all model. Different kinds of training are needed based on the educators' roles. For example, principals and teachers most likely do not need training in data system maintenance or troubleshooting, but the information technology staff do. Conversely, the information technology staff may not need training in how to modify teaching and learning practices, but the teachers and principals do.

The concept of collaboration is important in data-driven decision making. It rose to the level of an action step in the IES Practice Guide (Hamilton et al., 2009). Bringing educators together to examine data, led by a data facilitator, coach, or mentor, can only serve to build internal capacity within a school. Such collaboration can help to build knowledge and decrease the misuse of data (Means et al., 2011). Professional learning communities are major vehicles for this type of collaboration. They can also be called data teams.

Professional Workshops

Several organizations and individuals provide professionally delivered training on data-driven decision making. We describe a few of the most prominent groups, recognizing that it is not an exhaustive list. The inclusion of these models does not equate to an endorsement.

It is important to note that professionally delivered training needs to be supported within districts' financial infrastructure. Such training must be viewed by administrators as sufficiently useful, informative, and worthwhile to compensate for the costs. Thus, in a cost-benefit analysis, the benefits must outweigh the costs, even in these times of severe budgetary constraints. The provision for such professional development must be recognized as a good investment. This is part of a district's vision for data use—the expenditure of resources to support data-driven decision making. Most important, though, the professional development must be aligned to and customized to the needs of the district. It should not be a "canned" training.

Using Data

The Using Data Project at TERC was funded by the National Science Foundation and the Eisenhower Regional Alliance for Mathematics and Science Education to develop a training program to help educators use data in mathematics and the sciences (Love, 2002). The model has expanded into a more generic intervention that crosses content areas and grade levels (Love et al., 2008). Two fundamental components of the Using Data model is that schools should create data teams and appoint a data coach. The team focuses on the collaborative inquiry while the data coach facilitates the team's work and helps others to use data. The objective is to create a data culture within a school.

The intervention introduces teachers and school leaders to a causal analysis process through which they learn to frame questions, collect data, formulate hypotheses, draw conclusions, take action, and monitor results (Love, 2002, 2009; Love et al., 2008). Schools build capacity to use and interrogate data efficiently by training teachers, administrators, and instructional specialists to become school-level data coaches. These coaches work with teacher teams to facilitate a structured process of analyzing and questioning multiple sources of data. Data coaches then lead data teams and teachers through a process of data inquiry. The process includes five components: (1) building a foundation for data, (2) identifying student learning problems, (3) verifying causes of learning problems, (4) generating solutions, and (5) implementing, monitoring, and achieving results (see Love, 2002; Love et al., 2008 for details).

The Using Data model posits what they refer to as high-capacity data use strategies (Love et al., 2008). These are skills and knowledge thought to be essential in the effective use of data. They are contrasted with low-capacity data use strategies that are considered less effective ways to use data. There are thirteen dichotomous pairs. Table 4.1 presents the strategies. As can be seen in Table 4.1, there are fundamental principles of instruction, measurement, and methods that underlie the strategies. For example, a basic premise of measurement is that it is better to use multiple measures, rather than one from which to obtain a valid indication of performance. Further, it is better to use both formative and summative assessments, not just summative measures.

Data Wise

Data Wise (Boudett, City, & Murnane, 2006) is a professional development program from Harvard University that consists of a sequence of eight data use steps that focus on empowering teaching and learning. It is both a professional development program and a course at Harvard (Murnane, Boudett, & City, 2009). Data Wise was founded on the notion that schools should be learning organizations working toward continuous improvement. Data Wise helps schools to develop teacher collaboration through teams of administrators and teachers. Murnane and colleagues noted (2009) five practices that characterize the program:

Table 4.1   Using Data's Low- and High-Capacity Data Use
Strategies[11]

Low-Capacity Data Use	High-Capacity Data Use
• Misinterprets and misunderstands data	• Accurately interprets data and discerns what they mean
• Uses aggregated and disaggregated data only	• Regularly uses item-level data and student work
• Accepts achievement gaps as inevitable	• Responds to achievement gaps with immediate concern and corrective action
• Uses single measures to draw conclusions	• Uses multiple sources of data before drawing conclusions
• Uses only summative measures	• Uses formative and summative measures
• Blames students and external causes for failure	• Looks for causes for failure that are within educators' control
• Draws conclusions without verifying hypotheses with data	• Uses student work and data about practice and research to verify hypotheses
• Fails to monitor implementation and results; big surprises at the end	• Regularly monitors implementation and student learning; no surprises
• Responds as individual administrators and teachers	• Responds in teams and as a system
• Prepares for tests by drilling students on test items	• Aligns curriculum with standards and assessments; implements research-based improvements in curriculum, instruction, and assessment
• Tutors only those students just missing the cutoff for proficiency—"bubble kids"	• Differentiates instruction; provides extra help and enrichment for all who need it
• Tracks students into classes by perceived ability	• Increases the rigor of the curriculum for all students; assigns the best teachers to those who need them most
• Chooses strategies based on instinct or the latest educational fad	• Chooses strategies that are culturally proficient and research based and have a logical link to the intended outcome

From the Using Data Project, TERC. Published in Love, et. al (2008).

1. a system of interlocking teams;

2. meetings for collaboration;

3. time for teachers to observe one another;

4. teachers providing critical feedback to one another; and

5. teachers held accountable for self-improvement.

Boudett and colleagues (2006) describe an eight-step process of using data to improve teaching and learning. The first step is to prepare by building for improvement by organizing school structures to facilitate collaborative work, essentially building a data culture. They further prepare by building assessment literacy. The inquiry phase consists of the creation of graphical displays of data, or data overviews, and then having the faculty "dig into student data." By examining data, Data Wise means that educators should use multiple sources of data, triangulating on the different kinds of data. The fifth step involves the examination of instructional practices. The final phase is acting upon the organization learning process first through the development of an action plan, then by planning to assess progress, and finally by acting and assessing the action plan.

Victoria Bernhardt's Education for the Future

Education for the Future, located at Chico State University, is a model for professional development that focuses on helping education agencies to use data through systemic change for continuous improvement (http://eff.csuchico.edu/). The model sees schools, districts, and state departments of education as learning organizations in which systemic change can occur through the use of data (Bernhardt, 2008). The model builds capacity through workshops that bring together diverse staff members from education agencies. A data portfolio is created for the school or district that stimulates the consideration of where the agency is, where it should be, and how to attain the objective. Diverse data are considered: demographics, perceptions, student learning, and school processes (Bernhardt, 2004, 2008).

Wellman and Lipton's Data-Driven Dialogue

Wellman and Lipton (2004) present a model of the data-driven dialogue as a way of facilitating collaborative inquiry among educators. The objective of the model is to create structures around which data can be used in group settings. The authors lay out a three-step process that includes: (1) activating and engaging, (2) exploring and discovering, and (3) organizing and integrating. Activating and engaging is about making predictions and assumptions. Exploring and discovering focuses on analyzing data. Organizing and integrating is about theorizing, explanations, and making inferences. The model also notes four other components: (1) managing, (2) modeling, (3) mediating, and (4) monitoring. The model further lays out three principles of a data-driven dialogue. These include "conscious curiosity," "purposeful uncertainty," and "visually vibrant information."

The Oregon DATA Project

The Oregon DATA Project has been an effort based out of the Oregon Department of Education, with funding, in part, from the SLDS grants, and is a collaboration with several institutions of higher education in the state. These institutions include Western Oregon University, Portland State University, Eastern Oregon University, Oregon State University, the University of Oregon, and Southern Oregon University. The purpose of the project is to train educators throughout the state on the use of data. The model the project uses (see http://www.oregondataproject.org) is to first acquire input from the field about needs, then provide in-service training to existing teachers so that the implementation of data reaches a point of sustainability. The next step is the evaluation of use, followed by extending the work to pre-service candidates.

The project helps teachers to learn how to ask questions and to determine what data to examine. It helps to build capacity within the district and across people to promote sustainability, given the mobility of educators. It is grounded on the notion of team-initiated problem solving, using school-based teams.

It recognizes implementation barriers and notes the importance, not just of acquiring knowledge and skills, but also attitudes, beliefs, self-efficacy, and the concerns of educators. Interestingly, early evaluations of the project indicate that the concerns of educators must be addressed and allayed before dealing with issues of self-efficacy and knowledge acquisition (Airola, Garrison, & Dunn, 2011).

Training in Formative Assessment

Other forms of professional development also are relevant to data-driven decision making. These include how to use formative assessments and benchmarks. Two names come to mind immediately: Rick Stiggins and Margaret Heritage. The Assessment Training Institute (ATI; http://www.assessment inst.com), directed by Stiggins, provides team-based professional development on the accurate use of assessment to promote learning (Chappuis, Stiggins, Chappuis, & Arter, 2012). The focus is on formative assessment that enables educators to integrate instruction with assessment to promote assessment *for* learning, not assessment *of* learning. ATI conducts workshops to help educators integrate assessments into their practice to inform teaching and learning. As formative assessment has become more accepted, Stiggins has been hired to train entire districts in the use of these techniques.

Margaret Heritage, of CRESST, is one of the most prominent researchers working in the area of formative assessment. These assessments are those used during instruction to shape the process of teaching and learning. As the notions of formative assessments have begun to gain recognition of their utility and importance, Heritage has been helping education agencies, such as the Arkansas Department of Education (2007), to implement large-scale models of these assessments.

Summaries of Professional Development Programs

The professional development programs have some similarities and some differences. One contrast among the models is the delivery. Data Wise is a five-day program given at Harvard. School teams travel to Cambridge during a week in the summer when the training is offered. Education for the Future provides one- or two-day workshops, but recommends two days. The Using Data model is more flexible. Data facilitators go on site to schools and districts and can modify their training and workshops according to the needs of the client. Typically, Using Data includes both formal professional development sessions as well as continuous technical assistance delivered over time. Normally it consists of six sessions distributed over a year. Using Data also has an online version in which teachers engage in fifteen one-week virtual professional development sessions. They also have developed a Principals Academy, recognizing the important role of leadership in enculturating data-driven decision making. This model reflects three fundamental findings in the literature. First, Means and colleagues (2010) recommend continuous, rather than one-time training. Second, the IES Practice Guide (Hamilton et al., 2009) recommends that districts seek professional development providers that can adjust and align the training to the needs of the specific group of educators. Third is the key role the administrators plays in data use, either in schools or in the district.

We are not endorsing any one vendor or model. But we do agree with the Practice Guide recommendations that districts carefully examine their options, given limited funds, and work to customize the training with the providers so that the sessions meet the districts' needs, not just getting a one-size-fits-all model of professional development. These and other professional development programs vary in cost, duration, intensity, and focus. Districts need to determine what is the best for their needs, educational objectives, staff, and budgets. Districts also need to continuously support these efforts, not do a one-time event (Means et al., 2010). Further, making the investment as comprehensive as possible is more effective. That is, sending a few people to a workshop is not sufficient. The benefits will be minimal.

School-level teams or larger groups need to receive training on a continuous basis.

With our increasing abilities to collect data on student learning, the use of data has become and will continue to be a lifelong process throughout the career of educators. Acquiring knowledge of data-driven decision making and how it can impact practice should begin early in educators' training, with authentic examples of diverse forms of data. This knowledge acquisition will become more firmly embedded as educators enter the classroom or an administrative office, making actual use of real data. Experienced teachers who are adept at the use of data can mentor more junior colleagues as well as pre-service teachers. These individuals can serve as exemplars of data-driven practices. As noted above, graduate programs need to be encouraged to support strong data-driven models and provide a foundation for interpreting tools as well as results. This educational process is ongoing and continuous as the field changes. With the increasing diversity of data types and frequency of use, data-driven decision making can and must become an enculturated tool for all educators.

Reflect on How Professional Development Is Integrated Into Your District and Used

Are your workshops one-time deals?

Are you offered opportunities for continuous training?

Does your district offer you professional development opportunities or do you have to seek them on your own?

Are the providers internal to the district or external trainers?

Do they do a good job?

How might the training events be made more effective to impact your practice?

Data-Driven Skills

Chapter 2 described several theories or frameworks for data-driven decision making. These theories form the basis for understanding the skills needed for effective data use. Each of the frameworks has slightly different approaches. Some have more well-defined skills and knowledge outlined, whereas others are less specific. Table 4.2 outlines the components for each framework. Keep in mind that many of these frameworks are cyclical and iterative, meaning that there is not a strictly linear process, although the numbers in Table 4.2 indicate some degree of order. Multiple passes through the components may be needed and a decision maker may jump into the cycle at different points, depending upon the specific needs. Also keep in mind that some of the skills are quite similar although the frameworks may use different terms. We could try to chunk these skills into larger units to ease understanding, but we think it is important to illustrate that the research field cannot quite agree on common definitions of the components of data-driven decision making (see Mandinach & Gummer, 2011). The frameworks also have slightly different foci and purposes.

Mandinach, Honey, Light, and Brunner

As a by-product of a larger research project on data-driven decision making, Mandinach and colleagues (2008) developed a conceptual framework on how educators make decisions based on the use of technological solutions. A fundamental part of the framework was the hypothesizing and identification of the skills involved in the decision-making process (see Figure 2.1). The conceptualization specified the cognitive skills or processes that are needed as data are transformed along the data continuum from data into information and ultimately to actionable knowledge. Two skills are hypothesized to be needed at each of the three steps along the data continuum.

Table 4.2 Comparison of Data-Driven Skills Across Frameworks

Skills	Mandinach et al. 2008	Means et al. 2010	Means et al. 2011	Hamilton et al. 2009	Abbott 2008	Easton 2009
Collect	1		1	1		
Organize	2					
Analyze	3	4				
Summarize	4					
Synthesize	5					
Prioritize	6					
Decide	7					
Plan		1			2	
Implement	8	2			3	
Assess		3			1	
Reflect		5				
Prepare data			3	1		
Interpret			5	2		
Develop hypotheses				2		
Modify instruction			4	3		
Identify problem						1
Seek solution						2
Monitor progress						3
Research						4
Evaluate	9				4	
Comprehend			2			

The framework posits that the first skill needed in the data-driven process is to *collect* data. The user must determine what data are needed and collect those data elements. This may entail the collection of new data or obtaining existing data from repositories such as a data warehouse or student information system. The data then must be *organized* in some way that makes them understandable to the user. The organization of data is necessary because raw data need to be pulled together for sense making. The data are then *analyzed* in a way that they are transformed into information, rather than just raw numbers. The analytic process may yield information that is still too unwieldy and therefore there is a need for the user to *summarize* the amassed information. The summarization process enables a further transformation of the information into knowledge that the educator can use to form a knowledge base about the issue at hand. This requires a process of *synthesizing* the accumulated information. Finally, the user *prioritizes* the knowledge from which a decision is made, it is implemented, and its impact determined. These last three steps—decide, implement, and evaluate impact—were conceptualized as part of the feedback loop of decision making, rather than the specific cognitive skills that are needed in the process. But for the purposes here, they become fundamental skills or components in the data-driven process. Thus, we extend the skill set of the original framework to include the components of the feedback loop as also necessary cognitive skills.

Means, Padilla, and Gallagher

Means and colleagues (2010) posited a cyclical set of skills for data-driven decision making writ large. The first skill is *planning*. Educators must be able to plan out a course of action based on an issue with which they are confronted. The plan is then *implemented*. Educators must know how to carry out an intervention or potential solution strategy. They then must *assess* how their plan is doing. Is it working, not working, or needs to be modified? This is accomplished through the *analysis of data*. Finally, the educators must *reflect* on the outcomes and determine if they must go back to some earlier component of the cyclical process to collect more data, try a new plan, or the like.

The objective of this conceptual framework was not so much to outline the cognitive skills that decision making requires, but to identify aspects of educational technology and other components that contribute to effective educational data-driven decision making. The components include data systems, leadership, tools for generating data, social structures, professional development, and tools for acting on the data. Taken together with the five-part cycle above, they form a data-driven continuous improvement process.

Means, Chen, DeBarger, and Padilla

Unlike the conceptual framework developed by Means and colleagues (2010), a spinoff study was conducted in which five data-driven skills were reported (Means et al., 2011). This work is based on giving teachers several scenarios from which the skills were extracted and identified. The first skill is called *data location*. It means that one can find the right pieces of data in a table, a data system, or a data display. The second skill is called *data comprehension*. It means that one can understand what the data signify.[12] The third skill is called *data interpretation*, which is that one can determine what the data mean. The fourth skill is *instructional decision making*. This is the ability to determine instructional steps based on the data and the particular circumstances. The final skill is called *question posing*. It is slightly different from hypothesizing in that the authors define it as the ability to pose instructionally relevant questions that are answerable through data.

Hamilton, Halverson, Jackson, Mandinach, Supovitz, and Wayman

The focus of the IES Practice Guide was specifically on the use of achievement data to inform instruction. There are two key elements here. First, the report only examines instructional decision making, which differs from decision making more broadly construed. So the skills are operationalized based on classroom practices. Second, the focus on achievement data also delimited the skill set.

Hamilton and colleagues (2009) identify three processes (p. 10):

1. *collecting* and *preparing* "a variety of data about student learning";

2. *interpreting* data and *developing* "hypotheses about how to improve student learning"; and

3. *modifying* "instruction to test hypotheses and increase student learning."

These three processes focus on student learning data and are defined in a very broad manner. Like other frameworks, it begins with the collection of data but also includes the preparation and interpretation of data. It then jumps to the development of hypotheses. It is interesting that hypothesis generation follows data interpretation when the order could have just as easily been switched. The inquiry cycle concludes with the modification of instructional activity based on the data collected, interpretation, and the hypotheses that have been generated. Seemingly there may be a missing step that includes the analysis of the hypotheses to determine if the data confirmed or disconfirmed the assumptions. Those outcomes then could lead to the modification of instruction.

So what skills does this model promote? Teachers must know how to collect data and prepare them for analysis. They must understand how to interpret the data and form hypotheses based on the data. Finally, teachers must know how to align the data and assumptions made on them, and revise their instruction accordingly.

Abbott

Abbott's (2008) framework differs slightly from the others because it was written from the state level about school improvement, but it can be generalized more broadly. The broad conceptualization is a called a functionality framework for educational organizations in which there is a cycle of improvement and readiness for change that is fed by data within a context of distributed leadership. The author outlines what he calls a four-step linear process of evidence-based improvements. He outlines four skills that supposedly form a linear sequence. However, those skills or components are embedded within a cyclical model that begins with needs assessment and is followed by planning, implementation, and evaluation.

Abbott posits that decision makers first must assess the needs of the educational setting and determine what is happening and what issues need attention. The needs assessment is followed by a planning phase in which the decision makers chart out a course of action that is intended to address the identified problems. Abbott stresses the importance of identifying and planning with research-based strategies. The next component is the effective implementation of the identified strategies, and finally the evaluation of the impact of those strategies. The evaluation component then leads back to the needs assessment phase. Thus, decision makers must know how to *assess* needs, *plan* for future actions, *implement* those strategies, and finally *evaluate* the outcomes of the decisions.

Easton

Easton's (2009) framework is focused on using data collection and research to address issues and problems in real educational settings. His model was developed during his directorship of the Consortium on Chicago School Research (see http://ccsr .uchicago.edu/content/index.php; Bryk et al., 2010). The decision-making loop includes using data, evidence, and research to inform policy and practice. It is geared toward decision makers in classrooms, schools, and at the district level. It also can be extrapolated to the state and federal levels.

The first skill is for a decision maker to be able to *identify a problem*. This could be an instruction problem or a student learning problem for a classroom teacher. It could be an administrative problem for a principal or superintendent. The second skill is to be able to *identify possible solutions* that can be tested. Third, the educator needs to be able to monitor progress for continuous improvement. The final step is to be able to *target research* that can be fed back into the cyclical process.

An example that Easton (2009) gave is trying to find the causes of high dropout rates and seeking solutions to keep students in school. Easton noted that in Chicago there was a strong relationship between the number of absences students had in their freshman year and probability of dropping out. Similarly, there also was a relationship between the number of Fs students received as a freshman and dropping out. The problem in this example is not only a high dropout rate but also absenteeism and course failure. What educators then need to do is determine how to decrease the number of days that students miss school and the number of course failures. They then must implement the potential strategies to remediate the problem and monitor the progress being made. Targeted research can identify how well the strategies are working or not, and those results can help to adjust the solutions to make them more effective. This is a formative cycle of inquiry based on data-driven decision making.

Summing Up

As can be seen from the reviewed frameworks, using data to inform practice requires a set of skills that, with time and experience, can become internalized and used to help educators in their work. The skills, although named differently across the models, involve similar processes. Data need to be collected, organized, examined, analyzed, tied to practice, decisions made and implemented, outcomes determined, and then fed back into the cyclic process for additional steps within the sequence. The process is not linear. It is cyclical. If it were linear, once all the steps had been executed, the objectives would have been attained and it would be end game. But that simply is not the case. Education, and the decision making that informs policy and practice, is a never-ending and iterative process. There always will be more data to collect or examine; more problems, issues, or questions that arise to which data need to be applied; more decisions to be analyzed; and so on. Thus, the sooner educators become familiar with data-driven decision making and become data literate, the more effectively and efficiently data-driven practices can be implemented in educational settings.

Some Questions

Are there skills that the frameworks in this chapter outlined that you think don't make sense?

Are there skills that you think these frameworks have omitted?

What does your cycle of inquiry look like?

How linear or cyclical is your process?

CHOPS

When you think about your own classroom, school, or district, what do you see as the challenges for building capacity in data-driven decision making?

Which ideas in this chapter need to be implemented, but there are barriers?

What are those barriers?

What would be needed to remove them?

What do you see as the opportunities that are available, but are not effectively or efficiently used?

What is already being done toward improving capacity, but has not yet been achieved?

What are the available resources?

How could some of the resources be used to meet the challenges?

SOME HIGHLIGHTED REFERENCES

Blue Ribbon Panel. (2010). *Transforming teacher education through clinical practice: A national strategy to prepare effective teachers.* Washington, DC: NCATE.

Heritage, M. (2010a). *Formative assessment and next-generation assessment systems: Are we losing an opportunity?* Washington, DC: Council of Chief State School Officers.

Love N., Stiles, K. E., Mundry, S., & DiRanna, K. (2008). *A data coach's guide to improving learning for all students: Unleashing the power of collaborative inquiry.* Thousand Oaks, CA: Corwin.

Mandinach, E. B., Honey, M., Light, D., & Brunner, C. (2008). *A conceptual framework for data-driven decision making.* In E. B. Mandinach & M. Honey (Eds.), *Data-driven school improvement: Linking data and learning* (pp. 13–31). New York, NY: Teachers College Press.

Means, B., Chen, E., DeBarger, A., & Padilla, C. (2011). *Teachers' ability to use data to inform instruction: Challenges and supports.* Washington, DC: U.S. Department of Education, Office of Planning, Evaluation, and Policy Development.

Stiggins, R. (2005). From formative assessment to assessment FOR learning: A path to success on standards-based skills. *Phi Delta Kappan, 85*(4), 324–328.

GLOSSARY

Developmental continuum—The progression from a college student who is learning to become an educator, through to graduate students in education, and experienced teachers and administrators.

Learning organization—A concept developed by Peter Senge in which a complex organization, such as a school district, collects and examines data on itself to evaluate its performance, learn from the results, and make necessary modifications for improvement.

Summative assessment—A test that measures the culmination of learning from a course, a topical unit, a marking period, or a school year. Such tests measure student learning, knowledge, and skills for at a particular end point in time.

5

Using Data for Continuous Improvement[13]

Processes and Structures

We have touched on many of the components needed to implement and enculturate data-driven decision making in districts, schools, and classrooms in the previous chapters. In this chapter we focus on the processes and structures needed at the school level for data use to inform continuous improvement. We highlight four overarching, but interrelated, components in this chapter: (1) leadership, (2) data coaches, (3) data teams, and (4) the enculturation of data-driven practices. Jimerson and Wayman (2011) proposed additional components: (1) collaboration, (2) workable data systems, (3) time, (4) leadership, (5) triangulation of data, (6) data literacy, (7) shared leadership, and (8) a focus on problems of practice. Leadership involves both the role of the principal and the need for distributed leadership. The concept of distributed leadership means that others within the school take partial responsibility for the use of data, not just the principal. The data coach plays a fundamental role in building a school's capacity for data use. This individual is the go-to person for all things related to data. The data team also serves a key function in helping teachers throughout a school begin to implement data-driven practices and gain data literacy. The ultimate objective is for data-driven decision making to become enculturated throughout a school, not just residing among the data coach and data team. For this to happen, certain structures must be implemented. These structures rely on committed leadership, bringing us full circle in a highly systemic process.

COMPONENTS OF DATA USE

As a parenthetical comment about this section, we move back and forth between the school level and the district level. Much of what applies at the district level also applies at the school level. This includes the need for strong leadership (although most of the research here has been done at the level of the principal), the creation of a vision, the provision for resources, and other components of embedding data use in classrooms, schools, and districts. Although there is an implied and actual hierarchy or nesting of these levels, the levels comprise a complex system into which the components are interrelated (Mandinach & Cline, 1994; Mandinach et al., 2006).

Leadership

The literature is in agreement that a key component in making data-driven decision making that happens within a school is leadership (Armstrong & Anthes, 2001; Hamilton et al., 2009). Ideally, a principal will have embraced data, recognizing how data use can inform practice at the school and classroom levels. There are instances, however, where a principal may not be data-minded and may actually be an impediment.

This may result in two outcomes. First, the teachers may follow the principal's lead and not use data in their practice. Or second, there may be a move among the teaching staff to use data, thereby doing an end-around the principal. Data-driven practices may take hold despite the principal being a data nonbeliever.

We have noted a growing trend in which principals are increasingly data-driven. Some districts actually select principals based on their ability to apply data in their decision making (Long et al., 2008). In the district, every candidate for a principal's position must complete an authentic assessment in which they are presented with a fictitious set of data and asked to apply those data to develop a school improvement plan. In another district, the superintendent has made clear the expectation that principals must use data as a part of their everyday practice, thereby weeding out those who are not like-minded.

At the other end of the continuum, we have heard of instances in which the principal literally obstructed teachers from using data, making it almost impossible for them to obtain the kinds of information needed to inform practice. This is an extreme, and it is unclear how rare this is. A less extreme position is probably more common. That is, a principal may be neither data-driven nor an impediment, allowing the teachers to use data but perhaps not providing the kinds of supports and resources that create an effective data culture.

Distributed leadership may serve as an effective vehicle here (Copland, Knapp, & Swinerton, 2009; Love et al., 2008). This is a situation in which other staff members take the lead in helping the school staff to use data. People who function as leaders may include the assistant principal, a curriculum specialist, a teacher leader, or others who recognize the utility of data. A distributed model may be useful when the principal actually lacks data skills (Lachat & Smith, 2005). This means that there is shared responsibility for outcomes.

What Kind of Leader Are You?

Do you help your staff use data?

Do you have a vision for data use?

Do you make that vision explicit?

Do you provide support and resources for your staff to use data?

Do you encourage and facilitate data use?

Do you model data?

Do you use data when you speak to parents, the community, and others?

What steps do you need to take to become more data-driven?

How important is it for you to use data? For your staff to use data?

Do you provide professional development opportunities for staff?

Is there a clear message from your superintendent that you should use data?

What Do Leaders Do?

A primary function of the leader is to help provide a vision for data use (Hamilton et al., 2009), define the purpose (Datnow & Park, 2010), and expectations (Wayman, Cho, Jimerson, & Snodgrass Rangel, 2010; Wayman, Jimerson, & Cho, in press) for data use, and build agreement within the school. Principals set the tone for their schools. Superintendents set the tone for their districts. The more explicit the vision, the clearer the expectations are for the staff either at the school or district levels. The vision paves the way for the creation of a culture accepting of and expecting the use of data to inform practice (Long et al., 2008; Means et al., 2010). Principals and superintendents also make possible the resources needed to help establish the data culture, such as encouraging data use, appointing a data coach, setting aside time for collaboration, and modeling data use (Means et al., 2010; Wayman, 2005a).

As noted above, not every principal may be capable of modeling data use due to a lack of knowledge and skills or even a lack of interest or motivation. These principals should, however, recognize their limitations and accept the importance of data-driven decision making by appointing a data coach and invoking a model of distributed leadership (Long et al., 2008). Such principals should not be an obstruction to data-driven practices, allowing a staff member or members to take the lead in integrating data use into the school. Thus, the most important act a principal can take is to appoint a data coach to provide intellectual leadership in data-driven decision making and to give that individual the resources to engrain data use into the school culture. It is important to note, however, that the building of a school culture is the shared responsibility of everyone in that building. A culture implies a collaboration, not just a top-down mandate.

What Kind of Leader Do You Have?

Is there leadership around data from your principal? From your superintendent?

Does leadership provide resources for you?

Are there explicit expectations that you use data?

Does your district or school have a vision for data use?

Does your principal or superintendent model that vision?

The Role of the Data Coach

A data coach is an individual who takes responsibility for integrating data use into the school and modeling data use (Lachat & Smith, 2005; Love et al., 2008). According to Means and colleagues (2010), roughly two-thirds of schools have a data coach who helps staff analyze data and motivate them to use data. The coach's responsibilities may include creating a data team; facilitating data use; helping to collect, analyze, and interpret data; and providing training to other staff members within a school to create a teaming model of professional development. The data coach, also referred to as a facilitator or mentor, is perhaps the most important person within a school to make data use a reality. The data coach serves as an important part of continuous professional development within a school or a district.

The data coach may be a lead teacher, a content specialist, or an administrator. The data coach may even be a retired educator rehired to work with existing staff (Datnow et al., 2007). It must be someone who knows data, but he or she also must be someone who knows how to interact with staff in an effective manner (Hamilton et al., 2009; Lachat & Smith, 2005). This means that the data coach may not just be the typical statistics enthusiast, someone who knows only the numbers. On the contrary, the data coach should be an individual who can easily work with others and help staff translate the numbers into actionable pedagogical knowledge. This is a person who knows and understands classroom teaching.

Perhaps the best sources of information about the roles and responsibilities of the data coach can be found in the *Data Coach's Guide to Improving Learning for All Students: Unleashing the Power of Collaborative Inquiry* (Love et al., 2008). This volume provides a compendium of descriptions and activities for what a data coach must do to help a school use data effectively. The guide describes three main roles. First, the data coach models data use and attempts to spread data literacy throughout the school. The coach helps colleagues interrogate their data. Second, the data coach serves as a facilitator by convening meetings and guiding the collective inquiry process. Third, the data coach provides leadership to sustain data use within a school. The objective here is to enculturate or institutionalize data-driven decision making through the implementation of structures, the provision of resources, and training.

Love and colleagues (2008) have identified five specific components in which a data coach engages to help lead a school's data practices. The first component is to *build* the foundation for data-driven decision making. This involves a process of needs sensing. The data coach must examine and understand what are the needs of the school and how data can be applied to those needs. The coach also is fundamental in establishing the work of the data team. The second component is to *identify* the problems or student learning issues to which data can be applied. Once problems are identified, sources of data then can be determined. Third, it is necessary to *verify* the possible causes of the problems. Fourth, the data coach must *generate* possible solutions. These solutions should be based on knowledge of best practices and existing research. Fifth, the data coach must *implement* the solution plan and *monitor* its outcomes. This component includes the provision of information that enables formative, corrective actions, not simply waiting for an end result to determine impact.

It is clear that the data coach plays an essential role in a school's use of data. The data coach is seen as the knowledgeable go-to person on issues related to the use of data. Ideally, data must get used, but there is the potential that the data coach may become overburdened. This is a risk to pay for a successful coach. This is precisely why the data coach needs colleagues with whom to work, such as a data team and a model of distributed leadership.

Data Teams

The literature is clear that collaboration around data is an essential component in the implementation of data-driven practices throughout a school (Datnow & Park, 2010; Hamilton et al., 2009; Long et al., 2008; Wayman, 2005a). Collaboration emphasizes the need for shared ideas, common terms, the interrogation of data, and discussion of outcomes among colleagues so that educators can learn from one another. Collaboration enables educators to come together to discuss pressing problems around student learning so that teachers may share opinions about possible instructional strategies to remediate student learning issues. Such collaboration must be based on mutual trust in which colleagues can learn from one another, often recognizing that someone else may have a solution to a problem that another teacher may lack. It is about leaving the ego at the door and being open to input from others. Means and colleagues (2010) found that only 90 percent of schools report that educators feel comfortable collaborating this way and 59 percent know how to work with colleagues. As Mason (2003) notes, using data in classrooms is essential but it has not gone far enough. What also is needed is time for teachers to learn from each other about instructional strategies for particular problems. Thus, the collaborative process promotes shared responsibility for student learning.

A data team is a composite of individuals within a school who are tasked with collaborating to collect, analyze, and interpret data. Data teams learn to focus on and talk about data collectively. A team also is tasked with helping to increase the data literacy among other educators within a school, using a turnkey model. A turnkey model means that one educator trains other individuals, who in turn, train even more people. Data teams take various forms. They can be horizontal collaborations, that is, teaming at a grade level or a course level. They can be vertical, with teams across grade levels. They can be content-based, grade-based, course-based, or other forms of logical teaming. Data teams also can occur across schools within a district (Datnow et al., 2007).

Data teams help to think through the data that are needed to inform practice, often aligned with school improvement plans. They consider where to focus inquiry and the data they need. Thus, the team can impact planning and processes of data use throughout a school. Beyond the obvious data collection and analysis activities expected of data teams, these collaborations can be made responsible for developing common assessments, data-supported action plans, evaluating prepackaged data systems and tools, and helping to communicate results to other staff and stakeholders (Love et al., 2008). They help to supply the administration with the needed data for communication with parents and the community (Long et al., 2008).

Love and colleagues (2008) recommend that data teams spend at least forty-five minutes per week working together in what they term "protected" time. This time is maximized through three principles. First, the work of a team will be facilitated through the identification of a common purpose. Second, there must be clear objectives, measurable goals, defined roles and responsibilities, distributed leadership, and clear sets of questions to guide action (Hamilton et al., 2009; Lachat & Smith, 2005). Wayman and colleagues (2010) describe the need for common understanding, goals, and aims with shared conceptions reached through a process called "calibration." Finally, there should be an agreement to discuss the "undiscussables" (Love et al., 2008). That is, there are topics that are difficult and perhaps even embarrassing, but they must be put on the table for progress toward achieving continuous improvement to be made. Data teams also have other responsibilities and roles within a school. They may be responsible for data quality and for responding to data requests from other staff (Lachat & Smith, 2005).

Reflect on Leadership and Data Teams

How is data leadership in your school and district organized?

Where are the leaders?

Who are the leaders?

Where are there gaps?

Where are they in the leadership framework?

How are data teams formed?

Who makes the selection of the members?

What are the data team members' responsibilities?

Establishing a Data Culture

Leadership, data coaches, and data teams are key components in the establishment of a data culture. Earlier chapters and parts of this chapter have touched on the importance of these components and related issues. We now turn to some specific aspects about data cultures, such as issues of time, skills, collaboration, and the provision for formal structures that support institutionalizing data cultures. For the purposes of this discussion, we use the definition of a data culture drawn from the IES Practice Guide (Hamilton et al., 2009) since we both helped to define it:

> The data culture is a learning environment within a school or district that includes attitudes, values, goals, norms of behavior, and practices, accompanied by an explicit vision for data use by leadership, that characterize a group's appreciation for the importance and power that data can bring to the decision-making process. It also includes the recognition that data collection is a necessary part of an educator's responsibilities and that the use of data to influence and inform practice is an essential tool that will be used frequently. (p. 46)

Love and colleagues (2008) outline seven steps needed for developing a data culture:

1. enculturate the notion of continuous improvement;

2. build support from stakeholders;

3. strengthen collaboration;

4. empower a data coach;

5. organize a data team;

6. create time for collaboration; and

7. provide timely access to data.

We discuss some of these ideas in more depth under the structures section.

Setting the Stage

Two issues loom large as data use becomes enculturated into a school. The first is the kinds of data that educators want to use and have available. The second is the skill set that is part of the inquiry cycle of data use.

Kinds of Data

We have already discussed sources of data. The literature makes very clear the importance of using multiple sources of data (Datnow & Park, 2010; Hamilton et al., 2009; Long et al., 2008; Love et al., 2008). Using multiple sources of data is a fundamental principle of measurement. The more forms of data, the more accurate will be the information extracted from the data.

Take, for example, a student, Smackie, who takes a standardized test and was either ill or tired on the testing occasion. The resulting score may not truly reflect Smackie's understanding of the material. But including other sources of data will enable the teacher to gain a more comprehensive picture of what Smackie knows or does not know. Another common example is what to do with conflicting data. Often teachers are confronted with sources of data that tell a different story, perhaps the state summative test and more local assessments. Taken separately, no simple measure gives an adequate picture of the student. The triangulation, or bringing together of these multiple sources of data, is an effective data use strategy (see Figure 5.1).

Kinds of data vary. Love and colleagues (2008) outline a pyramid of data in which annual state summative assessments are at the top of the structure and classroom activities are at the base. In the middle are intermediate and more frequent assessments such as benchmark, formative, common, and diagnostic tests. Data other than assessments also can be used to form a comprehensive picture of a student's performance. For example, Long and colleagues (2008) describe a data warehouse in which a variety of data are housed and used for decision making. These might include demographics, attendance/absences, behavioral transgressions, health-related data, and familial circumstances. Knowing if the student has extended absences, suspensions, illnesses, or

Figure 5.1   Triangulating Multiple Sources of Data

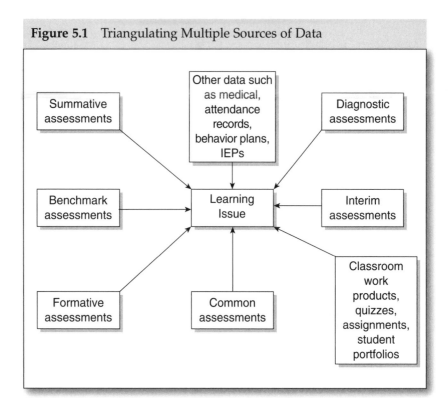

problems at home can provide valuable contextual informa-tion for a teacher and for schoolwide use of data.

Also of importance are the characteristics of the data in terms of utility. Mandinach, Honey, Light, Heinze, and Nudell (2005) describe some of these characteristics that make a dif-ference in how the data can be used. The one on which we focus is the timeliness of the data; that is, the feedback loop between time of administration and time of delivery of the data. We refer to state summative tests as producing DOA or autopsy data. By this we mean that there is a substantial delay in the feedback loop that makes the data less informative and useful to the teacher. Typically, testing is in the spring and the data reports are delivered in the fall for the new school year. This lag diminishes the utility of the data. In contrast, there are diagnostic data that can be delivered immediately to the teacher so that instructional strategies can be modified on the spot (Hupert et al., 2008). One might refer to these data as akin to periodic checkups.

The U.S. Department of Education (2010a; Gewertz & Robelen, 2010) is encouraging the development of new kinds of assessments that will ultimately replace the traditional model of tests. The new tests will assess complex skills and deliver results in a more timely manner. Time will tell what these assessments will look like and how they will impact the timeliness and utility of the data delivered to teachers.

Inquiry Cycle

Data teams, through the process of collaborative inquiry, implement a cycle of inquiry that becomes a regular part of school procedures. Armstrong and Anthes (2001) refer to this as part of the school improvement cycle in which data are used to solve problems and improve process. In earlier chapters, we discussed the various frameworks for data-driven decision making. Halverson, Grigg, Prichett, and Thomas (2005) outline six steps that schools use to work through data: (1) data acquisition, (2) data reflection, (3) program alignment and integration, (4) instructional design, (5) formative feedback, and (6) test preparation. Love and colleagues (2008) also note that schools can be organized around short cycles of collaborative inquiry to identify questions and seek solutions. They see data as the means by which to test assumptions and construct an understanding of students.

Collaborative inquiry requires certain skill sets and knowledge. First, teachers must acquire data literacy and collaborative inquiry skills. We have discussed at length the need for data literacy. Collaborative skills are also key. As we have noted, much data inquiry occurs in data teams or professional learning communities. Thus, it is important for educators to know how to effectively work with one another. Teaching is not a solitary occupation any longer. Second, teachers must have content knowledge, or pedagogical content knowledge (Shulman, 1986). Mandinach (2009a, 2009b) refers to the intersection of these two sets of skills as pedagogical data literacy— the ability to translate data into actionable instructional knowledge. Data literacy without the pedagogical components would mean that the teachers are able to look at the data and understand average performance or outliers. Pedagogical data literacy takes this a step further to help the teachers determine what are the appropriate instructional actions that need to be aligned with the student performance data. As Whitaker and Young (2002) note, teachers must be able to align data with instruction strategies and the curricula in ways that will produce the desired learning objectives. Third, it is helpful to understand and be sensitive to cultural proficiency (Love et al., 2008). Cultural proficiency means that teachers are aware of and take into account, through sensitivity, the differences across students and groups of students in terms of language ability, background, ethnicity, and other relevant demographic factors that may influence student performance and attitudes. Finally, data teams and data coaches must have leadership and facilitative skills. Think back to our previous comments on the importance of leadership and collaboration.

Reflect on Your Skills

Can you engage in collaborative inquiry?

Do you have data literacy skills?

Do you have pedagogical data literacy?

Do you understand cultural proficiency?

Where are there gaps?

What do you need to do to acquire the skills?

The Process of Enculturation

The creation of a data culture is about educators assuming internal responsibility for data use and collaborative inquiry for continuous improvement (Love et al., 2008). Datnow and

Park (2009) outline a six-step process for enculturating data within a school:

1. a foundation for data-driven decision making must be laid;

2. continuous improvement must be emphasized;

3. an information management system must be incorporated;

4. the right data must be selected;

5. capacity must be built; and

6. data must be analyzed and acted on to improve performance.

Enculturation is based on the notion that inquiry is an essential component of professional practices. The goal is a shared vision and understanding of objectives and strategies. Wohlstetter, Datnow, and Park (2008) and Datnow and colleagues (2007) note the need for explicit norms and expectations with measurable objectives in which there is an assumption that decisions will be made from the use of data. Further, school staff must develop an understanding of how data can be used to inform practice (Mason, 2002). Through iterative cycles of inquiry, educators must use data-informed questions to stimulate the process of continuous improvement (Copland et al., 2009; Mason, 2002). It is about matching the right solutions to the right questions. Part of the enculturation process is the sharing of data and strategies across teachers and even schools with a developed culture of trust and security (Datnow et al., 2007; Love et al., 2008). Educators need to know that it is both okay and safe for them to share information without the possibility of negative consequences.

What we have been talking about is developing schools into learning organizations (Ingram et al., 2004; Senge, 1990; Senge et al., 2000). Data-driven decision making is a fundamental principle of learning organizations across fields. Schools and districts are no different.

Some Questions

What are the essential elements of a data culture?

- Strong leadership and a vision for data use
- The provision of needed resources such as common planning time
- The provision for a data coach and a data team
- The provision of technology tools to support data-inquiry

What elements does your school have?

What elements are lacking in your school?

What other needs do you have to support data inquiry?

What needs to change?

Where are your sources of support?

Needed Structures

Structures are resources and supports that undergird the data culture. Without these structures, it would be very difficult for data use to take hold in a school. Perhaps the three most important structures found throughout the literature are provision of time for data inquiry, the need for collaboration, and the building of human capacity.

Time

Time is an educator's four-letter word. There simply is not enough of it. School calendars are structured with little flexibility to make changes. There is a perception that asking educators to use data will take more time. The payoff, however, is likely to be more effective time spent planning and implementing instruction, based on credible data from which to make decisions once data-driven inquiry has been enculturated and internalized. That is, the return on the investment of time spent is better structured instruction and more intimate knowledge of one's students. For some educators, data-driven decision making is seen as a tradeoff between data use and teaching (Ingram et al., 2004). Ingram and colleagues (2004) report that schools simply have not made the changes needed to integrate data use. How can data inquiry be integrated into a schedule that is already full and also constrained by union regulations that often restrict required meetings beyond typical school hours? This is true of meetings, but one could argue for the individual teacher, data-driven decision making should and must become part of the professional repertoire of skills and methods. Over time and with increased experience, data use will become a fully integrated part of teachers' practice.

There is no question, however, that time is an impediment. Mandinach (2009a, 2010, 2012) has asked educators about the challenges to data-driven decision making. Almost unanimously, respondents reported that the biggest problem is the lack of time. Lack of time involves a variety of interconnected issues and problems, such as:

- time for data meetings and collaboration (Datnow et al., 2007; Ingram et al., 2004; Lachat & Smith, 2005; Symonds, 2004; Wayman, Snodgrass Rangel, Jimerson, & Cho, 2010);
- the need to restructure the school day to incorporate such meetings (Armstrong & Anthes, 2001);
- teachers having to meet on their own time (Wayman, Cho, et al., 2010);
- the need for time to plan (Wayman, Snodgrass Rangel, et al., 2010);
- a lack of time for reflection (Means et al., 2010); and
- a lack of time to use data (Wayman, Snodgrass Rangel, et al., 2010).

In spite of the constraints of time, teachers find time for using data. Means and colleagues (2010) found that 78 percent of the teachers examine data on their own and 71 percent meet in teams. Finally, there is little remuneration for data work. There are few if any instances of teachers being paid for data work. Obviously there is some overlap here, but time is an issue. In contrast, Ingram and colleagues (2004) found more group decision making than individual decision making. Thus, the lack of time is both collaborative and an individual issue. And Means and colleagues (2011) found that data teams can compensate for the lack of individual data literacy.

Collaboration and Time

As we have emphasized, collaborative meetings to analyze and discuss data are absolutely essential. Teachers need time to come together around data. Schools must make provisions for shared time for collaboration (Wayman, Snodgrass Rangel, et al., 2010). There needs to be structured opportunities to reflect and discuss data and potential instructional strategies as well as share successes and failures (Symonds, 2004). Meetings are a time to receive constructive feedback from colleagues and share strategies. This might even include visiting and observing other classrooms to learn from colleagues.

Data team meetings are the most prevalent collaborative opportunities (Hamilton et al., 2009). There are formal meetings of collaborations in grade, content, or other groupings as described earlier. Other strategies include discussing data in full faculty meetings and convening data retreats (Halverson et al., 2005). Schools need regular, planned time for data inquiry. These processes may begin with standing professional learning communities and evolve into sources of data-driven decision making through regular weekly meetings. These should be formal, but they can also be informal and impromptu (Wayman, Snodgrass Rangel, et al., 2010). Wohlstetter and colleagues (2008) have noted the use of weekly, structured meetings in which topics around data are discussed, as well as daily planning meetings within grades and courses. This speaks to the need for organized structures at both the school and district levels to provide the support for collaboration. Educators will be left to use data on their own, making it all the more difficult to achieve enculturation.

Human Capacity

Schools and districts need to make provisions for helping their staff acquire data literacy. Principals typically are the first to learn to use data (Mandinach & Gummer, 2011) and then the teaching staff. Data coaches and data teams get trained and can use a turnkey model to help colleagues to use data. That said, there should be an emphasis on hiring teachers, principals, and district administrators who are data literate. Armstrong and Anthes (2001) report the need to provide supportive structures for such training.

As noted in Chapter 4, this could be accomplished through allowing staff to take formal courses, bringing in professional training providers, designating key internal staff to provide the professional development, or using a turnkey model within a school. As noted previously, ongoing and continuous professional development is preferred rather than a single event (Means et al., 2010) that can be integrated as an integral part of the collaborative time. As a cautionary note, the professional development must not be piecemeal. It must be well considered, avoiding uncoordinated workshops.

Wayman, Cho, and colleagues (2010) report the need for structured and differentiated training. This means that training should not be haphazard but implemented in a manner that meets the needs of the educators. It should also be customized according to grade levels, course content, and other relevant factors that may affect how data practices are carried out. The authors also note the need for modeling good practice. This means that the trainers should model good data-driven practice and instruction during the course of the professional development activities. They identify training on data skills, collaboration, and goal setting. For data coaches and data teams, there also needs to be training on how to lead data discussions with other staff. Hamilton and colleagues (2009) list several kinds of differentiated training, including teachers, principals, technology specialists, and other staff. The opportunities should be immediate and explicitly applicable to practice.

Other Structures

Other structures also have been identified. Related to the human capacity issue, hiring practices can be modified to include data expertise (Datnow et al., 2007; Long et al., 2008). Districts can begin to make hiring decisions in favor of applicants who are data literate and show a proclivity toward data use. We have seen districts that apply data use as a screening technique, particularly for principals.

An Example

The Charlestown School District hired a new superintendent who is very much focused on data. Mr. Polo begins to integrate a data culture throughout the district, stressing the importance for all administrators and teachers to use data to inform their practice. Openings for principals' positions emerge over time. In the hiring process, it is made clear that all candidates must be fully data literate and willing to establish data use in their schools. A large part of the hiring decision is based on the candidates' willingness to embrace the vision for data use and spread it in their schools. The same process for hiring also was used for teaching. Data has become encultured throughout the district, with new administrators and teachers reflecting the vision of Mr. Polo.

Of course the provision for technologies is important (Copland et al., 2009; Hamilton et al., 2009; Wayman & Stringfield, 2006). There is no way that educators can keep pace with the increasing amount of data. The technologies also should be varied (Wayman et al., 2007), provide timely access to the data (Armstrong & Anthes, 2001), and have the appropriate characteristics (Mandinach, Honey, Light, Heinze, & Rivas, 2005). That is, they should be accessible, comprehensible, flexible, have a reasonable feedback loop, have aligned data to classroom needs, and have a link to instruction.

Finally, incentivizing educators to use data may be an effective support (Hamilton et al., 2009; Mason, 2003). Money is always good, but there are other possible incentives, such as release time from a course. Schools need to be creative in these times of economic constraints.

Some Questions

What incentives have been provided by your district?

For teachers?

For principals?

For central administrators?

What incentives do you think would be helpful?

Consider both intrinsic and extrinsic incentives.

Caveats

With any potentially positive opportunity, there are always challenges and caveats that balance out the effort (Mandinach, 2009a, 2009b). Armstrong and Anthes (2001) note that one of the biggest challenges is helping teachers to understand how to align the data to instructional practice. As we have noted, data-driven decision making is more than just examining numbers or statistics. It is about transforming the quantitative and qualitative data into actionable knowledge. This is a very important issue. Data are meaningless in and of themselves. We must help educators to understand what to do with them to inform their practice. We also must help educators to become savvy consumers of data so that they can discern good data from erroneous data, thereby minimizing the misuse of data. This goes back to the human capacity issue.

Ingram and colleagues (2004) note cultural, technical, and political challenges to data use. The establishment of data-driven practices is not easy, especially if people are skeptical or resistant. Technical challenges refer to human capacity, technology, and having the needed infrastructure. Political challenges refer to the difficulty of enculturating a philosophy of education that may be costly or even counter to the leadership and vision.

Wayman, Snodgrass Rangel, and colleagues (2010) raise some other issues. A first is the issue of resistance. Some educators may find data-driven decision making too hard, too time consuming, or too labor intensive. This may diminish with experience, increasing expertise, and confidence in the data-driven inquiry process. They must know it works to be convinced to expend the time needed to integrate it into practice. They also found that principals are many times not prepared to help in the data-driven process. Finally, they raise a concern about the disconnect between teachers and principals' expectations. They found that principals often say one thing and do another, and teachers cannot articulate what the principals expect them to do. This is a major communication issue.

Mandinach (2010, 2012) and Long and colleagues (2008) also have observed challenges. The most pervasive challenges identified are the lack of time and the lack of human capacity around data-driven decision making. Another issue is the disconnect between the emphasis on summative assessments and the need for more instructionally valid data sources. Thus, there has been a move toward the use of formative assessments that are better aligned to teaching and learning (Arkansas Department of Education, 2007; Goertz et al., 2009a, 2009b; Heritage, 2007, 2010a, 2010b).

Reflect about your CHOPS. What are they? What are the biggest hurdles to overcome?

Time?

Compensation?

Lack of human capacity?

Poor leadership?

Lack of recognition?

No colleagues with whom to collaborate?

Too much emphasis on accountability and not enough on student learning?

No vision for data use?

Tests not sufficiently aligned to the curriculum?

Resistance from staff

What are some others?

CONCLUDING COMMENTS

Enculturating data-driven decision making is not easy. It requires many necessary components to make it work. It takes an explicit vision and leadership to reinforce that vision. It takes committed leadership from the superintendent and principals, as well as distributed leadership within schools. It takes a fundamental infrastructure that includes the technological tools to support data-driven decision making, as well as data literacy among the staff. We have discussed many of the support structures and resources that facilitate the development, implementation, and sustainability of a data culture.

It is not easy, but it may get easier with time and experience. It may be labor intensive and require the expenditure of money, time, and effort. The data-driven inquiry process is not about reinventing the instructional wheel. It is about helping educators to think more deeply and strategically about how instructional decisions are made. Mandinach (2009a, 2009b) has spoken of balancing the challenges and the opportunities. The list of challenges may be long and perhaps even daunting. This is the reality check. The list of opportunities, however, may be much shorter, but it is meaningful and important. Educators need to, want to, and must use data to inform practice. The objective is clear. Using data is about helping all students to learn and achieve. It is about using data to capitalize on students' learning strengths and remediate their weaknesses. It may not be easy at first. It will become easier with time. Ultimately, it must become part of educators' daily repertoires of tools and methods. Data-driven decision making can and will make a difference. Education can no longer rely on gut feelings and anecdotes. Remember, without data, you are only an opinion. And with bad data? Education must be evidence-based and informed by appropriate data. It is our hope and expectation that all educators will be armed with data to inform their practice as a regular component of their work. Then there will be true enculturation, based on the ability to build a culture that values data-driven instruction and practices. It would be a culture that recognizes that, with time and experience, data-driven instruction and inquiry becomes an embedded part of practice, not an add-on that takes time away from actual teaching. It becomes an integrated process where data inform instruction.

CHOPS

What challenges and opportunities currently exist for supporting a culture that values and effectively uses data to inform instruction and improve student learning? How do these challenges and opportunities relate to key ideas expressed in this chapter? For example, do they represent:

Strong leadership?

The use of data coaches?

The use of data teams or other collaborating groups?

Time for collaboration?

Involvement of other stakeholders?

What are the challenges to creating or sustaining a data-driven culture?

How can opportunities provide solutions to some of the challenges?

How can meeting the challenges provide new opportunities?

SOME HIGHLIGHTED REFERENCES

Datnow, A., & Park, V. (2010, May). *Practice meets theory of action: Teachers' experiences with data use.* Paper presented at the meeting of the American Educational Research Association, Denver, CO.

Datnow, A., Park, V., & Wohlstetter, P. (2007). *Achieving with data: How high-performing school systems use data to improve instruction for elementary students.* Los Angeles, CA: University of Southern California, Center on Educational Governance.

Knapp, M. S., Swinnerton, J. A., Copland, M. A., & Monpas-Huber, J. (2006). *Data-informed leadership in education*. Seattle, WA: University of Washington, Center for the Study of Teaching and Policy.

Lachat, M. A., & Smith, S. (2005). Practices that support data use in urban high schools. *Journal of Education for Students Placed at Risk, 10*(3), 333–349.

GLOSSARY

Data culture—An environment within a district or school that espouses the importance of using data to inform practice. The environment contains attitudes and values around data use, recognized behavioral norms and expectations to use data, and objectives for why data are to be used, informed by a district-level or school-level vision for data use.

Data team—A group of educators in a school or in a district that is designated to collaborate, examine, and use data to inform practice, and help other educators to use data in effective ways.

Distributed leadership—The idea that leadership in a school does not reside solely in the principal, but that management and leadership can be disbursed across a number of educators to create a shared sense of ownership, responsibility, and leadership.

6

Building a Culture to Use Data[14]

In this chapter we focus on how to use data for school-wide collaborative inquiry, the kinds of data that are used for continuous school improvement, and how teachers use data for making decisions about instruction to improve student learning. The concept of collaborative inquiry is fundamental to the use of data. Recall that Means and colleagues (2011) found that teachers working collaboratively showed evidence of greater data literacy than individual teachers. They can compensate for the lack of individual skills and knowledge. Collaboration has many benefits, but it must be supported by school leadership through a comprehensive vision for how data are to be used. A vision helps to guide how data are expected to be used. Therefore, without a clear vision, using data may be unsystematic and lacking effectiveness.

As noted in earlier chapters, schools need leaders with a clear vision for data-driven decision making (Hamilton et al., 2009). A strong vision that has widespread support sets the stage for which data are to be collected and how data are to be used. Leadership in schools should consider identifying educators who are knowledgeable about data use to facilitate data teams. Resulting from the vision is the need to support sustained professional development that provides administrators and teachers the opportunities to gain experience with and knowledge of how data can be used to inform instruction and for other decisions as well. Thus, the vision should include opportunities for professional learning around data-driven practices and training on the use of data systems that support the analysis of student learning data to inform instruction. The data systems must be able to integrate and supply multiple sources of data elements that are reflective of the vision, including student learning, school process, demographic, and perception data as well as administrative, teacher, course, disciplinary, transportation, attitudinal, and other sorts of data. Finally, structured time for collaborative discussion can facilitate sustained examination of the kinds of data that teachers can use to accurately and efficiently identify learning problems and inform instruction.

ORGANIZING FOR COLLABORATIVE INQUIRY AND DATA USE

The following section outlines the components that are important for the creation of a data culture based on collaborative inquiry and data use. Love and colleagues (2008) provide a training manual on the essential elements for the creation of data coaches and data teams. The intent here is to provide an overview of these elements, grounded in research. What the reader will notice is how interconnected the elements are and how they relate back to many of the issues discussed previously in this book.

A recommendation of the IES Practice Guide on data-driven decision making (Hamilton et al., 2009) states that there should be an explicit vision for how data should be used throughout a district and in schools. The vision typically includes provisions for a data coach and a data team. The data coach serves as a facilitator and mentor to other educators. The data team members may include school leadership and classroom teachers. It may be possible to include support professionals to provide input as a way to develop a shared vision with stakeholder involvement and support for effective school and district data use.

Data Use and School Vision

As we have noted previously, a vision for data use is an essential component for data-driven decision making to be enculturated within a school or district. Support for effective data analysis and interpretation relies heavily on the vision school and district leadership have for data use in schools and classrooms. School leaders must provide the essential conditions for making the vision happen. As noted in Chapter 5, the conditions include providing for structured time for data work, data coaches, data teams, and professional development opportunities. Structured time provides opportunities for collaboration. The data coach can carry out the vision for data use throughout the school with the assistance of a formal data team. Data coaches and data teams mirror the school's vision for data use. They should consider identifying group norms for collaborative discussions to ensure data transparency—that is, that the data are accessible and accurate. Teachers can analyze and interpret data to identify ways by which to improve instruction that are aligned to the vision and without concern for negative or punitive outcomes. This is especially true if a district is using data as the means by which to evaluate teacher performance. Teachers in classrooms need to be able to work with the data coaches as trusted advisors to help support their data use to meet the district's objectives without fear of retribution.

An Example

Mr. Schwarzkopf discusses in a data team meeting that he is having difficulty finding a way to help a particular student. This student, Bentley, has been struggling, and he has tried several instructional approaches with no success. Through Mr. Schwarzkopf's admission that he has been unsuccessful, he is seeking help from other data team members for possible successful solutions. Yet, if someone reports this lack of success to an administrator, who then uses that information for evaluative purposes, Mr. Schwarzkopf is not likely to be as forthcoming, trusting, and collaborative in the future. There should be no penalties for being open about needing help from colleagues in data team meetings.

How does such openness work in your district? Is there trust among colleagues? Is there fear of retribution?

Strategic Planning

Being planful about how data are to be used will facilitate a smoother integration of data-driven practices than if a school simply jumps right in without sufficient forethought. A strategic plan requires input from all relevant stakeholders and potential users. It should outline how data are to be used and how the plan is aligned with the more comprehensive school improvement plan.

A strategic plan will help data team members adopt and implement action steps for collaborative inquiry and professional learning that focus on critical teaching and learning concepts. The framework or plan can be strengthened by developing a shared understanding of key data; that is, the data that are needed to inform all sorts of practice. The shared understanding can minimize misunderstandings and increase the efficiency of data use (Wayman et al., 2007; Wayman, Midgley, & Stringfield, 2006).

The strategic plan is an important determinant for how schools will triangulate among different sources of data to support teaching and learning. The goals for data use should be attainable, measurable, and relevant to broader school and district objectives (Halverson et al., 2007; Hamilton et al., 2009; Leithwood, Louis, Anderson, & Wahlstrom, 2007), and the data must be reliable and valid. Further, the IES Practice Guide recommends that there is a written plan with four components (Hamilton et al., 2009). First, the plan should include action steps that are needed for instructional data-driven decision making. Second, the roles and responsibilities of data team members should be identified. Third, there should be a timeline for the strategic plan. Finally, the plan needs to specify how the action steps address the school's long-term objectives.[15]

A Strategic Plan for Data Use

Digit High School seeks to improve its dropout rate.

Action 1: Identify the indicators that are linked to the probability of dropping out.

Path to the Goal: Staff at Digit examine various data points to determine their relationship to dropping out or graduating.

Action 2: Two indicators are identified with the closest link to dropping out—number of freshman absences and number of freshman course failures.

Path to the Goal: Staff begin to identify students who are deemed at risk, based on the two indicators.

Action 3: Administrators at Digit develop remediation plans for students who have been identified as at risk, based on the two indicators.

Path to the Goal: Data are collected about the at-risk students over time to see if the remediation strategies are decreasing absences and course failures.

Action 4: Mid-course modifications are made based on additional data collected about the indicators and the outcome of the remediation strategies.

A strategic plan is not something set in concrete. It must be flexible, based on the changing needs and context of the educational environment. Once it is has been developed, there is a need for periodic review to determine its continued relevance to and alignment with school and district goals (Wayman et al., 2007). Implementing the plan is a formative and cyclical process in which the school and data team are actually using data-driven decision making to inform and modify the plan according to emerging needs.

Data Coaches and Facilitation of Teaming

The data coach is an integral part of helping a school and its educators use data in effective ways and carry out the strategic plan. Data coaches assist colleagues to integrate data use into the school, create collaborative data teams, and model effective data use (Lachat & Smith, 2005; Love et al., 2008). These individuals serve as facilitators by mentoring other teachers in the collection, analysis, and interpretation of data. They also identify professional learning needs of teachers. Data coaches should be able to motivate colleagues to use a data inquiry process as an integral part of improving teaching and helping students to master learning outcomes. This means knowing how to transform the data into actionable, instructional steps.

Data coaches tend to be experienced educators, content specialists, administrators, department leads, or educational consultants. They have to know how to use data and how to create conditions for effective data use in the classroom. This means helping teachers to reflect on improving teaching practices by collecting and preparing a variety of data, interpreting and developing hypotheses about how to improve student learning, and modifying instruction as needed (Hamilton et al., 2009). The coach works with teachers, using data to support school-level goals. The coach can help teachers to build their capacity to make instructional decisions by creating plans for improving student achievement.

Coaches, in collaboration with administrators and teachers, can help to create a safe environment for data use in which teachers do not fear using data to make decisions. They can provide assistance in terms of collecting and interpreting data as part of the data use cycle (Hamilton et al., 2009). One of the primary responsibilities of a data coach is to plan meetings and lead the data team in collaborative inquiry (Love et al., 2008).

In an ideal world, the responsibilities of the data coach can be shared. Different educators can and should assume leadership through a rotation of roles and responsibilities. This sharing will build increased and distributed capacity across a number of individuals so that the sole responsibility for data use within a school does not reside with one person. The broader the distribution of leadership, the deeper data use can become, the better institutionalized, and sustained. Given the mobility rate among educators, developing a model of distributed leadership can help to sustain data use in a way that would not be possible with only one data leader.

Examples of Successful and Unsuccessful Data Coaches

Ms. Staci understands how to use data. She also is good at establishing rapport and working with others. Ms. Staci is able to model how data can and should be used. She knows how to transform data into instructional action. She is adept at working with other teachers, helping them to understand the instructional ramifications of data inquiry. Ms. Staci also can help train other educators to use data. She patiently works with others and explains to them the meaning of a data analysis and its potential for improving instruction.

Ms. Jazz also knows how to use data. She is considered by her colleagues to be a "data nerd." That is, Ms. Jazz always is tinkering with numbers and taking pleasure in looking at data. What Ms. Jazz does not do, however, is communicate well with colleagues. She gets impatient with others who do not immediately grasp the essence of a data analysis. She expects them to "get it" just like she "gets it." As Ms. Jazz's frustration increases, the other educators in her building become less likely to see her assistance.

Both Ms. Staci and Ms. Jazz know data, but a key to being an effective data coach is more than just being a data nerd. It is about being a mentor to colleagues and communicating effectively to help them improve their data literacy.

Motivating Analysis and Use Data

There are many ways to motivate educators to analyze data and validate interpretations about student learning. Districts can provide structured time for professional development to teachers, administrators, and support staff. They can offer continuing education credits, graduate credit, degree programs, stipends, and honoraria. They can also provide technology solutions, online mentoring, access to experts, online courses, certifications, leadership roles, support staff, and school-based training. These resources can serve to incentivize educators. The outcome can be seen in an increased willingness and capacity to engage in data-driven practices.

There are also intrinsic motives for data-driven decision making. Educators participating in data teams tend to be more willing to engage in the collaborative process, sharing information, and exhibiting data literacy skills (Means et al., 2011). In fact, teachers' self-efficacy and collective efficacy improve when they believe they can impact student learning in a positive manner (Woolfolk Hoy, Hoy, & Davis, 2009). Teachers become part of the process, rather than pawns in a process, thereby increasing their sense of professionalism.

Data Literacy

What is data literacy? We see data literacy as the ability to use data to inform practice, whether as a classroom teacher or an administrator. Data literacy is about transforming the data into actionable knowledge. Recall that we defined pedagogical data literacy in an earlier chapter. Data literacy is one's knowledge about data-driven decision making. The inclusion of the pedagogical component is the merging of educators' data skills and knowledge with their understanding of pedagogical content knowledge (Shulman, 1986) so that they can apply their data and pedagogical literacy to facilitate instructional change. A parallel can be drawn for administrators who apply their knowledge of administrative functions, in conjunction with data skills, to inform their practice.

A data coach must model data literacy to help teachers attain an understanding of terminology and potentially effective uses of data. A fundamental part of data literacy is for teachers to understand not just the uses of data, but also the limitations of using certain types of data for different reasons. It is about knowing the right tool for the right task. For example, a nurse does not choose a pair of pliers to remove a splinter when a tweezers will suffice. Similarly, a diagnostic item tied directly to the curriculum is a better gauge of understanding than a NAEP assessment or even the total score on a state summative measure. Part of pedagogical data literacy is for educators to understand the importance of using multiple sources of data, to drill-down to the item level to examine performance, and to be able to transform the data into actionable knowledge of how to differentiate instruction for students with varying needs (Love et al., 2008; Mandinach et al., 2008). Refer back to Table 4.1 that outlines the thirteen high-capacity data use strategies. These are actions fundamental to data literacy. Also refer back to Table 4.2 that summarizes the skills hypothesized in various theoretical frameworks as essential to data-driven decision making. These skills form the foundation of data literacy.

There are many definitions of data literacy. Mandinach (2009a, 2009b, 2010) has spoken widely about the need for pedagogical data literacy, or the need to transform data into actionable instructional knowledge. Hamilton and colleagues (2009) define data literacy as "the ability to ask and answer questions about collecting, analyzing, and making sense of data" (p. 47). Based on the current literature, this was the definition agreed upon by the panelists who wrote the IES Practice Guide. Because data-driven decision making is an evolving field, no doubt the conceptualization of what it means to be data literate will also continue to evolve. Even the skills and knowledge may also evolve as the field matures. But they are the fundamentals of data literacy that will always be with us.

Examples of measurement-related skills might include: (1) the ability to determine if data are drawn from valid and reliable instruments, (2) the ability to determine how much error there is in an instrument, (3) understanding the limitations of instruments, and (4) determining if the interpretation made and the data use are appropriate. These fundamentals won't change when the ways we conduct measurement change. The analyses, uses, and interpretations will only be as good as the tools or instruments from which the data are collected.

Contrasting High and Low Data Using Schools

As an example, we highlight two middle schools in the same large urban district in Alabama.

Leo Middle School is in the downtown section of the city. Its students are diverse and from lower-income families. The school is led by a data-minded principal who wants all of his teachers to use data. The principal, Mr. Turbo, has appointed a data coach and there are grade-level and course-level data teams. The data teams regularly meet to discuss student outcomes and to examine student performance. The teachers highlight particularly challenging student cases in these meeting, trying to understand what strategies might help these students. Teachers feel free to share possible strategies with their colleagues. There is an open and trusting culture that follows Mr. Turbo's vision for data use.

Libra Middle School is in an affluent section of the city. Its students are less diverse than the prior school. Mr. Quincy, the principal, has no vision for data use. In fact, when one asks the faculty if there is a data culture in the school, teachers shrug and say that they do not regularly look at any data. They get the state summative test scores, but those results do not influence what they do instructionally. Teachers do not discuss student performance in collaborative settings, and teacher meetings are rarely used to discuss test results or instructional practices. When asked if they use data to inform their practice, teachers, such as Ms. Pepper, respond by saying that it is not something they typically do because Mr. Quincy does not communicate any importance to data use.

Questions

What lessons can be drawn from these schools?

What changes might you make in the schools?

Schoolwide Action Planning Through Teaming

The data use planning process should involve all stakeholders. It should be aligned to the performance objectives for the school and be informed by the school's overall improvement plan. As noted previously, the principal should identify data coaches or data facilitators who have a solid foundation in instructional data analysis and interpretation, the ability to motivate others, and the skills to use data for improving instruction. The data coaches and the data teams work with school leadership to develop and implement an action plan. The work of the data coach facilitates the enculturation of data use throughout the school.

There are essential conditions for establishment of a data culture. There should be ongoing training of school-based data coaches and facilitators and periodic grade-level or content area team planning meetings. As has been noted, teachers need dedicated and structured time for collaborative discussions about data analysis and interpretations. It is also helpful if there are external professional development opportunities available, in addition to having internal personnel providing training. Not every school district has an in-house expert that can deliver the kinds of professional development that are needed. Districts may need to hire external expertise to assist in data training. For example, very small schools or districts may lack the internal staff and must seek help from professional developers or experts that can work with their educators.

School-based data teams use a collaborative inquiry process to identify critical teaching and learning concepts. They develop actionable plans with measureable goals and identify testable hypotheses. Teams can also stimulate teachers to explore new ways to help students learn through discussions among colleagues that seek to identify learning strengths and weaknesses. For example, the Shadow Elementary School data team has identified that their students are struggling with phonemic awareness. The data coach, Ms. Lisel, may bring together the teachers of the relevant grades and their literacy expert to first examine the data and try to understand what skills the students are lacking and how pervasive the problem is. The team may drill down to items and student work products to examine trends in student performance. Ms. Lisel then can facilitate a discussion about potential instructional strategies with which some teachers have had success and that the team members are willing to try with their own students. Ms. Lisel will reconvene the team to examine data on a periodic basis to monitor progress and modify instructional strategies further if needed.

Based on our experiences, when teachers collectively use a systemic data inquiry process to analyze and interpret student data, they no longer work competitively and in isolation. They instead discover ways to share information and support one another. They have access to a much broader range of innovative instructional strategies to solve student learning challenges, create student-centric learning environments, and exceed the learning needs of all students.

Do you work in isolation or collaboratively with other educators?

Do you prefer to work alone, behind the closed doors of your classroom to solve the problem of a challenging student? Or do you prefer to consult with other teachers to see if they have also encountered similar problems, and if so, how did they solve those problems?

Are you willing to share successes and challenges with your colleagues?

Do you have a data coach who can help lead you through this collaborative process?

Forms of Data Use for Teachers

We have mentioned different kinds of data throughout the book. These data also can be reported in different ways to facilitate interpretation. For example, aggregate, disaggregate, and item-level data all have different uses and interpretations. Assessments such as summative, formative, diagnostic, interim, and benchmark are used continually during the data inquiry process by teachers to provide them with opportunities for validating interpretations of evidence of actual student performance. Curriculum and assessment technologies that display these data enable teachers to gain a deeper understanding of the learning standards and develop stronger curricula, instruction, and assessments for classroom use. Such understanding can be used to target instruction based on an individual student's knowledge of core concepts.

The instructional inquiry cycle can provide teachers with feedback loops of data from various measures of student learning data to assist them in testing hypotheses about student performance. Feedback cycles can provide rapid responses to inform instruction by testing hypotheses through a process that includes identifying student learning issues, verifying causes of the problem, generating instructional solutions, implementing actions, and monitoring outcomes (Love et al., 2008).

Summative Assessments and Technological Advances

Summative assessments are assessments *of* learning (Nichols & Berliner, 2007; Stiggins, 2005). They provide a summary or evaluation of what students have learned. They occur at the end of a unit of study, quarter, or school year. Most often, teachers assess students by giving tests, quizzes, writing prompts, student portfolios, and lab activities. They assign letter grades or scores to measure student achievement and are related to an expected state standard. Many times, teachers and administrators determine the effectiveness of a program and whether their school is achieving AYP on state improvement goals used to compare schools and districts for accountability purposes through the examination of summative data. State summative assessments are primarily designed to provide data to administrators, teachers, and parents about student achievement based on state curriculum learning standards. Educators often question the utility of these assessments to help them modify their instructional strategies.

Districts administer annual summative assessments to students typically during the third quarter of the school year. These assessments create a situation in which teachers feel compelled to focus enormous amounts of classroom instruction on rote memorization of facts and test preparation to meet accountability targets prior the testing. The results of the state assessments are made available to classroom teachers, administrators, and parents during the fall of the next school year on published school report cards. They deliver autopsy data in fixed reporting formats. This creates a problematic situation. Teachers are unable to create useful queries, graphs, or reports for comparison purposes from these fixed formats. The results therefore are not particularly useful in providing information as part of an assessment and instructional feedback cycle that can inform or modify daily teaching and student learning activities. Taken alone, these data may not be particularly useful for instructional purposes. However, examined with other data sources, teachers can triangulate among different forms of data to provide a more comprehensive picture of how students are performing, which can lead to instructional modifications. The closer the data are to the instruction, the more informative the data can be in terms of determining instructional next steps.

Technology to Support Assessment Data

As noted in Chapter 3, technological applications are being developed to support the use of assessment results and data-driven decision making. Data systems and mobile computing devices can help districts and schools implement technology-based assessments. These systems and assessments can provide more timely data so that teachers can make instructional modifications as needed, rather than with substantial delays. The tighter the feedback loop between instruction and assessment, the more informative the assessments will be in helping to make instructional adjustments (Mandinach & Snow, 1999).

Technology-based assessment systems provide graphical displays, query capabilities, and analytic tools. They have the ability to generate reports about teacher instruction and student learning to monitor results. The reports can be useful for understanding areas of strengths, weaknesses, trends, and patterns of achievement. They can be used to identify students and subgroups that need additional support or specific interventions, and for setting schoolwide, grade-level, content area, classroom, or departmental goals, and developing action plans based on student performance.

Some assessment technologies assist educators in using summative results. For example, the technologies can provide comprehensive reports with drill-down capacity so that teachers can examine results at different levels and at different levels of aggregation. They can produce individual reports, whole class reports, reports for different subgroups of students, and at the level of entire tests or subsections. However, evolving technologies are beginning to emphasize interim assessments. Assessment technologies that focus on more frequent measures give teachers the ability to transform the teaching and learning process. They provide immediate access to standards-based curriculum and assessment results that are administered in regular intervals with rapid feedback cycles.

What summative assessments are administered in your school?

How are the data from these assessments used to improve instruction and learning?

Formative, Diagnostic, and Interim Assessments

Formative measures are assessments *for* learning (Heritage, 2010a, 2010b; Nichols & Berliner, 2007; Stiggins, 2005). These assessments enable teachers to use the results to modify instruction and student learning to encourage continuous learning on a daily, weekly, or monthly basis. Data analyses and interpretations of formative assessment results seek to empower teachers to modify instructional methods based on real-time data with rapid feedback cycle loops to inform classroom practices. The data can have an immediate impact by customizing feedback to meet individual student learning needs soon after the assessment has been completed. Teachers can use diagnostic assessments on a daily basis to determine students' learning deficits and to structure a remediation strategy to address the learning weaknesses. They provide specific diagnoses of what skills or knowledge students have or lack. Such data are used to inform frequent instructional changes based on results that identify the individual needs of students. These assessments focus on individualizing instruction to ensure students are achieving to the best of their ability and not on high-stakes summative accountability testing administered after learning has occurred.

How do you use formative assessments?

Do you use formative assessments in your classroom?

Does your school use formative assessments?

How are you integrating formative assessments into your practice?

Teachers are not the only users of formative assessment data. Students also are part of the process. They should monitor their own progress using such assessment data to manage and modify their own performance. Teachers should involve students in a collaborative process of setting goals in which students receive timely, specific, and constructive feedback on assignments to help them understand their performance and ways to improve (May & Robinson, 2007). This is the second recommendation in the IES Practice Guide (Hamilton et al., 2009). Most students have the ability to monitor their own progress. In doing so, they transition from being passive to active learners. Formative assessment informs the students, as well as the teachers, about learning progress, and can provide personalized instruction and guidance to support the customization of students' learning needs.

Interim assessments are tests that are given within a school or across schools in a district at scheduled intervals over a school year. The purpose of these assessments is to monitor progress over time. Interim assessments have an added advantage. They can be used and compared across content areas and grade levels due, in part, by the frequency of use by teachers. These assessments help teachers to reflect on the effectiveness of their instructional practices and curriculum alignment through item analysis. They can help teachers to monitor the progress of their students throughout the school year, identifying areas of weakness and strength to optimize instructional effectiveness by providing results and progress in achieving mastery of outcomes related to standards.

For example, a teacher can identify a problem with students who are struggling with three-column addition, as determined by a common school-level interim assessment compared across grade levels. The data teams can then collaboratively discuss targeting students with different learning styles or profiles. They can facilitate small-group instruction using base ten math manipulatives activities to provide hands-on, concrete experiences for building a conceptual understanding of place value to address the students' needs.

Given the frequency of these interim assessments, teachers working together in data teams can triangulate data by comparing multiple measures of common assessment data to analyze and identify student learning needs. They can share and reflect on practice as critical friends. This process helps teachers to reflect on their instructional practices based on evidence from student assessment results to determine the effectiveness. Teachers in data teams can share ineffective instructional practices and develop agreement on common feedback strategies of student work samples as well as proven instructional strategies based on research and data-driven evidence. These results can be used to facilitate group discussions to ensure students receive the academic and developmental support needed to accelerate achievement.

It is essential for classroom teachers to have access to and examine multiple measures of assessment data. Such analyses of performance data can help to stimulate student learning and performance. Interim data can be used to measure instructional effectiveness, reflect on ways to improve practice, and provide insights for ongoing data team discussions. The key for teachers is to recognize which data to use for what purposes, noting that all sources of data have validity for different uses and interpretations. Some data are more instructionally valid than others, but the triangulation of data sources and forms of data is an essential component of data-driven decision making (Love et al., 2008).

Valid Uses of Data: Comparing Valid and Invalid Uses[16]

The SAT is typically used, among other data, by college admissions officers to make decisions about which students to admit to their colleges or universities. Yet, in many cities and towns, the SAT is seen as a proxy for the quality of a school district. The assumption is that the higher the SAT scores, the better the school district. Therefore, real estate agents use SAT results to sell property, saying that the better the SAT scores, the higher the property value. The use of the SAT for admissions purposes is a valid use of the data. It is the reason the test was developed. The use of the SAT, as a proxy for real estate values, is not a valid use of the test. It most likely was not an intended purpose in the development process of the test.

The lesson to be learned here is that data must be valid for the purposes for which they are intended, reliable, and practical; that is, they must be useful and informative. Having bad data may be worse than having no data at all. The key for educators is to be able to determine if data are good or bad, and then make their interpretations on the good data, and use the bad data with appropriate skepticism and caution.

Other Sources of Data

Assessment data are not the only forms of data that are relevant to inform educational practice. Other forms of data may include: (1) demographic; (2) accountability; (3) special program; and (4) financial, personnel, programmatic, and administrative data, among other sources (e.g., school profiles). We briefly touch upon four categories of those data sources and their uses.

Student and school demographic data include information about the composition of students being served by a school or district. For example, a data warehouse might include the number of registered students, the ethnicity of the students, the languages spoken and language status, gender, date of birth, parental information, and the like. Related data might include attendance figures, absences, excused absences, and enrollment figures. Mobility might fall within this category, including first day of enrollment, transfer, withdrawals, reentries, and a stability rate. Demographics also might include suspensions, demerits, and behavioral referrals. For example, when analyzing the impact of a new reading program, it is important to examine not only student progress in the program by performance measures, but to also analyze the attendance rates of students in relation to program outcomes.

Schools and districts are required to collect substantial data for accountability purposes. *Accountability data* are required by state and federal regulations and are delivered to state departments of education on a periodic basis. The data are then transferred to a national repository for education data, called ED*Facts*. There are hundreds of data elements required for collection, but not all are relevant or readily useable at the local level. Perhaps the most important data elements for a district are graduation and dropout rates. Other important data may be special status data such as English Language Learners, special education, and free and reduced-price lunch status percentages.

Special program data can help educators to understand the special needs of their students. For example, it is important for teachers to know if their students have learning disabilities, are eligible for Title I, require exceptional education programs, or qualify for gifted and talented programs. These data can help teachers by providing essential background information about their students. Similarly, it is important for teachers to know the home status of their students. All kinds of background data can be informative for teachers to provide essential contextual information about a student. For example, it is important to know if there is an incarcerated parent, a single-parent family, if the student is the sole supporter of the family, if a student is a single mother, if there has been family or child abuse, if there have been substantial behavioral or legal transgressions on the part of a student, or if there have been medical issues within the family or on the part of the student. These sources of data can be combined or triangulated with other data to form a more comprehensive understanding of students.

Administrative, personnel, programmatic, course, and financial data can inform practice at the school and district levels. Personnel data are those about the staff, such as teacher credentials and licensure information, degrees, years having taught, and certifications. Programmatic data might include data about the performance of new interventions, curricula, or programs. These data sources all provide different kinds of information to users. They typically are made available based on the role the educator plays within the district. Course data refer to those that provide information about course offerings and common course identifiers.

Supporting Teacher Data Use

Adopting a systematic framework for implementing the data inquiry process can help teachers to develop an understanding about how to use multiple sources of data about student achievement. Several frameworks have been described in previous chapters. The common theme among these frameworks is their cyclical or iterative structure (see Figure 6.1). Data are collected and interpreted based on hypotheses, which in turn inform how instruction or other decisions can be made. The actions are implemented and then examined for impact. The outcomes are assessed in terms of the need for additional steps that are needed and subsequent actions taken.

Figure 6.1   Cyclical Process of Instructional Decision Making

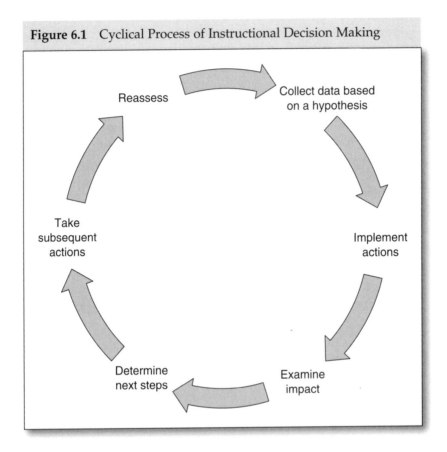

The cyclical process informs how educators handle decision making. Every student comes to school with different learning experiences, and it is the responsibility of the teachers to use a variety of data to identify the best ways to help each student demonstrate mastery of learning outcomes. Just as a doctor examines a patient to gather a variety of data to monitor growth and diagnose diseases, illnesses, or injuries, teachers should instruct, assess, collect, analyze, interpret, monitor, and triangulate a variety of data about student learning and performance to monitor growth and identify learning needs through the cyclical data inquiry process.

The data process is impacted by the ability of educators to access the needed data and then know what to do with the data once they have been obtained. Many school districts now have data systems that provide teachers access to a variety of data about student performance. However, teachers must be trained on how to use the systems to examine data and determine what data to access. This data process is facilitated by the development of hypotheses about ways to improve student learning. Teachers and administrators then create testable hypotheses about learning to increase student achievement, how to use data to set learning goals, and how to modify instruction based on evidence. They may then need to access additional information and reexamine their thinking about the hypotheses. Take for example the dropout rate problem discussed previously. In that example, educators hypothesized that part of the cause for dropping out was related to excessive absences and course failures. If the district was able to find ways to keep the students in school by making the instruction more interesting or relevant, the student might also be less likely to fail their courses. As remediational strategies are put into place, additional data can be collected and modifications to the strategies made.

Collecting, Preparing, and Examining Student Learning Data

Teachers need to consider the strengths and limitations of data types when collecting, preparing, and examining student data. For example, summative assessments occur at the end of a unit of study, quarter, or the school year. They are primarily designed to provide data about achievement or performance after instruction has concluded. The state results are based on curriculum standards in fixed reporting formats after students have progressed to the next grade level. These summative data may have utility, but they may not be the most informative for instructional purposes. The data are seen as measurement of the culmination of learning, rather than to inform the process of instruction.

Such annual assessments can provide useful information about trends, patterns, and student achievement progress of subgroup populations over time and in relation to state standards.

The item analysis of specific skills on annual assessments can reveal gaps in student learning across grade levels, schools, districts, and the state that need to be addressed by data teams and for school-level goal setting. When used as the only form of data upon which to make decisions, however, these assessments become high stakes.

Data analysis and the interpretation of multiple summative and formative assessment results can help teachers to focus on specific questions they might have about student learning. This comprehensive evaluation process also can assist in prioritizing the types of data teachers need to gather for further analysis to identify student learning problems, verify causes, identify patterns, and provide instructional solutions (Herman & Gribbons, 2001; Huffman & Kalnin, 2003; Lachet & Smith, 2005; Supovitz, 2006). These data not only provide evidence of what is missing, but also what is working to meet standards or can be improved to exceed standards.

Interpreting Data and Developing Hypotheses

Classroom-level performance data can help to identify students' strengths, weaknesses, and readiness levels. These data can be used to evaluate subgroup progress and determine which students or groups of students need additional support of interventions (e.g., response to intervention). Useful classroom data include a variety of sources, such as written work, projects, presentations, classroom responses systems, in-class work, homework, attendance records, online coursework, behavior plans, and IEPs. These are data that teachers already have and regularly use to make decisions.

Hypotheses or teachers' critical questions about student learning can help to identify possible ways to improve student learning by using ongoing assessment data to verify whether or not teachers need to make instructional changes. For example, looking at a variety of schoolwide and classroom-level data, teachers can identify if the proficiency levels of students are rapidly declining or increasing as they attempt to master a specific concept. The data can help determine curricular alignment. There could be an increased number of test items about the concept on the annual summative assessment. Teachers might hypothesize that realigning the school curriculum by creating instructional materials to include relevant activities to address the topic in a different way will increase student understanding and mastery of the content. Examining the data can help to validate the hypothesis or critical questions and determine future curricular and instructional modifications.

Developing a Hypothesis and Following It Through

Ms. Kaycie, a social studies teacher, is helping her students to understand the nature of conflict throughout history. She has her students select a conflict on which to report. Students select the American Revolution, the French Revolution, the U.S. Civil War, World War I and II, the Vietnamese War, and the Gulf War. The idea that Ms. Kaycie is trying to get across to the students is the systemic nature of conflict and that there are many similarities among all of these historical events. Students only view the conflicts as isolated events in history, rather than based on common principles. Ms. Kaycie develops a few critical questions about why the students are failing to grasp some of the common factors, and then initiates some classroom activities to illustrate the similarities between, for example, why the American colonists revolted and why the French stormed the Bastille. Students begin to understand some of those common ideas and apply them to other conflicts in history.

Summing Up

Organizing for collaborative inquiry and implementing a vision for districtwide and schoolwide data use requires substantial work and dedication. Given the potential for improved student learning, many policy makers and others feel that the data-driven practices must now be implemented throughout the educational system (Blue Ribbon Panel, 2010; Duncan, 2010a, 2010b; Easton, 2009). Yet a balance must be struck. Like many professions, there is always an art and science to teaching or leading in education (Gage, 1978). There must be a balance between the science and rigor of using data and the art of applying experience.

For effective data use to occur in a district, school, or in a classroom, a number of components must be in place. And note that much of our discussion has been at the classroom level. But classrooms are embedded in schools that are embedded in districts. The components of data-driven decision making cross levels of a school system. They have been discussed here and in previous chapters. In particular, there must be a vision for data use, leadership, a systematic process for data inquiry, and an ongoing cycle of instructional improvement. Communication and collaboration among educators is a key element in this process. This process also runs across groups of educators and teams of educators. Communication and data teaming provide teachers with structured time to work together and create plans for how they will ultimately improve student achievement. Data team meetings provide opportunities for teachers to collectively analyze, interpret, and discuss the data needed for making instructional modifications likely to improve student learning outcomes.

Schools leaders need to provide dedicated and structured time for data teams to collaborate. Teachers working together in data teams create and test hypotheses about student learning. They reflect on the instructional effectiveness of teaching solutions and diagnose and solve student learning issues with the invaluable input from classroom teachers. Teachers share student learning experiences and instructional insights during the data inquiry process. They evaluate the effectiveness of instructional interventions throughout an ongoing and cyclical process in which they collect, prepare, analyze, and interpret a variety of data to confirm or challenge evidence of student learning and mastery.

These are fundamental steps to effective data use, along with the development of an explicit vision at both the district and school levels, the creation of a data team at the school and possibly the district level as well, the designation of a data coach, and the slow and ongoing process of institutionalizing a data-driven culture. As has been noted in previous chapters, educators should be provided professional development opportunities on an ongoing basis. The data-driven process must be supported by resources provided by school and district leadership. The process is complex and labor intensive, but the potential benefits make it all worth the time and effort.

Some Fundamental Steps and an Implementation Plan

Create a vision for data use

Make the vision explicit

Develop or purchase technology tools to support data-driven decision making

Appoint a data coach

Develop a data team

Provide appropriate training and professional development

Provide common planning time

Encourage data use throughout the district or school

Create incentives for data use

Make hiring decisions based on educators' ability to use data

OUR HYPOTHETICAL SCHOOLS

Transforming Learning and Teaching Through Data-Driven Decision Making: Low-Performing Subgroup Population

The Maximilian Elementary School has been dealing with enrollment issues. Rather than attending their own local schools, Maximilian has been receiving students from underachieving, overpopulated, and low socioeconomic areas. This trend has been a concern for educators and the community. These conditions have resulted in emerging weaknesses at

Maximilian in reading, mathematics, and writing proficiency based on annual state tests, as well as on interim and benchmark assessments.

In preparation for the incoming numbers of students, the principal of Maximilian, Ms. Ethel, hired additional classroom teachers who have experience in coaching for effective data use, and improving literacy, math, and writing skills. Ms. Ethel selected a data coach, Mr. Frederick, with a proven track record of achieving student performance gains with subgroups and solving student learning problems based on evidence and collaborative action planning. The foci of Mr. Frederick's efforts for the new school year included collaborative action planning, systemic data use, intervention strategies, progress monitoring, and implementing best practices grounded in research in each of the traditional curriculum areas.

Maximilian's classroom teachers were unfamiliar with the process of using data to systematically monitor student progress and customize instruction according to the needs of each student. The teachers also were reluctant to spend time in collaborative planning meetings. Time was a major challenge. The teachers then began to work with Mr. Frederick to share effective strategies for data use and formative assessment strategies that involve making modifications to instruction based on student performance trends. The data use process began to evolve and become much more meaningful.

Mr. Frederick worked initially with teachers in grade-level teams to identify key weaknesses in third- and fifth-grade writing skills with students, creating narrative essays. Based on an analysis of state and other test results and the development of testable hypotheses, teachers collaboratively reviewed writing samples to develop a common understanding of student performance (both ideal and real), graphic organizers, and writing checklists. The teachers developed scoring rubrics with clear expectations to be applied across grade levels. As a result, students received consistent feedback from classroom teachers about their writing skills. The feedback was clear and constructive advice on what was needed to improve.

The computer teacher, Ms. Beamer, has supported classroom instructional efforts. She has demonstrated to students how to use word processing software, graphic organizers, and how to create their own portfolios of writing samples to examine growth.

Teachers facilitated classroom writing communities with structures and organization that help to support the students. They created structured time for writing. The teachers provided the students with good samples of effective writing, allowing students to work together during the drafting and revision process. Students therefore were able to share their texts with one another as they wrote, during mini lessons, response groups, and sharing sessions.

After the third-quarter progress reporting period, results indicated that third-grade students had increased from 80 percent to 94 percent in writing proficiency; fifth-grade students had increased from 87 percent to 98 percent in writing proficiency on the annual high-stakes state test results. Similar improvements were noted on more local tests. Maximilian Elementary School saw dramatic improvements in students' writing performance, even with the addition of the low-performing subgroups of students from neighboring schools. More important, grade-level teams of classroom teachers saw substantial improvement in students' writing ability that carried through to the end of the school year in action planning meetings.

At the beginning of the following school year, Mr. Frederick, Ms. Ethel, and Ms. Beamer met with teachers to identify professional development needs based on a variety of data about student learning profiles. Teachers were given an option of professional development opportunities being provided on site by internal trainers. Graduate credit was offered as an incentive. The graduate courses that the teachers selected were based on two books, *Best Practice: Today's Standards for Teaching and Learning in America's Schools* (Daniels, Zemelman, & Hyde, 2005) and *Methods That Matter: Six Structures for Best Practice Classrooms* (Daniels & Bizar, 1998). The participating teachers were able to learn about promising practices that they could implement in their classrooms.

The power of structured teaming, professional learning opportunities, a systematic data use process, clear goals for action planning, and data analysis can be seen in the gains in writing that began to occur at Maximilian in the previous school year. Teachers continued to work in grade-level and content area teams to conduct ongoing analyses of a variety of performance data. Ms. Ethel, her leadership team, and Mr. Frederick at Maximilian have used weekly meetings to provide extended times for teacher teams to meet, and to create improved learning opportunities for students by explicitly discussing instructional challenges and solutions in collaborative settings.

It had been a full school year since students from neighboring schools entered Maximilian Elementary to relieve the overcrowding in their neighborhood schools. Now teachers feel more confident in implementing school improvement strategies and formative assessments that enable them to make adjustments to their teaching in response to assessment evidence. Students receive rubrics to understand expectations and clearly articulated constructive feedback about their learning with advice on what to do to improve (Black & Wiliam, 1998b). Teachers receive the support of Mr. Frederick, the data coach.

Ms. Ethel held a two-day school improvement planning institute during the fourth quarter of the second school year with all staff members of the school. The administrative leadership team including Mr. Frederick and the literacy and math coaches worked closely with Ms. Ethel to organize classroom teachers into grade-level and content-area teams. These teams systematically analyzed a variety of assessment data about student learning to identify areas of strengths and weaknesses. The reason for identifying strengths and weaknesses was for everyone to see what needed less attention and to create more of a focus on the skills on which students were struggling.

Teachers worked during the institute in teams to analyze a variety of assessment evidence and student work from which they created testable hypotheses. They noticed, however, that there were no common or interim assessments being used to monitor student progress in reading and mathematics on a quarterly basis. So, they decided to systematically use common assessments developed by the district during a previous administration. Teams of classroom teachers aligned the assessments to daily instruction. They also used the assessments in their plans to monitor student progress.

Teachers co-created thematic project-based learning units that integrated all content areas and grade levels. These units provided relevant experiential learning opportunities to motivate student learning with embedded assessments for monitoring progress. A wide range of teaching strategies were integrated into project-based learning activities to address student learning needs such as:

- oral presentations with props;
- narrative, expository, and persuasive essays;
- original poetry slams;
- classic books discussions with interpretive questioning;
- science experimentations;
- research papers;
- rebus stories;
- original works of art;
- musical performances and skits; and
- math problem-solving activities.

Additionally, after teachers and coaches reviewed individual student achievement relative to learning standards in reading for students in grades 3 through 6, they decided to administer schoolwide literacy assessments for every student at the beginning of the following school year. Early literacy assessments would provide a baseline for literacy skills at every grade level to monitor student progress quarterly. For additional support, the district purchased and made available early literacy assessment software on a mobile device. This software provided quick and accurate results, easy-to-interpret reporting, and analyses with targeted teaching activities. Teachers were further supported because the software could link to the district's data system and to the web. It provided additional resources, such as graphical representations, reporting and analysis tools, and links to appropriate instructional activities.

The Maximilian Elementary School data and literacy coaches worked closely with the district to receive training on the early literacy assessment administration. They created distributed leadership and professional learning models throughout the school. These structures helped to ensure that classroom teachers were empowered to lead action planning and data team meetings to maintain a systemic approach to the formative, common, and diagnostic assessments and data use.

During the last day of school, the improvement institute teams of teachers and coaches brainstormed about intervention strategies for solving student learning problems. These problems were identified by using the various sources of assessment data. Teachers wanted to know which instructional intervention strategies were the most effective in producing learning gains. The data are helping the educators to understand their students' performance and helping them to structure subsequent instructional steps. Maximilian is a success story in terms of creating a culture of data use.

Lessons Learned From Maximilian Elementary School

What lessons can you draw from this hypothetical school?

What does it tell you about collaboration and data teaming?

What resources did Ms. Ethel provide to the school to support data inquiry?

What services did Mr. Frederick provide as the data coach?

How did Maximilian integrate multiple sources of data into practice?

How did Maximilian use technology to support data-driven decision making?

Did Maximilian implement a cycle of inquiry?

Were professional development opportunities offered to the teachers?

Were coaches involved in the data inquiry process?

Were data applied and linked to a strategic plan or a school improvement plan?

Were the interventions implemented based on research evidence?

How did students become their own data-driven decision makers?

Was Maximilian able to sustain its data work?

Data Wars, Mixed Messages, and Course Corrections

The Gryffin School District in central New Jersey has been struggling with data, educators are confused, and there have been recent leadership changes. A few years ago, Gryffin had a superintendent who was very much data-minded. Ms. Delilah was a long-term leader who established the idea that using data is important. She helped to raise money for the development and implementation of a district data warehouse, student information system, and assessment system. Her staff, administrators, and teachers knew that data were important. Most educators were on board and followed Ms. Delilah's lead. They were using data, some more effectively than others, but they were using data.

Ms. Delilah's idea of data use was to use all sorts of data, not just state achievement data. She wanted the staff to have a comprehensive picture of each student, not just their performance data. So teachers and administrators began to use attendance data, behavioral data, health data, attitudes, and other sources of data that might help them understand the students. The principals, who had access to the data warehouse, were charged with leading the process of examining data. The teachers had access to the assessment system so that they could create and administer tests and then examine the results.

Unfortunately, nothing is permanent in education. Ms. Delilah was forced to take a medical leave of absence that ultimately turned into retirement. The acting superintendent, Mr. Rudy, replaced her. After two years with the new regime, there was an apparent new and different philosophy and direct messages to the staff. Because of achievement gap issues in Gryffin, recent declines in performance, and a high mobility rate among students, Mr. Rudy's emphasis became one of a total focus on raising the level of proficiency, as measured by the state achievement tests, particularly for the students closest to the cut scores. The message had come down from the school board that actions must be taken to achieve AYP at all cost. It wasn't that he didn't care about the extremes, but he wanted the students at the upper end of the "partially proficient" group to move up to "proficient" at all cost. Students who were found to be at the low end of the "partially proficient" group or "advanced proficient" increasingly became less and less of a focus for the teachers.

To try and meet Mr. Rudy's emphasis, Gryffin's technology coordinator, Ms. Joy, was asked to work with the data system vendor to develop a new component for the data warehouse that aligned curricula with test item coverage. This component analyzes the item coverage in the state assessments and estimates potential performance increases if teachers focus on improving particular skills. Teachers were directed to use this tool around which to structure their instruction. For example, if teachers focused on reading comprehension, they could maximally expect a 17 percent gain in test scores, or a focus on vocabulary might bring an 11 percent gain. Teachers began to play the game—if I focus on X, my score with rise Y percent. The alignment component of the data warehouse became every teacher's best friend. Teachers began to structure their instruction solely around what topics would achieve the biggest potential gains in test scores.

Some students benefitted from this approach, but others suffered. Some students who had been deemed "proficient" the year before regressed. Some "advanced proficient" students did not perform as well. Little improvement was observed among the students most at risk.

Teachers soon became frustrated at the apparent all-consuming focus on teaching to the items and components of the tests, to the detriment of their students. They felt that they were no longer providing instruction, but instead were involved in data-driven test preparation. They had little class time for enrichment activities, to help students at the extremes, and no flexibility in their instruction.

An additional constraint emerged from district administration when Gryffin began discussing the possibility of linking student performance to teacher evaluations. Gryffin's administration presented this as a way of motivating teachers to improve instruction and student performance. The calculation that the district was going to use was, again, focused on the state assessments, and not any other tests or other metrics. Teachers became afraid for their jobs. The teachers' union began to consider its options. Suddenly the whole idea of using data to inform practice was being turned against the teachers—to hold them accountable, based solely on a single test score. Gryffin's administrators also became concerned because they did not want to a create a situation of such pressure that educators were forced to take dire measures like what happened in the Atlanta cheating scandal (Samuels, 2011; Severson, 2011), where educators actually changed students' answers to increase performance because they felt such pressure to produce high levels of student performance.

A positive result was that Gryffin vowed to not become another Atlanta. The district began to rethink its districtwide improvement strategy. It hired an educational expert, Dr. Beauregard, who was brought in to help Gryffin think through what is really important for its students, teachers, and stakeholders. Dr. Beauregard began helping the district consider the importance of meeting the needs of all students, not just a subset of students at the expense of others. She helped Gryffin think through the kinds of data that would be most informative for them to meet their evolving objectives. This included the use of multiple sources of assessments, not just the state summative tests. It also included attitudinal data, process data, and perceptions. Dr. Beauregard suggested professional development to help administrators and teachers understand how to use data to inform the kinds of decisions they need to make. She also suggested other ways to improve the working environment to help educators achieve their goals, without fear of retribution or job loss, including the introduction of working teams of educators and more purposeful uses of the data warehouse.

Gryffin had taken a wrong turn, but it is now changing course. The district may well be in the position to make some fundamental philosophical changes, midcourse corrections, and be on the road to improving the system for its students, educators, and its community.

Lessons Learned From the
Gryffin School District

What lessons can you draw from this hypothetical district?

How does Gryffin differ from Maximilian?

What challenges did Gryffin face and how did the district handle them?

What could the administration at Gryffin do differently?

What do you think will happen at Gryffin going forward?

How could Gryffin have made better use of data?

What sorts of data should Gryffin have considered using?

What could the district have done to better support the teachers?

CHOPS

What challenges and opportunities currently exist for using data? How do these challenges and opportunities relate to key ideas expressed in this chapter? For example:

Does your school provide time for collaboration?

Is collaboration expected? Encouraged? Discouraged? Not allowed?

Does your principal and/or superintendent make explicit a vision for data use?

Are there resources to support data use?

Do you receive conflicting messages about the importance of data use?

Is there a strategic plan for data use?

Do you have a data coach? Is that coach effective in helping others to use data?

Have you received any professional development around data use?

Do you have access to technological tools to support data-driven decision making?

SOME HIGHLIGHTED REFERENCES

Herman, J., & Gribbons, B. (2001). *Lessons learned in using data to support school inquiry and continuous improvement: Final report to the Stuart Foundation* (CSE Technical Report 535). Los Angeles, CA: UCLA Center for the Study of Evaluation.

Leithwood, K., Louis, K. S., Anderson, S., & Wahlstrom, K. (2007). *Review of research: How leadership influences student learning.* Minneapolis, MN: University of Minnesota, Center for Applied Research and Educational Improvement.

Stiggins, R. (2005). From formative assessment to assessment FOR learning: A path to success on standards-based skills. *Phi Delta Kappan, 85*(4), 324–328.

Wayman, J. C., Cho, V., & Johnston, M. T. (2007). *The data-informed district: A district-wide evaluation of data use in the Natrona County School District.* Austin: The University of Texas.

GLOSSARY

Collaborative inquiry—The process by which groups of educators come together to pose questions or hypotheses, collect and examine data, and use the results to inform their practice.

Formative assessments—Tests that can provide feedback to educators are periodic intervals so that the feedback can inform the teaching and learning process and allow the educators to make appropriate modifications to instruction.

Hypothesis—An assumption or question posed in order to examine its accuracy or its logic, based on the collection and analysis of data and evidence.

Reliability—The consistency of measurement. For example: (1) the same test given twice should yield the same results; (2) two observers, looking at the same activity, should see and rate that activity the same way; or (3) that different groups of items to measure the same concept should yield the same results.

Strategic planning—The consideration of long-term objectives and determining steps, over time, that will achieve those goals.

Triangulation—The bringing together of disparate sources of data or information.

Validity—The extent to which a test or work product measures what it purports to assess. Validity is not only a property of the test but also of the interpretation and use of the results.

7

Differentiating Instruction Using Formative Assessments[17]

Differentiating instruction is a fundamental concept in education. The premise is that teachers provide different forms of instructional methods, materials, and assessments for different students based on their cognitive, affective, physical, and cultural needs. The concept is not new. Differentiation focuses on differences in readiness, interest, opportunities to learn, and other factors. It has been called many things over the years such as adaptive instruction (Corno, 2008; Snow, 1980) and is similar to the notions of aptitude treatment interactions (ATI; Cronbach, 1957; Cronbach & Snow, 1977). In ATI, students with different aptitudes have been found to respond differently to different instructional methods. Higher ability students may perform relatively better than lower ability students with certain instructional paradigms. In contrast, lower ability students may benefit relatively more from different forms of instruction than higher ability students, thus causing an interaction effect. With differentiated instruction, it is contingent upon teachers to determine which students may perform better with which types of instruction, thereby differentiating how instruction is delivered in the classroom according to individual and group needs.

Using data to inform differentiated instruction is central to the teaching and learning process. It is essential to collect a variety of data about student learning that will inform how to determine instructional steps. Teachers must interpret the data to develop questions about how to improve student learning, analyze the multiple measures to verify causes of learning problems, and modify instruction to test solutions to increase student learning (Hamilton et al., 2009). They must align the data with individual students' needs to be able to map out a course of instruction appropriate to each student.

Teachers should use data to determine their own instructional strengths and weaknesses, adjusting instruction to fit students' diverse needs. When reviewing student performance on lessons, homework, activities, quizzes, or quarterly examinations, teachers should identify how many and which students failed to understand a particular skill or concept. The teacher must decide what to do next when determining whether or not students have learned the concepts or attained understanding of the desired knowledge during the instructional and assessment process.

Multiple forms of differentiated assessment data should be used to identify instructional problems and determine appropriately aligned solutions for differentiation according to the learning needs of the students. These assessments should be aligned to the standards and the curricula. The standards, particularly now with the movement to Common Core Standards (see http://www.corestandards.org/) help teachers identify priorities for instruction. Frequent formative assessments can be used to diagnose students' learning deficits and to determine whether or not learning goals have been achieved. Data from the assessments can serve as a roadmap to guide instructional actions, serving as powerful resources to inform the instruction and assessment cycle (Supovitz & Klein, 2003).

FORMS OF DIFFERENTIATION

Instructional differentiation is a whole class approach. In this section, we explore some of the ways that data can be used to inform instruction for both small groups and individual students. We provide examples of differentiated instructional practice.

Using Data for Small-Group Instruction

Effective classroom teachers use formative and differentiated assessments on a frequent basis to structure instruction. The combination of instruction aligned with formative assessments creates feedback loops that can be used to identify students' learning gaps, inform planning, and guide instruction. The objective of this cyclical process (see Figure 7.1) is to

Figure 7.1   Cycle of Instruction, Assessment, and Data Inquiry

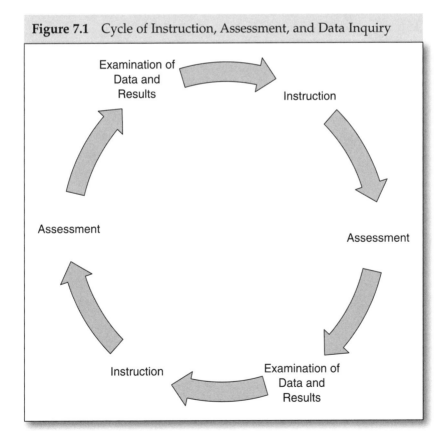

increase achievement by providing constructive suggestions on ways by which students can improve their learning related to the standards.

Teachers collect and examine a variety of measures. These measures include not only formative assessments but also summative, interim, benchmark, and diagnostic measures. Teachers then analyze the data, interpret the results, verify the hypotheses, and group students according to ability levels for differentiating instruction. During small-group instruction, teachers and students can work together to identify differentiated learning needs based on evidence from the assessment results. Teachers constantly adjust instructional practices, structuring learning opportunities to expand the skills and knowledge of students. They monitor progress using a variety of assessments. This section provides an example of how using data to differentiate small-group instruction can be implemented.

An Example

In the Peebles School District in Nevada, Mr. Houdi groups his fifth-grade students according to performance levels on the state summative reading assessment. He verifies the causes of student learning problems using a school-level common benchmark assessment before placing them into reading groups. During instruction in small groups, Mr. Houdi works with three students (Gracie, Rosemary, and Annie) who are at the same skill and ability level to examine their current fluency assessment data in relation to the standards and benchmarks. Mr. Houdi discusses their assessment data to let Gracie, Rosemary, and Annie know they are below level for their grade. He uses a bar graph to demonstrate where they need to be and explains that working together in the small group, with daily practice afterwards, will help them improve their fluency rate. This will help them to achieve their goal of fluency proficiency for their grade level.

Mr. Houdi discusses with Gracie, Rosemary, and Annie their strengths and weakness to set learning goals. He provides them with explicit instructions about the targeted knowledge and skills they will acquire if they work hard, pay attention to instructions, and practice reading aloud daily in teams. Mr. Houdi shows the students a description of the reading selection for the session. It includes an embedded mis-cue analysis note-taking assessment that he will use for the guided reading instruction to monitor their progress during each of the small-group sessions. Mr. Houdi models the guided reading passage to ensure that the students have a clear understanding of what they are to do and how they are to perform. He demonstrates reading strategies such as pausing after punctuation to increase the rate of fluency, interpreting meaning from a reading passage, and reading with expression based on the characters' actions in the story.

Gracie, Rosemary, and Annie begin by taking turns reading the passage aloud three times, pausing for specific feedback from Mr. Houdi on ways to improve. Before reading the passage a fourth and final time, Mr. Houdi provides constructive feedback on how to increase their fluency rates as well as models how to read with expression by interpreting the characters' emotions. He also dis-cusses how the students might feel if they were in the same situation in the story. The three students become motivated to read aloud and realize that during the final reading of the passage, Mr. Houdi is tak-ing notes to assess the progress of their small-group session. Mr. Houdi discusses the students' noticeable improvement in fluency rates, reading expression, and comprehension. He then solicits their feedback on what they need for continuing practice that focuses on pausing for punctuation, reading with expression, and slowing down their reading rate. Mr. Houdi and the students agree on the goals for the next session and identify the next reading passage that will be used for daily practice during their classroom group meetings.

This example shows that the teacher customized his instruc-tion to the specific needs of the two students. He worked with them in a small-group setting, monitoring their progress through the use of various sources of data. The original assign-ment to the small group occurred because of the students' level of performance and reading ability. That is, the teacher differen-tiated the group assignment and instructional remediation based on the learning needs of these particular students.

As can be seen from the example, students can become engaged and prepared to learn in small groups when they have sufficient understanding of the skills they need to acquire and are given specific, targeted, and constructive feedback about how to master those skills and concepts. The data that support such feedback ensue from frequent formative assessments to monitor strengths and weaknesses that provide ways to empower students as self-directed learners (Black et al., 2003).

When teachers use formative assessment data to help inform their work with their students, role changes occur in the instructional process such that students become partners in learning (Durán, 2010). Differentiated instruction and the use of data are achieved by students and teachers who collect and examine the results of formative assessments to inform the learning process. They interpret data to identify performance issues and work together as partners in the learning process, enabling the customization of instruction based on the needs of students and groups of students.

Using Data to Individualize Instruction and Remediation

Whether differentiating instruction for groups of students or individual students, data should play a fundamental role in informing practice. Just as in the previous section, data from various kinds of assessments provide the information a teacher needs to make a decision about the instructional steps needed for particular students. Instruction, therefore, can be individualized and differentiated based on the profile of students' strengths and weaknesses.

Using data to individualize instruction and provide remediation begins with process of collecting various kinds of data, including formative assessment data. These data can serve as evidence to identify students' learning issues. The data can be used to monitor progress throughout the course of instruction so that instructional modifications can be made to close achievement gaps and reach desired goals (Heritage, 2010a, 2010b).

For individualized instruction and remediation to be effective, both teachers and students must be involved in a systematic inquiry process. One strategy is to engage the students in their own learning process. The collaborative process involves examining and monitoring formative assessment data to set learning goals. The goals should have timely feedback loops to motivate learning, inform instruction, monitor progress, and improve academic achievement while it is occurring. The following example demonstrates instruction for individualizing and remediating student learning needs.

The Tapawingo School District, with a 77 percent minority population, has progressed from being designated a low-performing school district to a model school district. The graduation rate has improved from 51 percent in 2004 to 83 percent in 2010. During that time, Tapawingo began using a formative assessment model. The formative assessment process created a situation in which teachers and students became partners in reforming individualized instruction and providing remediation interventions. Students became involved by providing input to the school data team planning meetings, small-group instruction, and individualized remediation.

Joyce, a twelfth-grade student, is participating in a data team at Jackson High School. Joyce provides valuable perceptions by participating as an equal partner as the team collects and analyzes formative assessment data to identify achievement gaps that have been discovered in advanced algebra courses. Formative assessment results indicate that students are having difficulty finding the product of two binomials across grade levels. Joyce speaks during a team action planning session. She identifies a potential solution that is an outcome of working closely with Mr. Willy to interpret results on a recent algebra quiz that showed a gap in understanding mathematical terminology. The gap indicated that students did not know how to apply understanding of definitions to solving equations with a product of two binominals.

During an individualized remediation session with her math teacher, Joyce and Mr. Willy both discovered that she did know the definition of "foil" but did not know how apply it to the multiplication of more complex binomial problems. With support from Mr. Willy during individual remediation sessions, Joyce was able to demonstrate how to apply mathematical terminology from simple one-step problems to multiplying more complex two-step binomial problems.

Further analyses of additional formative assessment data across all of Jackson High School's algebra classes revealed that the majority of students had memorized the definition of "foil." However, they did not know how to apply the mathematical term to the multiplication of two binomials. As a result of the collaborative discussion about critical success factors in student learning, all mathematics teachers decided to administer common formative assessments that could be used to compare performance across classes. The teachers would offer ongoing individual remediation sessions to struggling students after school. The teachers administered a survey to determine what would encourage students to participate in the after-school remediation sessions. The survey results indicated that an appropriate incentive would be to provide snacks so that students might be encouraged to seek additional support in algebra.

Having student data team members in this district is quite unique. They are partners in helping to close achievement gaps between current and desired goals. Many of the students in the Tapawingo School District who were struggling are now meeting proficiency and continuing to take more advanced mathematics courses, with success rates rapidly increasing. These formative assessments that the teachers have been using are key sources of information for the data team members to make instructional corrections and individualized modifications. The teachers and students are working as partners to build the necessary data literacy skills. These skills are being used to identify important achievement patterns in student learning, inform next steps in instruction, identify solutions, solve problems, and empower students to be self-directed and lifelong learners. The process is helping students to succeed and prepare for the future.

**How do you include students
in your learning activities?**

What might be some strategies for engaging students in their own learning?

Do you have discussions with your students about learning expectations?

Have you set explicit objectives that the students understand?

Have you developed a rubric for scoring student work and shared the rubric with them?

Do your students help to analyze their own work products so they better understand their performance and misconceptions?

ORGANIZING INSTRUCTION

In the past, assessments and technologies have not always been aligned in ways to directly inform instruction. But developments have helped to close and tighten the feedback loop between instruction and assessment by including appropriate data and by being supported by technologies (see Figure 7.1).

The Future

There is little doubt that using data can help teachers to structure instructional practices. Collaboration among teachers, administrators, and students and the sharing of information can facilitate data-driven conversations. Teachers and students can help each other to identify the form of instruction that may be best aligned to particular students' learning needs. Teachers hopefully will gain experience over time in how to differentiate instruction that is grounded in data and evidence and become more adept over time, but that is not a given. They also will benefit from targeted professional development opportunities in which they can improve their pedagogical data literacy skills and their assessment literacy. Assessments are evolving and therefore will require teachers to continue to supplement their knowledge of how to apply the ensuing data to their classroom practices.

Technological advances in assessment systems also will play an essential role in supporting differentiated instruction. As described in Chapter 3, new applications and systems are being developed that will facilitate data-driven instructional practice. These tools will enable teachers and students to visualize student performance data in ways never before possible. The tools will facilitate the examination of trends and relationships. They will enable teachers to explore causes and effects and relationships, recognizing that correlations do not imply causality. The applications will simplify analyses that were once solely the domain of statisticians. At the same time, the pace and ease with which data are provided also present new challenges.

In advanced research, scientists and others study complex systems that generate massive amounts of data. A wide variety of new tools have been developed that allow data to be interpreted holistically and display patterns, structures, trends, and more to examine and display findings. These disciplines have given rise to the new visual data analysis tools that can be implemented in educational settings. Take, for example, Inspiration and InspireData (see http://www.inspiration.com/Inspiration and http://www.inspiration.com/InspireData). Inspiration and InspireData, for students in grades 6 through 12 and 4 through 12, respectively, facilitate the exploration of data. Such exploration and analyses can assist data teams to use pattern-making skills to facilitate their work to find meaning from complex sets of information. The analyses can help teachers to identify patterns of skills and performance that can lead to differentiation.

Another example is a software tool called TinkerPlots (see http://www.keypress.com). TinkerPlots can be used by teachers and students in grades 3 through 8 to provide graphical and visual representations of data. TinkerPlots was originally designed for students but has been used to help teachers examine visual trends in data through interactive, graphical representations (Rubin & Hammerman, 2006). In TinkerPlots, teachers can examine data from their classes to identify how groups of students are performing, determining differences and trends, and then structure instruction according to needs.

Visual analysis tools provide the capability to engage in rich graphical interpretation available to virtually anyone and can support the process of differentiation. And they need not be complex. TinkerPlots is simple enough that the software is easily used by students. So are Inspiration and InspireData. These tools can be applied to teaching and learning situations to help teachers better understand the complex relationships in the learning process. The tools can help teachers to analyze all kinds of assessment results, identify patterns of performance among and across students, and can inform the teaching and learning process.

Most teachers are faced with the challenges of analyzing school-level and classroom-level accountability data and other data to inform instruction. This is often done in isolation and with a limited understanding of how to actually use assessment data. That is, teachers tend to look at their own data and do not discuss the data with colleagues. They are on their own to understand student performance and group trends. Many teachers have received limited training in assessment and the application of results to classroom practices. Teachers need guidance about how to collect, examine, and interpret such data for the purpose of making decisions to inform instruction and student learning.

An essential component of differentiating instruction and using formative assessment is participation in professional learning communities, social networks, and online learning environments. Teachers will increasingly use online formative assessments in the future to inform instruction and empower students to become self-directed learners by providing timely and specific feedback. More important, teachers will work collaboratively to develop hypotheses about ways to improve student learning, share their repertoire of effective instructional strategies online, and increase their instructional effectiveness in differentiating student learning needs. Teachers will use online formative assessment systems that provide feedback loops to ensure that instructional effects can be measured. They will adopt common practices and share the same expectations for student involvement in performance. To be more effective at differentiating instruction to solve the specific learning needs of all students, every education system needs to build the capacity of the current and future teaching force with respect to formative assessment skills as well as pedagogical data literacy skills and implement formative assessments and other sources of student performance data to inform differentiated practices (Heritage, 2010a, 2010b).

SUMMING UP

In the United States, some states have already begun implementing formative assessment systems with feedback loops aligned to digital curricula to inform teaching and student learning (see, for example, Arkansas Department of Education, 2007). Using formative assessments for learning will create a paradigm shift in classrooms, from teacher-directed to student-centered learning environments, where data can directly inform the instructional process. These environments focus on identifying gaps in knowledge and solving the individual learning needs of students by involving them as partners.

One strategy is to engage students to become their own data-driven decision makers. Students need to be more actively involved in experiential, relevant, and participatory learning activities that use social networking for collaboration with peers and their teachers. These activities provide specific and constructive feedback from teachers to help students monitor their progress toward mastery.

Teachers in the United States have unfairly become the scapegoats for all the problems in education (Berliner, 2006,

2009). They have been forced to teach to high-stakes account-ability tests that measure achievement and performance after it has occurred, with minimal professional learning and the necessary supporting resources that can facilitate the improve-ment of student learning (Nichols & Berliner, 2007). Knowledge and skill in data-driven assessment, based on valid and reli-able formative assessments, can move the emphasis from assessments *of* learning to assessments *for* learning by imple-menting a systemic process of formative assessments to inform teaching and improve the student learning process based on individual needs. Formative assessments will enable teachers to truly differentiate instruction to meet the needs of all students (Heritage, 2010b; Heritage & Yeagley, 2005).

Applying Formative Assessment Results

Think about a formative assessment tool you have used in your classroom or school.

Examine the results of that tool and determine how instruction needs to be differentiated based on student readiness levels.

What types of formative assessments could be used to differentiate instruction based on students' cultural backgrounds, personal experiences, or prior knowledge?

What types of formative assessments could be used when instruction is differentiated based on student interests and choice of assignments or projects?

Plan for "differentiated assessments" for each of these three approaches to learning:

- differentiated assessments given different levels of readiness;
- differentiated assessments given different student back-grounds and experiences; and
- differentiated assessments given different levels of student interest.

What common characteristics do these differentiated assessments share? How would they inform the teaching?

CHOPS

What challenges and opportunities currently exist for using formative assessment and the resulting data? How do these challenges and opportunities relate to key ideas expressed in this chapter? For example:

Does your school use formative assessments?

Do formative data reflect the feedback loop in this chapter?

Do they seem usable in elementary schools? Middle schools? High schools?

Do they seem usable in classes where there are no high-stakes tests? Where there are high-stakes tests?

SOME HIGHLIGHTED REFERENCES

Black, P., Harrison, C., Lee, C., Marshall, B., & Wiliam, D. (2003). *Assessment for learning: Putting it into practice.* Maidenhead, UK: Open University Press.

Cronbach, L. J., & Snow, R. E. (1977). *Aptitudes and instructional methods: A handbook for research on interactions.* New York, NY: Irvington.

Heritage, M. (2010a). *Formative assessment and next-generation assessment systems: Are we losing an opportunity?* Washington, DC: Council of Chief State School Officers.

Nichols, S. L., & Berliner, D. C. (2007). *Collateral damage: How high-stakes testing corrupts America's schools.* Cambridge, MA: Harvard Education Press.

GLOSSARY

Aptitude treatment interaction—The theory that different learners benefit differently from different forms of instruction.

Benchmark assessments—Tests given periodically (monthly, quarterly) across the school year to measure progress through the curriculum.

Diagnostic assessments—Tests where the items are tightly linked to instruction and can provide a diagnosis of whether students know or don't know specific content, so that instructional steps can be prescribed to remediate deficiencies.

Interim assessments—Tests that are administered regularly throughout a district across a school year. Results can be examined at the class, school, or district levels to determine progress over time.

8

CHOPS

Learning From Examples and Closing Thoughts

We conclude this volume with a presentation of examples drawn from our experience working with educators who are trying to use data to inform practice, or in Sharnell's case, actually implementing data-driven practices in classrooms, schools, and throughout districts. We highlight both positive and negative examples because we recognize that people must learn from both the effective and the less effective. In previous chapters, we have referred to the balance between the challenges of using data and the opportunities for data use. Ellen often refers to the CHOPS when she speaks (Mandinach, 2009a, 2009b, 2010). The *CH* refers to the challenges and the *OP* to the opportunities. In any endeavor, there will always be challenges, issues, problems, and caveats. Nothing is simple and straightforward. There will be bumps in the road that must be circumvented. This is true of data-driven decision making. But also like other endeavors, data-driven decision making is full of opportunities and the promise to impact educational practice in a positive way (Duncan, 2010a; Easton, 2009). The opportunities may be fewer than the challenges but, in the opinion of many educators and policy makers, the former far outweighs the latter. Helping all children to learn by using data to remediate weaknesses and capitalize on strengths is what education is all about. It is an objective worth pursuing. It is why we become educators.

This chapter explores the CHOPS through a series of examples drawn from practice. For practical purposes, we have categorized the examples into five topics, in no particular order: technology, data choices, data use, leadership, and enculturation. As has been seen in the prior chapters, these topics are all interrelated and systemic in nature. There will be overlap. Our goal is to draw practical lessons from the examples, learning from the less effective ones and capitalizing on the more effective ones. We will then conclude the volume with some final thoughts about change management and schools as learning organizations.

PRACTICING DATA-DRIVEN DECISION MAKING

Technology

Data Dashboards

A nonprofit charter management organization called the Corona's Best Start Schools in South Dakota, serving approximately 7,600 students from grades K–12, is trying to prepare students to succeed. Corona's objective is to provide opportunities for students to succeed and to pursue higher-education goals. The organization has been tracking teacher effectiveness and student mastery of state standards for years using data dashboards. The data dashboards provide achievement data that enable educators to evaluate student performance. The data help principals to identify when teachers need support and when teachers need to reteach specific concepts to students. The dashboards enable educators to track student performance on the state summative assessment as well as common benchmarks over time.

Further, the dashboards can help educators to identify progress in achieving proficiency in math, science, and English language arts. Tracking such data provides key information on increases and decreases in proficiency across time. The dashboards provide teachers and instructional coaches with the needed data to identify individual student needs and target instructional support. These data give the educators information that helps them to identify potential strengths and weaknesses in their own instructional practice, leading to self-reflection and improvement of their own practice.

Data dashboards provide real-time, quick turnaround data to educators on essential data components. They highlight the targeted data elements so that educators can be alert to changes in student performance. This enables the educators to make instructional modifications that are sensitive to particular students' needs or the needs of groups of students. Because the dashboards provide such readily available data, they also can serve to help educators recognize when something they are doing is working or not working, thereby leading to continuous improvement on the part of the educators. Thus, a data dashboard can provide essential data that are immediately available in a display mode that alerts educators to the needs of students.

Interoperability

In 2005, a state department of education created an implementation plan for a statewide data system. The goal was for the data system to connect several different software systems and/or databases at the SEA level and within local school districts. The project is based on Schools Interoperability Framework (SIF) interoperability standards (see http://www.sifinfo.org/us/index.asp). The purpose of SIF is to ensure that computer systems can communicate with one another, creating a seamless transfer of data between and among systems. Many kinds of data are to be communicated across the systems, including student records, electronic transcripts, demographics, student performance, and other accountability and compliance data.

Every data system is different. But data must be standardized in order for them to be communicated accurately. To that end, the National Center for Education Statistics (see http://nces.ed.gov/dataguidelines/definitions.asp) and the Common Education Data Standards Initiative (see http://www.commondatastandards.org/) have sought to define common definitions and standards across data elements so that systems can easily interface with one another. Standardization of data elements helps to decrease the ambiguity in their meaning, with different people assuming different definitions of the same data. Common standards, definitions, and the capability for data tools and systems to communicate with and transfer data from one platform to another are essential technological and structural elements that undergird effective data use at all levels of the education system, whether at the federal, state, or local levels.

Handhelds

In the Puck School District, a small district in New Mexico, teachers are given handheld tools through funding from Reading First that enable them to administer the DIBELS early childhood literacy assessment to their third-grade students. This is in lieu of the paper-and-pencil version of the assessment. The teachers were trained through the Reading First funding to administer the assessment and interpret the results. Teachers give each child the assessment and obtain the results immediately to determine what each child knows and where they need help. The data are uploaded to a website where the teachers can trace the trend of each child's performance over time, and make comparisons across children, and even across classes. The teachers have immediate results right in the palm of their hand, without waiting for test results to be scored and reported. Access to the data is role-based. For example, Ms. Luanne, the teacher, can examine all of her students' performance. Ms. Allison, the principal, and Mr. Hootie, the reading specialist, can examine data by grade and examine all students, classes, and grades to identify trends and areas of strength and weakness.

The handhelds are one such emerging tool that provides ready access, easy-to-use solutions to teachers (see http://www.wgen.net/). Wireless Generation has developed an application for the DIBELS as well as an early childhood mathematics assessment on the handhelds. The tools integrate the assessments with the accumulation of data, immediately analyze the student responses, and provide feedback on student performance. The complete integration of assessment and feedback enables the teachers to gain information about their students' performance in real time, diagnose weaknesses, and determine what instruction to implement (Hupert et al., 2008; Penuel & Yarnall, 2005; Sharp, 2004; Sharp & Risko, 2003).

User-Friendliness

Teachers at Razoo Middle School in South Carolina feel compelled to ask their assistant principal, Ms. Suki, to run queries about their students and classes because they are deterred by the level of complexity and the user-unfriendliness of the district data systems. Even straightforward questions, like the number of behavioral referrals a particular student has had or how many unexcused absences have occurred for an entire class throughout the year, are sent to Ms. Suki. The system simply is not easy to use. There has not been sufficient professional development around the data system or provisions made to support data interrogation.

User-friendliness is an essential component of any technology tool. If it is too complex, it will not be used. Educators need a system that is simple, user-friendly, and accessible. This is true of a data warehouse, a student information system, an assessment system, an instructional management system, or any other type of data-related tool. Tools are supposed to be helpful, not an impediment. The easier to use, the more use there will be. The more difficult, the tool is likely to go unused.

Firewalls

The Francis Parish Schools, a large district in Louisiana, has a powerful data warehouse, but it is only accessible from district computers on district property. Firewalls for security prevent other access. Teachers and administrators can access files from their classrooms, offices, and schools, but they cannot access the system from home, when they have time in the evenings.

Anytime, anyplace access has become an important characteristic of good technologies. Educational data warehouses or systems are no different. In order to increase work efficiency, it is essential to provide users with ready access in places and at times where it is convenient and there is a need. If teachers prefer to run queries on their classrooms and students from the comfort of their home, after school hours, then access should be made possible. If an administrator wants access while on a business trip, that kind of access also needs to be made possible. The fundamental principle here is that for technologies to be used maximally, ready access must be provided or users will balk. Only so much work can be accomplished within the constraints of the actual academic day and on district property. This is an important security issue. The security of data must be preserved. Large companies solve this security all the time. Districts must do the same.

Levels of Aggregation

The Pookie School District, a large district in Florida, has built a data warehouse that contains data aggregated at the student level. That is, the student is the primary variable level in the system, not the class, school, or district. It is easy for a teacher or administrator to run a query about each or any student, but it is not easy to run a query at a class or grade level. For example, Ms. Maggie, a teacher, wants to know how many absences a particular student has. This is easily accomplished. But if Ms. Maggie or an administrator wants to know how many absences there have been for an entire class or grade, the issue becomes more complicated. A request to the Research Department must be made, requesting that the data for all students in the class or the grade be aggregated in order to produce an answer.

Data systems must be flexible in their capabilities to aggregate data. Educators will have questions about individual students, subsets or groups within classes, entire classes, courses, grades, schools, and even the district. The data system must be able to easily produce analyses and reports at all of these levels, and not require special requests made to data managers, statistical analysts, or researchers. Flexibility in analysis and reporting is essential.

Unintegrated Systems

Maizie Schools, a large district in Colorado, has a number of systems to support data-driven decision making, but none of them communicate with one another and were purchased in a piecemeal manner. The systems were acquired at different times and for different purposes. Staff in the district has become frustrated at the overlap of functions, the lack of communication, and the lack of integration among the tools.

The IES Practice Guide (Hamilton et al., 2009) makes clear the need to consider the landscape of needs when either developing or purchasing a data system. In the past, systems have had specific functions, causing a lack of integration and even overlap in functions (Wayman et al., in press). Now suites of tools are available commercially that provide integrated functions and almost one-stop shopping. The vendor can customize (not to the extent of a home-grown system) the system according to the needs of the district. These suites of applications help to reduce redundancy of effort as well as user confusion.

Alignment of Data to Data Needs: The Disconnect

A state data system director referred to the "disconnect." Mr. Vinnie was asked what he meant. The answer was telling. Mr. Vinnie said that the state data systems collect a tremendous amount of data from school districts that the SEA then reports to the U.S. Department of Education, primarily for federal accounting purposes. The SLDSs are huge repositories of data, but that they fail to meet the needs of the districts, thereby creating a disconnect. The SEA has data, but not the data that districts and schools need to make instructional decisions.

The disconnect is a problem. Data systems, no matter how powerful, must contain the data that users need to answer their questions. The state systems arguably may not be the place for instructional data, but they do need to be aligned to the needs of stakeholders in the districts. Many small districts do not have the capacity for their own data systems, and the question has always loomed about the role the state systems should play. Should they be a proxy for a local system, for those districts too small or too poor to have their own technological capacity?

District data systems must be aligned to the needs of the stakeholders. One of the action steps in the IES Practice Guide notes that districts initiating a system should consult their stakeholders about their needs and integrate the appropriate data elements into the system, whether commercially purchased or homegrown (Hamilton et al., 2009). Ideally, the data system's architecture will allow for the inclusion of additional data elements as needs emerge from various users and stakeholders.

Data Choices

DOA Data

Students in New York take their state summative assessment in the spring of a school year to provide information about how much they have learned on targeted skills and knowledge. The scores of the assessment are not delivered to educators until the beginning of the following school year. Educators feel that these data are less than useful, in part, because of the delay between the time of administration and the time of delivery. The students have changed over time, and the data are not deemed particularly informative. They have been called dead on arrival or autopsy data.

Feedback about performance must be given in a timely manner or it lacks maximum utility. The more time that passes between when an assessment has been given and when data are returned to educators, the less informative the results become. Students change daily in their knowledge and skills. So having a delay of months, weeks, or even days decreases the utility of the results. Tools such as the handhelds described previously provide immediate feedback on how students have performed and what they know (Hupert et al., 2008). The idea underlying computer-based testing is to provide more rapid turnaround of scores to test takers. One of the objectives of the new modes of assessments being developed by the two consortia of states under the auspices of the U.S. Department of Education is to ameliorate the delay between testing and results (Gewertz & Robelen, 2010; U.S. Department of Education, 2010a).

Creation of a Common Assessment

Fritz High School in Massachusetts has been using innovative technology-based assessment practices since the school was founded in 1996. Instruction at the school emphasizes project-based learning in which students are given complex, interdisciplinary problems. Students typically work in teams or groups. The projects are designed to cover required content standards and core learning outcomes that cut across academic content areas. These include collaboration, critical thinking, oral and written communication, use of technology, and citizenship.

The common framework assesses student work across grades and classes, thereby providing teachers with informative and comparative data that drill deeper than only a summary grade. In any topical or skill area, assessments cross all courses, providing teachers and students with information about learner strengths and weaknesses with multiple data points. An essential component here is that students have access to their own performance data through online grade books and electronic portfolios. Students and teachers can access data on each course, on learning outcomes, and work products.

Students receive performance ratings from peers as well as teachers. Additionally, students do self-assessments that require them to think about their learning experiences. These self-assessments stimulate reflection on what materials have been learned, interest, relevance, and the instructional process.

There are a couple of key points that can be learned from this example. First, the creation of common assessments puts teachers on the same page. They have a common metric from which to determine what students know and don't know. This is not so much for evaluative purposes, but for comparisons to determine the instructional steps that need to be made based on what is deemed to be working or not working. An administrator can look across classes within a grade—or in this case, even across grades—to understand trends. It enables teachers to drill down on specific topics, skills, or knowledge sets to help a student or groups of students.

The second point drawn from this example is the importance of having students become their own data-driven decision makers. This is the second recommendation in the IES Practice Guide (Hamilton et al., 2009). The more students can take ownership of their own learning, the better instructional interactions will be possible. Teachers can have productive conversations with students who understand instructional objectives and learning goals, and can self-assess. The students and teachers both benefit, as does the entire instructional process.

Getting the Right Data in the Right Hands

To encourage teachers to make formative use of assessment data, the Duncan Public School District, a K–12 public school district in Oregon, developed an electronic curriculum assessment resource tool. This web-based system allows teachers to access everything, from lesson plans to assessment tools. Teachers can use the tool daily to help them manage the assessment process, analyze the data, and link assessment data with instructional resources. The tool is a searchable database that provides access to district-approved resources and curricula, aligned with specific standards, benchmarks, and indicators. Teachers can create assessments using combinations of common assessment items. The items were developed by district teachers and designed to provide diagnostic information. The assessments are designed to help teachers diagnose student misconceptions and skills. The tool also enables teachers to link to a large library of instructional resources, including supplementary materials, lesson plans, and worksheets. The data system stores student assessment results, including classroom assessment, benchmark, and state assessment results.

The right data need to be in the right user's hands. The alignment of data to user needs is an essential component in effective data-driven decision making. Teachers need a variety of data that will inform their instructional practice. These may include classroom activities, common assessments, benchmarks, and even the state summative test. The alignment of data to the purpose of use is about validity; that is, the type of interpretations that will be made from the form of data and how they will be used. The summative tests may not be sufficiently aligned with curricula from which instructional decisions can be made, but these scores may be informative for other use and other users. A curriculum supervisor may have certain data needs, while principals and central office administrators have other needs, even of the same data source. Thus, the same results will have different uses and different interpretations depending on where within a school system the user resides. But the right data must be in the hands of the right users for valid interpretations to be drawn and decisions made.

Triangulating Data Sources: Summative,
Formative, and Diagnostic

Ms. Dory, a teacher at Misty High School in Wisconsin, is trying to understand what a student, Leda, knows and does not know about a particular content area. Luckily, Ms. Dory has several sources of information from which to gain this understanding and then consider what instructional steps to take. Each assessment provides a slightly different picture of

Leda, so Ms. Dory pulls together all the sources and begins to examine carefully the content of the assessments and results. This analysis provides a more comprehensive picture of Leda's knowledge.

A thorough understanding of what students know and are able to do guides teachers in developing instruction that is best suited for their students' learning needs. Teachers should compare multiple measures of data, such as summative, formative, interim, and diagnostic assessments, to validate performance data and clarify data analysis findings to answer questions they have about student achievement and reflect their instructional effectiveness. This process is commonly referred to as "triangulating data."

Summative assessments measure individual student achievement relative to the state standards and provide accountability information. State assessments provide an overall indication as to whether or not students have gained proficiency in specific content areas. The results reported after the school year has ended give parents, teachers, and schools one measure of student learning and school performance. As noted in previous chapters, summative assessments administered once a year generally do not inform daily instructional practices and individual student learning needs due to the timing and results reporting. Summative assessments given quarterly can be useful in measuring student achievement on content covered in courses, inform instruction, help to identify early interventions for students, and evaluate curriculum planning.

Formative assessments are used more frequently in districts and schools by classroom teachers to inform planning for individual student instruction, setting goals for learning needs, and monitoring progress over time. Formative assessments are not just the instrument but are the process of assessment (Heritage, 2010a, 2010b). Schoolwide formative assessments used by teachers in classrooms across grade levels and content areas have been found to be effective and the most underutilized assessments in schools and districts (Supovitz & Klein, 2003). States, districts, and schools are using web-based adaptive formative assessments to provide immediate feedback with curriculum content. These assessments automatically adapt to each student's instructional level based on their responses. The results and individualized learning plans help teachers create solutions to improve student performance and monitor progress.

Diagnostic assessments are used by educators to assess students who are struggling in a content area. Such assessments help teachers to identify specific learning weaknesses and strengths. Teachers subsequently can group students according to mastery of skills and plan for instruction.

By using summative, formative, and diagnostic assessments, teachers have an opportunity to examine the impact of their teaching on student progress, identify specific learning needs, and reflect on their practices to adjust instruction in response to those needs. But no one measure is sufficient. It is the triangulation of the multiple measures that brings strength to understanding a student's understanding and performance, before instructional remediation can be prescribed.

Data Use

Failure to Use Multiple Data Sources

A teacher in the Treat School District in Mississippi, Mr. Frankie, examines the scores from a recent test and determines that certain students have mastered the material satisfactorily, based on the single set of test results. Mr. Frankie moves on to a more complicated topic that builds on knowledge of the prior topic to which the test results refer. He finds that the students are really confused because they seemingly lack the skills and knowledge on which they had previously been assessed and passed.

No single source of data can provide a definitive answer. There may be problems with the measurement or the students may have guessed right or wrong, giving an inaccurate depiction of what they know or don't know. Using multiple sources of data helps to provide a more valid picture of performance.

Drilling Down: Item Level Versus Total Score

Ms. Katy, a teacher at the Tigger Elementary School in California, is given her class's test scores. She looks at the total scores and makes instructional decisions based only on those data. Ms. Katy does not look at section scores, nor does she drill down to the level of the item, information that may provide additional insights into the learning needs of the students.

A total test score gives you only the overall picture of how a student performed on an assessment. Ideally, there are more fine-grained sources of information, such as scores on individual sections of the test, or even item-level performance. A section score can provide information on whether a student has experienced difficulty with a particular topical area covered within the assessment. Item-level data can give even more minute information. Examining the patterns of correct and incorrect responses can give the teacher a wealth of information about what a student knows and does not know. If there are multiple questions on the same topic, the teacher will have an even more reliable estimation of how a student performs on that one topic. Thus, the more fine-grained the level of analysis, the more informative the test results will be. Drilling down to the item level can help the teacher isolate students' learning weaknesses, much more so that simply looking at a total test score.

Differentiating Instruction or Teaching to the Middle?

Ms. Bella, teacher at the Spunky Middle School in Ohio, looks over the distribution of performance for her class and notes that there are a few students who are very far below the level of others, and another group who are far more advanced than the majority of the class. She tries to determine what the best instructional strategy for the class as a whole might be. Ms. Bella figured that the advanced students will succeed no matter what and the struggling students may make limited progress regardless of what she tries. So Ms. Bella decides to target the majority of the class by going for the middle.

Every student can benefit from instruction, but it must be customized and sensitive to individual needs. Regardless of how advanced the best-performing students are, there are instructional strategies that can help them to achieve even more. They should not be ignored. They should be stretched with increasingly challenging material and tasks. Teachers can't give up on the most struggling students, as they require substantial attention and specialized instruction that focuses on remediating their learning challenges. This may mean private tutoring, extra work, teaming with more advanced students, or other tactics. Even the middle of the class may require more fine-grained instructional modifications based on individual student learning needs. Differentiating instruction requires the teacher to have a good idea about the needs of each student or student group and be able to align appropriate instructional strategies to those needs. For example, Ms. Bella realizes after giving a pretest that the students vary in their understanding of how to organize a persuasive essay. She also knows that not all her students are fluent in English and that some students have literacy skills well above the current grade level. How does she approach a new unit of study on persuasive writing?

Conflicting Data, Conflicting Interpretations

Mr. McGregor, a teacher at the Edelweiss Middle School in New Hampshire, gets the benchmark test scores back for his class which indicate that a number of students have scored below proficiency level. Mr. McGregor expresses surprise because these same students have performed well on in-class assessments and exercises. He is perplexed at what the conflicting data might mean and which test scores he should believe.

Conflicting sources of data always present difficulty in interpretation. What do you believe? Are the tests an accurate depiction of what students know and don't know? Did the students have a bad day when they took the benchmark? Were they tired, hungry, or unmotivated? What was individual performance like? What was the performance of the whole class? There are infinite possible explanations. One of the fundamental guiding principles of using data is that, when possible, one should use multiple sources of information because the truth lies somewhere in the midst of all the data. Indeed, the students could have underperformed on the benchmark, performed better on classroom exercises due to less test anxiety and pressure, or perhaps the benchmark differed significantly from the curriculum topics the teacher targeted. Reliance on only one source of data can lead to an inaccurate depiction of what students know, just as having multiple sources can create a level of conflict and therefore confusion. It is, however, better to have too much than too little data; the more data there are, the more reliable the information and the more valid the interpretations that can be drawn from the data.

Too Much Data

A new teacher, Ms. Nicole at Sparky High School in Oklahoma, takes over a class and is struck by the sheer amount of data about her class. There are state assessments, benchmarks, interim assessments, classroom exercises, portfolios, diagnostic information, disciplinary data, demographics, and other data. Ms. Nicole feels like she is literally drowning in data and cannot make sense of it all. She doesn't know which way to turn, how to prioritize, and what to believe.

Data is a new four-letter word for many teachers. In reality, data should be beneficial for teachers as tools to inform their practice. But as is often the case, too much of a good thing is not ideal. One of the IES Practice Guide's action steps deals specifically with the plethora of data confronting educators (Hamilton et al., 2009). The report suggests that one strategy for dealing with too much data is to formulate specific questions that can guide a teacher's examination of the data. Targeting specific questions or hypotheses about students' performance can narrow the focus of inquiry. They can help to structure course of instructional actions that may bring the teacher back to reexamine the data for additional information.

Sample Questions

Are some students struggling and not others?

Are there particular subgroups of students that seem to be having difficulty?

Can you identify any common characteristics causing the students to have difficulty?

What data might be the most informative to help you understand student performance?

Can you drill down to items or other work products that might be informative?

Bubble Kids

Teachers and administrators at the Dudley Middle School in Alaska receive class reports for the state summative assessment with test scores arrayed for each student according to their proficiency levels: "below," "approaching," "meets," and "exceeds." The cut score for proficiency differentiates those in the "approaching" group from those in the "meets" group. The score is 300. There are a few students whose scores are 295 through 299, just below the cut score. There are also a few students whose scores are 300 through 305, just above the proficient mark. In an effort to increase the number of students who achieve proficiency, the teacher, Mr. Ralph, then focuses much of his efforts on those students just under the cut score, hoping to move them to proficiency.

This instructional strategy is called focusing on the "bubble kids." They are the students right on the cusp of passing. This strategy is flawed in two major ways. The first involves a fundamental principle of measurement, called error of measurement. The students scoring 295 may not be all that different from those scoring 305, yet in terms of accountability, the difference is great: proficient versus not proficient. The second issue involves the instructional strategy. Focusing solely on the students who are most likely to get pushed into the proficient category ignores the fact that those who have already achieved proficiency may regress on the next test. The strategy also ignores the need to focus on all children, based on their individual needs, regardless of where along the continuum they fall. This means helping the most struggling students progress as far as they can, while helping the most gifted students achieve even higher levels of performance. The focus on bubble kids is a strategy founded in the push for accountability, not in the philosophy of helping all students to progress toward continuous improvement.

Too Much Data Alignment

The Sophia School District in Wyoming has, as part of its technology tools to support data-driven decision making, an application that calculates the potential score increase on the state summative assessment, the Proficiency Assessments for Wyoming Students (PAWS), if teachers focus on particular skills in their instruction. Take for example the eleventh-grade mathematics assessment, with its standards and subscales— algebra, geometry, measurement, data analysis and probability, and number operations. The system will align the PAWS with the curriculum standards and estimate that if teachers spend more time on five subscales, the potential gains in results will be 8, 5, 3, 4, and 10 percentage points, respectively. So the teachers, feeling pressure to improve their students' performance, primarily on algebra and number operations, concentrate their instruction on those skills because they may likely achieve higher scores based on the probabilities provided by the data system.

There are a few lessons to be learned from this scenario. First, the technology can be helpful up to a point. The technology points out to the teachers where students' strengths and weaknesses may be based on the PAWS, but it does not go beyond that summative assessment. Second, the PAWS may or may not be well aligned to Sophia's curriculum. Thus, there may be a misalignment and the data may not be reflective of the outcomes of the instructional process. Third, the PAWS is only one test, and a summative one at that. It may not be instructionally sensitive, and therefore may not provide the teachers the kinds of data that can help them modify their instruction. Other measures, in addition to the PAWS, are needed.

Leadership

Different Messages From Different Leaders

Ms. Zoe, a principal at the Dusty High School in Idaho, has been around for a long time and tends to make decisions based on her experience and through pressure from her parents and stakeholders. A new superintendent, Ms. Duffy, comes into the district and tries to eschew the notion about decisions made through political pressure. Instead, Ms. Duffy invokes a model of data-driven practices. The teachers in the school are conflicted. They have been working for years with Ms. Zoe and understand her mode of operation. Yet now Ms. Duffy insists that everyone begin to use data to inform all decisions—from the classroom to the central administration.

Having a consistent vision is important. Ideally, principals will be on the same page as the superintendent. What has been happening recently, in instances such as depicted in this example, is that the principal may decide to leave because her vision is not aligned with the superintendent. In other cases, the superintendent is able to convince the principal of the benefits of data and the principal slowly begins to appreciate data-driven practices. Alternatively, the principal may not serve as an impediment to her staff, allowing them to embrace the district vision for data use.

Nonbelieving Principal

The Atticus School District in Alabama has explicitly stated that all principals should be using data to inform practice. To that end, the district provided each principal with a powerful computer that facilitates access to the district's data warehouse. One principal, Ms. Dallas, is not data literate nor does she have an inclination to use the district data warehouse. Ms. Dallas gives her computer to her administrative assistant so that she cannot access the data warehouse. The donation masks her unwillingness to access the data warehouse, and her dislike for data. Her staff perceives the lack of leadership around data and fails to make any progress in implementing data-driven practices throughout the school. After all, if Ms. Dallas is not using data, why should the teachers?

Leadership around data is essential. The message Ms. Dallas gives to the staff is important in communicating the values and objectives of the school. If the principal does not value data use, the message comes across explicitly, and the staff will be less likely to embrace data-driven practices. If Ms. Dallas communicates the importance of data, staff will be stimulated to follow suit. Never underestimate the power of the principal. The teachers take their cues from the leadership.

Another lesson to be learned here is that data-driven decision making can occur without a data literate leader. It may take more effort on the part of the teachers, but it can be done. Teachers need to be convinced data-driven decision making is an important component of their work, that there is payoff to data use, and that data use will not negatively affect them in any way.

Another lesson to be learned here is that data literacy and technological literacy are separate entities. Ms. Dallas, although not technologically literate, might well have been a data-savvy principal. Conversely, Ms. Dallas also could have been technologically savvy but not data literate. However, in this district, the expectation for principals was for them to use data in their practice and regularly use their data system to examine various sources of data. So in this case, some minimal level of technological literacy was needed to access the data system and to promote data literacy. With emerging technologies, both technological and data literacy may be increasingly coupled. The technology is a tool by which the data inquiry process can be facilitated.

Principal Preparation Development

The Henry Public Schools, a large urban school district in Texas, lost more than one-third of its principals. Because of this shortage of administrators, the district decided to focus its efforts on building leadership capacity to drive the effective use of data for continuous improvement through the use of technology. A year-long principal preparation development institute was developed with face-to-face quarterly meetings and online course modules that created cohorts of professional learning communities. A major component of the institute emphasized school improvement planning grounded in inquiry-based data use. The institute included scenarios with analysis of pivot tables, spreadsheets, charts, graphs, state school report cards, principal leadership competencies, technologies for accessing data systems, online courses modules, and participation in online professional learning communities through wikis and blogs. The program trained over 400 principals. Throughout the process, participants involved assistant principals and used the distributed leadership model to encourage lead teachers who were data coaches to become involved. The institute reinforced Henry Public Schools's clear vision for enculturating data use to inspire and increase the effectiveness of school leaders.

As has been noted in previous chapters, principals make a difference, and their leadership and vision for data use are important components that help to institutionalize data-driven practices. The literature is clear about the role of principals in a data culture (Hamilton et al., 2009). This example shows the importance of training principals to lead in a data-driven school. It also shows that distributing the leadership to assistant principals, lead teachers, data coaches, and others is a useful strategy. Having a data-minded principal makes a difference.

Teacher Leadership

Cassie Public Schools, an urban district in Minnesota, requires every school to identify lead teachers to be designated as data coaches. These individuals participate in a professional learning program and build their capacity to implement a sustainable model of effective data use for school improvement. The lead teachers are expected to facilitate data-driven practices that are embedded in daily instructional practices. They use a distributed leadership model in which they meet with grade and content area data teams. This process involves all classroom teachers in communicating, collaborating, and creating common assessments embedded in relevant project-learning modules. The lead teachers identify structured time, schedule team meetings, identify multiple measures of assessment data for analysis, and facilitate action planning.

This model for building the capacity of lead teachers ensures continuous data-driven improvement efforts are sustainable. Leadership does not reside in just one individual, but several. They are teachers, not administrators, therefore colleagues may resonate more to the process and the work than if it were to come from an authority figure. Having several lead teachers also ensures that there is broader distribution of the process and does not rely solely on the shoulders of one person, especially given high rates of teacher turnover in schools across the country.

The Importance of the Superintendent

The Wildcat School District in Michigan is located in a fairly affluent area. Wildcat, however, has an achievement gap issue. The small number of students from minority ethnic groups are struggling and achieving at low levels. The superintendent, Mr. Sebastian, is convinced that implementing certain programs, including the use of data to specifically focus instructional strategies on these students, will help to decrease the achievement gap. The parents, community, and school board are concerned that a large amount of funds will be devoted to a small number of students without any promise of payoff. Mr. Sebastian intercedes and explains how data-driven practices will be introduced that not only will help the struggling students, but it also will benefit the more affluent students. The school board approves the strategy and allows Mr. Sebastian to implement the interventions.

A superintendent can make or break a school district. The superintendent in this example had an explicit vision for data use and an articulated plan of action on how to address a pressing educational problem. It may not have been the most popular idea, but it was grounded in an educational philosophy that all children should be given a chance to succeed and that data would serve as the foundation from which to determine the progress that each child and all groups of students were making. Having real data can make a difference when unpopular or difficult decisions must be made. It is hard to argue with hard evidence, in contrast to political pressure, opinions, and anecdotes. The superintendent sets the tone for the district. The vision is essential.

Leaders Modeling Data Use

Ms. Joseph, the principal at the Pepper High School in Maine, is preparing for a meeting with the public about how her school is performing. Ms. Joseph spends time on the district data warehouse examining data. She has a huge binder of printouts that is at her disposal. She is prepared for just about any question the stakeholders and parents might ask because she comes to the presentation armed with data.

It is important for leaders to model the use of data in front of teachers, parents, and the public. Presenting information that is backed by evidence shows that data-driven decision making is valued. It models data-driven practice. It is no longer acceptable for a leader, whether a principal or a superintendent, to respond to questions by using gut feelings or only anecdotes. Just as a doctor would not present clinical findings to a patient based on gut feelings, but rather on the data from an examination, an educational leader's presentations or decisions must be grounded in hard evidence. Principals must have data readily available for meetings with teachers, parents, and students, just as superintendents must make evidence-based presentations to the public, school boards, and other stakeholders.

Enculturation

Collaboration Versus Going It Alone

Ms. Ruth, a teacher in the Lowell Elementary School in Hawaii, is facing a difficult decision about how to reach a particular student, Eddie, given his learning disabilities. Eddie continues to struggle and the teacher has reached the limits of her experience and knowledge of what might be effective instructional strategies. Ms. Ruth feels alone and a failure. She seeks guidance from a host of experts who have been trained to deal with the complex of learning disabilities. She presents the case to her grade-level team.

Teachers often work in isolation in their classrooms. But isolation does not have to be the typical mode of operation. Colleagues and collaborators abound. Teaming to help students with disabilities is a common source of support for teachers. The teams closely examine data to understand a student's status and what strategies might be used for instructional, behavioral, and other decisions. Data form the basis for decisions on IEPs. Further, data teams serve as an important source of information and feedback. Creative ideas can be shared about successful instructional strategies.

Professional Learning Communities

Teachers in the Loren Middle School in Virginia come together within their school to discuss instructional methods, student learning issues, review course content, and examine student data. Team meetings are a regular, weekly event, led by Mr. Mizzou, the data coach. Teachers bring issues to the table and discuss potential action steps. The teachers feel supported because they are working with and learning from colleagues through the teaming process.

Professional learning communities are not new, but they now are garnering substantial attention. The literature is clear about the importance of collaborations around data use (Feldman & Tung, 2001; Hamilton et al., 2009; Love et al., 2008;

Supovitz & Klein, 2003). Data teams are a form of professional learning community.

The National Staff Development Council introduced a new tag line, "learning forward" (see http://www.learning forward.org/index.cfm). One of its foci is on data-driven professional learning communities. The website contains videos of teachers demonstrating a data-driven, distributed leadership model. Its contents include common planning time, identified roles and responsibilities, participation in team meetings, discussions about assessment results, work samples, common assessment development, online collaboration, lesson creation, and grade-level action plans. The Doing What Works website   (http://dww.ed.gov/Data-Driven-Instructional-Decision-Making/topic/index.cfm?T_ID=30)   for   the   IES Practice Guide also provides invaluable videos, materials, and resources for teachers collaborating on data-driven practices.

Leave the Ego at the Door

Ms. Martha, a teacher at the Gericho Elementary School in Illinois, is experiencing difficulty finding an effective strategy to address a particular student's learning issue. Ms. Martha has tried several ideas, none of which seemed to work. The student, Sam, continues to struggle and the teacher's level of frustration increases. Ms. Martha is hesitant to present the issue at the weekly data meeting because she does not want to look inept in front of her colleagues. At the next data meeting, she sucks it up, takes a deep breath, and presents the problem to her colleagues. Ms. Martha notes how she has tried to reach the student with limited success and asks for concrete advice. The team discusses the case and admits that Ms. Martha has tried viable solutions and acknowledges that this is a difficult situation. A teacher who had Sam in the prior year then volunteers that she had similar problems with him, but then describes the strategy that she found worked fairly well and suggests that Ms. Martha try the instructional approach. Ms. Martha now is armed with a strategy that has worked for

Sam in the past. She has gained insight from a colleague who struggled in the same way with the same student.

As we have noted earlier, a fundamental principle of collaboration is learning from colleagues who may have more experience with, insights to, or knowledge around a particular instructional strategy, student, or challenging issue. The ability and willingness to exchange ideas and learn from colleagues is critical. This often means that teachers have to leave their egos at the door and admit that they are stumped, others may have a better perspective, and that they need help. That is, they just have to suck it up. Trust is an essential element here. So is the fear of evaluation, or looking stupid or ridiculous. Building a positive and accepting environment takes time, but it will evolve over time with the right foundation, objectives, support structures, and open and accepting attitudes.

Common Planning Time

The Dakota School District in Vermont recognized the importance of providing common planning time for its teachers, but it had to find a time block that would not run counter to union regulations. Dakota considered convening meetings before school, after school, and during lunch periods, but it found no easy solution. Yet it was committed to the idea of providing teachers time to work together and have professional development time within the academic calendar. Dakota then decided that the only way to accomplish this goal was to reconfigure the academic week to provide a protected block of time for such activities. They blocked out one afternoon a week, removing instructional time from those hours. The instructional hours were redistributed throughout the week, and the designated afternoons became the time for teachers and administrators within each school to come together for common planning time, team meetings, and professional development.

One of the ways that districts can show their commitment to the enculturation of data is to provide common planning time for staff to collaborate and discuss data, instructional strategies, and other pressing issues that they face on a daily basis. The provision for such common time essentially communicates the message to all educators that collaboration and discussion among colleagues are expected and seen as essential components of the work environment. Teachers are not expected to function in isolation, but to seek support and guidance from colleagues, administrators, and experts. It gives teachers an opportunity to share successes and consult on less effective cases. The common planning time provides opportunities for administrators to work closely with their staff and understand the challenges they may be facing with classes or individual students.

Too Much Reliance on the Data Expert

The school's assistant principal, Mr. Gabriel, at the George Middle School in Washington, was the go-to person for all things data related. Every time a teacher has a query about a particular student or class, the teacher asks Mr. Gabriel to access the district's data system and provide the needed answers. No one else in the school knows how to access the data system and much of the assistant principal's time is spent running the queries for his principal, guidance counselors, or teachers. Mr. Gabriel is one tired data wonk.

What would this school do if the go-to data person left? Who would be available and knowledgeable to run the queries? The IES Practice Guide (Hamilton et al., 2009) recommends that there is a data coach, mentor, or facilitator in each school. This person should be knowledgeable about data and be able to communicate easily with others. But too much reliance in this one individual is not good. There is a fundamental difference between this example and the objective of having a data coach. Part of the role of the data coach is to help colleagues use data, not do the data mining and analysis for them. The ultimate goal is to have all educators knowledgeable about data-driven decision making, but that one or two staff members may be the data leaders. What the assistant principal and data coach should have been doing, instead of running the queries for the staff, would have been to work with the colleagues to help them slowly understand how to run the queries on their own or with limited guidance. This is the turnkey model that many schools have used.

Too Little Time

The Micah Middle School in Georgia is now requiring that its teachers use data to inform practice. The initial reaction from the educators is that this requirement is one more thing loaded on to a number of tasks that necessitate more time that they simply do not have. The principal, Ms. Belle, hears comments like: "Where am I going to find the time to use data?"; "How much time will it take to access the data system to find the answers I need?"; "I should be focusing on instruction, not number crunching"; "Using data is not in my contract"; and "There is no time for it or I will have to give up some other activity."

Time is an educator's best or worst friend. However, it seems that there is simply not enough time to devote to everything that needs to be done. Some educators perceive that the use of data will require more time and effort in an already time-constrained schedule. Using data will have to replace some other activity. Others maintain that once data-driven practices become a normal part of an educator's repertoire—part of an ongoing cycle of instruction, data, and assessment—data-driven decision making will become engrained in common methods and practice. We firmly believe that data use will become a generic tool that educators can use to make decisions, if there is a supportive environment, the appropriate resources, and readily available technology tools. Data and the supporting technology can actually help to increase productivity and streamline work processes, not necessarily adding to time commitments.

Fear of Retribution

A first-year teacher at the Quill Elementary School in Pennsylvania, Ms. Sydney, attended a training session on an assessment system at a district site. The session showed her how to interpret her students' performance results. After careful review, Ms. Sydney wondered why her students had not achieved mastery despite having taught a particular skill to her second-grade students on three separate occasions. After a moment she paused and said, "Maybe, I need additional professional development to help me to become a better teacher and meet the individual needs of my students." In the next breath Ms. Sydney uttered, "Do you think I will be fired for my students' poor performance assessments results?" Fear of retribution is what many teachers face when student assessment results are used to evaluate teacher performance and teacher quality.

Data use should be safe and transparent to build the capacity of teachers to improve practices and student achievement. Adding the evaluative component can be a dangerous and feared practice. Especially for new teachers, there is so much they have to learn. Examining student performance results should provide learning opportunities, chances for self-reflection, and help teachers to understand where they might need to make modifications in practice. The process might indicate when they need to seek help from experts and colleagues. It should not be about fearing the loss of a job or blaming the teacher, for there is so much beyond the control of the individual teacher (Berliner, 2006, 2009).

Getting Trained

Effective teachers are a determining factor as to whether or not students' learning needs are being met. A Maryland district, the Sedona Public Schools's approach to building the capacity of teachers to use data effectively is to initially implement a data team model in the school. The model provides a common, structured time for getting teachers trained on their new data assessment system and focuses on using an inquiry process to analyze multiple measures of student performance data with action planning. Sedona's belief is that their greatest capacity is to accelerate student achievement and continuous school improvement by building better teachers through increasing professional learning in data-driven decision making.

Getting educators trained in data-driven practices is fundamental to the creation of a data culture. Training can come in different forms. A district can hire an external professional development provider to come in and provide training, with some necessary customization to the specific needs of the site. A specific individual within a district can be tasked with providing internal training. Principals often receive training before teachers and are expected to return to their school and train their teachers, using a turnkey model. Data teams are formed which are then tasked with helping colleagues learn data skills. Teachers may take a course at a local university or enroll in a virtual course. Yet it is not clear how widespread course offerings are for teachers and administrators (Mandinach & Gummer, 2010, 2011). There is no one right process, but fundamental to all of the models is the notion that training is necessary. Educators cannot invoke data-driven principles by the seat of their pants. They must be trained in the concepts; that is, they must gain pedagogical data literacy.

Using Data Is Good Practice, Not a New Fad

Mr. Max, a teacher at Isabella High School in North Carolina, assigns an in-class exercise to his students. The teacher makes the rounds of his classroom, noting how each student is responding to the problem. Some students, such as Shlomo and Chai, are doing really well with the problem and finish quickly, while others are having a bit more difficulty. Some students ask questions. Other students take a good deal of time, thoroughly considering their responses. A few students look totally stumped or distracted. Mr. Max collects not only the work products but also valuable data about how each student approached the exercise by carefully observing how the students solved the problem, the questions they asked or did not ask, and the relation to past performance.

Data-driven decision making has been given much attention by policy makers. It is seemingly a new fad. The push toward accountability and invoking the medical model that demands hard evidence have suddenly created an emphasis in education on data-driven decision making. But as we have noted earlier, data-driven decision making is not new. It has been around a long time. Good teachers have been using data for many years. The practice just may not have been recognized as data-driven decision making.

In this example, Mr. Max collected the end product of each student's work. But equally informative, he collected important data about the students as they worked on the problem. The questions they asked provide data on students' knowledge and understanding, just as would the questions that were not asked. Data-driven decision making is not just about the product of student work, but it is also of the process by which students perform. Good teachers are constantly collecting data on their students by observing, questioning, and listening. In some sense, the teacher's brain is a data warehouse, a repository of many kinds of data that may not easily be quantified into a technology-based tool. Data-driven decision making most definitely is not new. Teachers recognize the fact that policy makers are putting a new twist on something old, especially with the proliferation of different data sources and the technological tools to assist in the mining and analysis of the data.

Hiring Practices and Building Capacity

Mr. Grady is applying for a principal's position in the Jasper School District in Delaware, which is known to be data-driven. Mr. Grady goes through the usual sets of interviews with the superintendent, school board, teachers, and other stakeholders. His credentials are excellent. He has fine references from his other jobs, and a degree from a top university. Mr. Grady is asked to develop a school improvement plan based on a fictitious set of data and is given four hours in which to examine the data and write the plan. The four hours come and go, with the candidate struggling to understand how the data can be transformed into a viable action plan. When queried about the plan, Mr. Grady admits that there was little useable information that could be drawn from the data, preferring to use instinct and experience to make decisions. He does not get the job.

An increasing number of administrators, both superintendents and principals, are attempting to reform schools and districts through the use of data. A new superintendent arrives and makes clear that data and hard evidence are to be used to inform decisions and practice, including hiring practices. Existing principals and teachers who may not be like-minded become uncomfortable with the new philosophy and seek jobs in other districts. The district slowly evolves into an increasingly data-driven organization as new hires arrive and the nonbelievers leave. Making hiring decisions based on a candidate's ability to use data is one way to ensure that new teachers and administrators are data literate. Making promotion decisions on the proclivity toward data use can help to weed out those who do not use data.

Deep Enculturation Versus Changing Leadership

The Tiger Schools in Tennessee had a superintendent for many years that was firmly data-driven. Data informed every phase of district activity. When Mr. Scooter retired, a new superintendent, Ms. Angel, arrived with new ideas and new philosophies, and she placed less emphasis on data-driven practices. Some staff members were confused and concerned about what they should do in terms of using data to inform practice. Many continued with practice as usual, using data as if no leadership transition had occurred.

Educational leaders change all the time. Superintendents come and go, as do principals. With new administrators come new and different philosophies. Staff must take their cues from the administration. Frustration often reigns when deeply engrained modes of operation, philosophies, and methods are forced to change when a new administrator arrives with very different views. What is all the more frustrating is when the staff is convinced of the worth of a deeply enculturated belief system or method and the new administration wants to try something different. This is why one often hears educators say, "Ah, this is only a passing fad. If I close my door and wait, this too shall pass." Data-driven decision making is not a passing fad. If educators firmly believe in and have evidence of the effectiveness of a practice—and it is engrained in the culture—it is likely to be sustained through changes in leadership.

Systemic Reform

A superintendent, Ms. Rogers, in Kansas wants to make her district completely data-driven as part of a move toward systemic reform. She views the district as a learning organization in which data are to be used to turn around the less successful schools, and to inform and enhance the more successful schools. She tasks her staff to find professional development opportunities to train not only the principals, but all educators, including central administration staff. The school board fully supports the effort. The ultimate goal is to help all students to learn, but other goals also are important. Ms. Rogers also sees data as stimuli for creating increased communication among staff, higher staff satisfaction, and increased efficiency throughout the district. Data become the conduit for systemic reform.

School districts are complex systems of many interdependent components. They can be seen as learning organizations that constantly are changing, morphing, and evolving in response to many internal and external constraints. One of the fundamental components of learning organizations is data-driven decision making (Senge, 1990). Schools and districts are no different. Every day and every minute, educational agencies are making small course corrections based on incoming data. Whether it is a teacher making an instructional modification or a superintendent making an administrative decision, data must be the foundation for these decisions. Reform takes time and it requires recognition of the interdependencies among the complex components of a school district. Just as you can't turn an ocean liner on a dime, the same holds for schools and districts. Reform requires patience, sustained leadership, and real data from which to make hard decisions about course corrections.

Evidence That Data Use "Works"

The Kimberly School District in Connecticut is committed to participating in a randomized controlled trial to see if training teachers to use data will improve teachers' classroom practices and ultimately student performance. Everything was prepared for the study and everyone from the district, the researchers, the professional developers, and the funding organization were enthused about the prospect of the study yielding informative research results and, more important, helping the teachers and students of the school district. The research design was set and everything was good to go. Then two things happened. First, the district experienced a major economic issue that caused them to close a number of schools and merge others. Second, the superintendent who committed to the study left, and an acting superintendent stepped in who was not nearly as enthusiastic about the study. Kimberly eventually pulled out of the project because they did not feel that the challenges of participating in a rigorous study and meeting the needs of the researchers and data collection were balanced sufficiently by the possible benefits to the students and teachers of the district.

Educators and policy makers have been seeking concrete evidence that using data "works"; that is, using data makes a difference in what teachers do in their classrooms and those differences improve student performance. The IES Practice Guide (Hamilton et al., 2009) indicates that the level of evidence for the five recommendations is "low." This means that there have been few, if any, gold standard (randomized controlled trials) studies conducted around data-driven decision making. Such studies are notoriously difficult to conduct in real school settings. They are costly and labor intensive. They require a lot in terms of commitments on the part of districts and educators. Implementing an experimental design, although providing the highest level of scientific evidence, is confronted with a plethora of challenging practical realities. These challenges include having enough schools, teachers, students, or whatever the level of analysis might be, to provide sufficient statistical power; withholding the intervention or treatment to the control group; possible cross-group contamination; establishing commitments on the part of the participants over a multiyear timeframe; dealing with turnover of key administrators who have committed to the study; attrition of teachers, students, and even schools and districts; and the imposition of the sheer burden of the data collection required of a long-term study. These are all realities in the real world of education and research. Researchers and policy makers must be attuned and sensitive to them. They must be respectful of the educators and the context in which they are working. Conversely, educators must understand what they are committing to when they agree to participate in such studies. Incentives must be provided, and the participants must have a full understanding of why the study is being conducted and the potential benefits to the district and to research. Policy makers must be realistic about the issues involved in the conduct of research studies when they demand that education be held to the gold standard of scientific rigor.

PUTTING THEORY INTO PRACTICE: THE CATCH-22

Ironically, both of us have been asked numerous times by educators about the low level of evidence around data-driven decision making when we have conducted workshops. They want to know what "low" means in terms of the credibility of the recommendations and action steps to implementing data-driven practices. "Low" has now been re-termed "minimal," but it still carries the same connotation. Should educators believe the recommendations or ignore them as ideas for which there is no evidence of effectiveness? These are difficult issues because education should be evidenced-based yet research must mirror practice. It is hard to conduct good research when the practice has not been sufficiently implemented or enculturated to study. Data-driven decision making is an emerging field. It is also hard to impress upon consumers of research that just because the level of evidence is deemed as "low" that there are not important lessons to be learned from the amassed research. On the contrary. Implementation research can be highly informative here. Further, educators who are demanding higher levels of evidence must be willing to participate in research efforts and cooperate in order to obtain the needed evidence. Yet participating in a rigorous research study is not a trivial commitment. We have a Catch-22 here.

Another important lesson to be learned from this example is the importance of communication between researchers and practitioners. When conducting rigorous and long-term projects, there needs to be a comprehensive discussion of the needs and objectives of the work. The practitioners need to understand fully the requirements of the commitment to participate. And researchers need to understand, appreciate, and be sensitive to the needs of the educators and the educational setting. Compromises need to be made. Provisions must be put in place for transitions in leadership and therefore commitments to a project. The best strategy is to bring all interested parties to the table for a face-to-face meeting before a project is launched so everyone fully understands the needs and the constraints of others, and that there is a shared respect for and commitment to the research project. Further, the educators must feel that they are getting something from the study, not just being a lab rat for the benefit of the researchers. Open communication is needed.

CHANGE MANAGEMENT: USING DATA TO IMPROVE EDUCATION

Education is changing around the world. In all countries, the message comes from the very top, as evidenced by President Obama's (2009) view of what education should be. Secretary Duncan (2009a, 2009b, 2009c, 2010a, 2010b) has made clear that education should be about continuous improvement and that data-driven decision making is an essential component in the educational process. Data and evidence must be used to inform practice, and human capacity around data use must be built, reinforced, and sustained. But building such capacity will not happen quickly and without cost and the need for structural changes. Education is a complex system and change does not come easily. The recommendations for the clinical preparation of educators by NCATE's Blue Ribbon Panel (2010) are an important first step toward building the infrastructure needed to help educators acquire pedagogical data literacy.

We have recognized throughout this book that implementing and enculturating data-driven decision making is not easy and can be quite costly and labor intensive. At the same time it can be rewarding and has the potential to make tremendous improvements in student learning and classroom practice. Using data, however, is not a panacea nor is it a one-size-fits-all solution that can be simply dropped into an educational setting. As Heritage and Yeagley (2005) note, data-driven decisions also must be made with thoughtfulness and examined for "common sense and reasonableness" (p. 333). Data-driven practices can go a long way to help make decisions, but data and evidence must be balanced by human judgment (Jamentz, 2001). Flexible adaptations are needed to implement and embed data-driven practices into classrooms, schools, and districts.

We have shared with you, particularly in the examples in this chapter, the CHOPS, the challenges to and opportunities afforded by data-driven practices. We acknowledge that there may be many challenges, but we firmly maintain that those challenges are more than compensated for by the overarching opportunities provided to educators and students through the effective use of data. It is no longer a question of *IF* and *WHY* educators should use data, but *WHEN* and *HOW*. Data use has become a professional imperative. As we have said, you would not want your doctor making important clinical diagnoses and decisions without adequate evidence or most up-to-date knowledge in the field. Educators must follow the same professional code of conduct. There is much to say for experience informing practice, but it must be done in parallel with information.

The use of data requires a change in mindset and even a philosophical shift. We discussed the philosophical shift that has occurred in the U.S. Department of Education from accountability to continuous improvement. Such shifts are trickling down to state departments of education, districts, schools, and classrooms, and being imported by other countries (e.g., Australia). Using data to inform practice is about helping all students improve over time and helping schools and districts to do the same, not just about meeting compliance and accountability requirements. This shift may be less apparent to some educators, depending on where they are in the educational system and the extent to which leadership has embraced the idea of continuous improvement. The shift requires a change in mindset among teachers and administrators. There must be a recognition that all children can succeed, that education can make a difference if it is customized to the needs of the students, and that data and hard evidence can inform practice in a way that can modify work processes, whether administrative or instructional, to make course corrections toward that goal of continuous improvement. Some course corrections may be proximal, minute, and fine-grained; others may be more distal and broader. But the iterative feedback loop of using data is a fundamental tool in this improvement process.

Schools and districts are learning organizations. They require data from which to learn and make decisions. And educational agencies are highly systemic in nature. There are many working parts that are all interconnected in very complex ways. Organizational change requires a systems perspective (Mandinach & Cline, 1994; Senge et al., 2000), recognizing that decisions or changes in one part of a system have consequences for other components. Feedback loops are formed. Part of learning and improvement is being able to make sense of data, understanding the data in ways to make informed decisions, and then analyzing the outcomes of the decisions to determine further action steps. This is data-driven decision making in action, whether in a classroom or in an administrative office.

We also recognize that changing old habits is not easy. The change process is not trivial. Many educational pundits have commented that data-driven decision making is just another passing fad, something that will disappear if one waits long enough. Teachers and administrators can just close their doors, avoid the tsunami of data, and assume that this too shall pass. It is not a fad. Data-driven decision making has had different names, different emphases, and different appearances. But it is basically still the same thing. Evidence, information, or data trump anecdotes, political pressure, and gut feelings. After all, without data, it is only an opinion. So educators' mindsets must change and be aligned to this philosophy.

Throughout this book, we have emphasized the systemic nature of enculturating data-driven decision making, including the need for leadership, an explicit vision, the appropriate structures and resources to support data-driven practices, the appointment of a data coach, the creation of a data team, collaboration, the technological infrastructure, and *TIME*. Let us add to that list now the concept of patience—patience with one's colleagues, patience with the change process, and patience with one's own learning curve. It takes time to learn to use data effectively. It takes time to learn from colleagues and students. It takes time, effort, and support for the enculturation process to take hold. But think of the end goal: helping all children, despite weaknesses and challenges, and in addition to their strengths and advantages. Remember the CHOPS, but consider the OPS first and foremost. It is an endeavor worth pursuing.

Endnotes

INTRODUCTION

1. Ellen would like to thank Ashley Lewis for contributing the concept of CHOPS. It evolved through our collaboration on an earlier project.

CHAPTER 1

2. The director of the Institute of Education Sciences, appointed in 2009.

CHAPTER 2

3. See Evidence That Data Use Works among the CHOPS in Chapter 8.
4. See Means et al. (2010), page 3.
5. Adapted from Hamilton et al. (2009), page 10.
6. See Abbott (2008), page 269.

CHAPTER 3

7. See the technology examples among the CHOPS in Chapter 8.
8. Note many of these tools are defined in text. We define again some of the most prevalent applications.

CHAPTER 4

9. Thank you to Hilda Rosselli for taking the time to describe what she has done to integrate data-driven decision making into Western Oregon University's College of Education.

10. Ellen acknowledges the contribution of Edith Gummer in helping with issues around the standards.

11. Used with permission from the Using Data Project, TERC.

12. These distinctions are the authors'.

CHAPTER 5

13. See Leadership CHOPS in Chapter 8.

CHAPTER 6

14. See Data Choices and Data Use CHOPS in Chapter 8.

15. See Example 6 on page 30 of the IES Practice Guide (Hamilton et al., 2009) for a school improvement plan.

16. Ellen sometimes uses this example when speaking, given her experiences as a research department staff member at Educational Testing Service.

CHAPTER 7

17. See Differentiated Instruction CHOPS in Chapter 8.

References

Abbott, D. V. (2008). A functionality framework for educational organizations: Achieving accountability at scale. In E. B. Mandinach & M. Honey (Eds.), *Data-driven school improvement: Linking data and learning* (pp. 257–276). New York, NY: Teachers College Press.

Ackley, D. (2001). Data analysis demystified. *Leadership, 31*(2), 28–29, 37–38.

Airola, D., Garrison, M., & Dunn, K. (2011, July). *Are data-based decisions promoted through state longitudinal data systems (SLDS) happening at the teacher level?* Presentation made at the You Want It When? Balancing Timeliness and Quality conference: DC STATS-2011. Bethesda, MD.

American Recovery and Reinvestment Act of 2009. (2009). Public Law 111-5. Retrieved from http://www.gpo.gov/fdsys/pkg/PLAW-111publ5/content-detail.html

Anderson, C. (2006). *The long tail: Why the future of business is selling less of more.* New York, NY: Hyperion.

Arkansas Department of Education. (2007, October). Arkansas educators learn what "formative assessment" really is. *Education Matters for Administrators, 1*(4), 3.

Armstrong, J., & Anthes, K. (2001). How data can help: Putting information to work to raise student achievement. *American School Board Journal, 188*(1), 38–41.

Association for Supervision and Curriculum Development. (2008/2009). Data: Now what? [Special issue]. *Educational Leadership, 66*(4).

Bailey, A. L., & Heritage, M. (2006). *Formative assessment for literacy, grades K–6.* Thousand Oaks, CA: Corwin.

Baker, E. L. (2003). *From unusable to useful assessment knowledge: A design problem* (CSE Technical Report 612). Los Angeles, CA: University of California, National Center for Research on Evaluation, Standards, and Student Testing.

Berliner, D. C. (2006). Our impoverished view of educational reform. *Teachers College Record, 108*(6), 949–995.

Berliner, D. C. (2009). *Poverty and potential: Out-of-school factors and school success.* Boulder, CO, and Tempe, AZ: Education and the Public Interest Center & Education Policy Research Unit. Retrieved from http://nepc.colorado.edu/publication/poverty-and-potential

Bernhardt, V. L. (1998). *Data analysis for comprehensive schoolwide improvement.* Larchmont, NY: Eye on Education.

Bernhardt, V. L. (2004, November/December). Continuous improvement: It takes more than test scores. *ACSA Leadership,* 16–19.

Bernhardt, V. L. (2008). *Data data everywhere: Bringing it all together for continuous improvement.* Larchmont, NY: Eye on Education.

Bettesworth, L. R. (2006). *Administrators' use of data to guide decision-making.* Unpublished doctoral dissertation, University of Oregon, Eugene, OR.

Black, P., Harrison, C., Lee, C., Marshall, B., & Wiliam, D. (2003). *Assessment for learning: Putting it into practice.* Maidenhead, UK: Open University Press.

Black, P., & Wiliam, D. (1998a). Assessment and classroom learning. *Assessment in Education, 5*(1), 7–74.

Black, P., & Wiliam, D. (1998b). Inside the black box: Raising standards through classroom assessment. *Phi Delta Kappan, 80,* 139–148.

Blackboard K–12. (2010). *Learning in the 21st century: Taking it mobile!* Washington, DC: Author.

Blanche, A. (2008, April 23). N.Y. court upholds school cell phone ban. *CNET News: News blog.* Retrieved from http://news.cnet.com/8301-10784_3-9926538-7.html

Blue Ribbon Panel. (2010). *Transforming teacher education through clinical practice: A national strategy to prepare effective teachers.* Washington, DC: NCATE.

Booher-Jennings, J. (2005). Below the bubble: "Educational triage" and the Texas Accountability System. *American Educational Research Journal, 42*(2), 231–268.

Boudett, K. P., City, E. A., & Murnane, R. J. (2006). The "Data Wise" improvement process: Eight steps for using test scores to improve teaching and learning. *Harvard Education Letter, 22*(1), 1–3.

Breiter, A., & Light, D. (2006). Data for school improvement: Factors for designing effective information systems to support decision-making in schools. *Educational Technology and Society, 9*(3), 206–217.

Bruff, D. (2007). Clickers: A classroom innovation. *National Education Association Advocate, 25*(1), 5–8.

Bruff, D. (2009). *Teaching with classroom response systems: Creating active learning environments.* San Francisco, CA: Jossey-Bass.

Bruff, D. (2010). *Classroom response systems ("clickers")*. Retrieved from http://cft.vanderbilt.edu/teaching-guides/technology/clickers/

Brunner, C., Fasca, C., Heinze, J., Honey, M., Light, D., Mandinach, E., & Wexler, D. (2005). Linking data and learning: The Grow Network study. *Journal of Education for Students Placed at Risk, 10*(3), 241–267.

Bryk, A. S., Sebring, P. B., Allensworth, E., Luppescu, S., & Easton, J. Q. (2010). *Organizing schools for improvement: Lessons from Chicago*. Chicago, IL: University of Chicago Press.

Carter, D. (2009, July 6). Cell phones used to deliver course content. *eSchool News*. Retrieved from http://www.eschoolnews.com/2009/07/06/cell-phones-used-to-deliver-course-content/

Chappuis, J., Stiggins, R., Chappuis, S., & Arter, J. (2012). *Classroom assessment for student learning: Doing it right—using it well*. Boston: Pearson.

Chen, E., Heritage, M., & Lee, J. (2005). Identifying and monitoring students' learning needs with technology. *Journal of Education for Students Place at Risk, 10*(3), 241–267.

Cheesman, E., & Winograd, G. (2008). Classroom response systems: Perceptions of learning style, age, and gender. In K. McFerrin, R. Weber, R. Carlson, & D. Willis (Eds.), *Proceedings of the Society for Information Technology & Teacher Education International Conference 2008* (pp. 4056–4062). Chesapeake, VA: Association for the Advancement of Computing in Education.

Choppin, J. (2002, April). *Data use in practice: Examples from the school level*. Paper presented at the meeting of the American Educational Research Association, New Orleans, LA.

Coburn, C. E., & Talbert, J. E. (2006). Conceptions of evidence use in school districts: Mapping the terrain. *American Journal of Education, 112*, 469–495.

Coburn, C. E., Touré, J., & Yamashita, M. (2009). Evidence, interpretation, and persuasion: Instructional decision making in the district central office. *Teachers College Record, 111*(4), 1115–1161.

Confrey, J., & Makar, K. (2002). Developing secondary teachers' statistical inquiry through immersion in high-stakes accountability data. In D. Mewborn, P. Sztajn, & D. White (Eds.), *Proceedings of the twenty-fourth annual meeting of the North American Chapter of the International Group for the Psychology of Mathematics Education PME-NA24* (pp. 1267–1279), 3, Athens, GA.

Confrey, J., & Makar, K. (2005). Critiquing and improving data use from high stakes tests: Understanding variation and distribution in relation to equity using dynamic statistics software. In C. Dede, J. P. Honan, & L. C. Peters (Eds.), *Scaling up success: Lessons learned from technology-based educational improvement* (pp. 198–226). San Francisco, CA: Jossey-Bass.

Copland, M. A., Knapp, M. S., & Swinerton, J. A. (2009). Principal leadership, data, and school improvement. In T. J. Kowalski & T. J. Lasley II (Eds.), *Handbook of data-based decision making in education* (pp. 153–172). New York, NY: Routledge.

Corno, L. (2008). On teaching adaptively. *Educational Psychologist, 43*(3), 161–173.

Council of the Chief State School Officers. (2008). *Educational leadership policy standards: ISLLC 2008.* Washington, DC: Author.

Council of Chief State School Officers, Interstate Teacher Assessment and Support Consortium. (2011). *InTASC model core teaching standards: A resource for state dialogue.* Retrieved from http://www.ccsso.org/Documents/2011/InTASC_Model_Core_Teaching_Standards_2011.pdf

Cronbach, L. J. (1970). *Essentials of psychological testing* (3rd ed.). New York, NY: Harper & Row.

Cronbach, L. J., & Snow, R. E. (1977). *Aptitudes and instructional methods: A handbook for research on interactions.* New York, NY: Irvington.

Daniels, H., & Bizar, M. (1998). *Methods that matter: Six structures for best practice classrooms.* York, ME: Stenhouse Publishers.

Daniels, H., Zemelman, S., & Hyde, A. (2005). *Best practices: Today's standards for teaching and learning in America's schools* (3rd ed.). Portsmouth, NH: Heinemann.

Data Quality Campaign. (2007). *Measuring what matters.* Washington, DC: Author.

Data Quality Campaign. (2010a). *DQC 2009–2010 annual survey results: Action 9.* Retrieved from http://www.dataquality campaign.org/survey/compare/actions

Data Quality Campaign (2010b). *2009–2010 survey results by state.* Retrieved from http://www.dataqualitycampaign.org/

Data Quality Campaign. (2011a). *Data for action 2010: DQC's state analysis.* Retrieved from http://www.dataqualitycampaign.org/

Data Quality Campaign. (2011b). *Data for action 2010: DQC's state analysis: State analysis by action: Action 9.* Retrieved from http://www.dataqualitycampaign.org/stateanalysis/actions/9/

Datnow, A., & Park, V. (2009). School system strategies for supporting data use. In T. J. Kowalski & T. J. Lasley II (Eds.), *Handbook of data-based decision making in education* (pp. 191–206). New York, NY: Routledge.

Datnow, A., & Park, V. (2010, May). *Practice meets theory of action: Teachers' experiences with data use.* Paper presented at the annual meeting of the American Educational Research Association, Denver, CO.

Datnow, A., Park, V., & Wohlstetter, P. (2007). *Achieving with data: How high-performing school systems use data to improve instruction for elementary students.* Los Angeles, CA: University of Southern California, Center on Educational Governance.

Dede, C., & Dieterle, E. (2004, May). *Ubiquitous handhelds: Sifting knowledge through our fingertips.* Presentation at the Harvard Graduate School of Education Technology in Education Open Seminar, Cambridge, MA.

Delisio, E. R. (2002). Schools, states review cell phone bans. *Education World.* Retrieved from http://69.43.199.47/a_issues/issues270.shtml

Dieterle, E., Dede, C., & Schrier, K. (2007). "Neomillennial" learning styles propagated by wireless handheld devices. In M. Lytras & A. Naeve (Eds.), *Ubiquitous and pervasive knowledge and learning management: Semantics, social networking and new media to their full potential* (pp. 35–66). Hershey, PA: Idea Group, Inc.

Duncan, A. (2009a, March 10). *Federal leadership to support state longitudinal data systems.* Comments made at the Data Quality Campaign Conference, Leveraging the Power of Data to Improve Education, Washington, DC.

Duncan, A. (2009b, June 8). *Secretary Arne Duncan addresses the Fourth Annual IES Research Conference.* Speech made at the Fourth Annual IES Research Conference, Washington, DC. Retrieved from http://www.ed.gov/news/speeches/2009/06/06-82009.html

Duncan, A. (2009c, May 20). *Testimony before the House Education and Labor Committee.* Retrieved from http://www.ed.gov/print/news/speeches/2009/05/05202009.html

Duncan, A. (2010a, July 28). *Data: The truth teller in education reform.* Keynote address at Educate with Data: STATS-DC 2010, Bethesda, MD.

Duncan, A. (2010b, November 16). *Secretary Arne Duncan's remarks to National Council for Accreditation of Teacher Education.* Retrieved from http://www.ed.gov/news/speeches/secretary-arne-duncans-remarks-national-council-accreditation-teacher-education

Durán, R. P. (2010, June). *Comments regarding the presentations by Margaret Heritage and Caroline Wylie on professional learning communities to support formative assessment in the classroom* [PowerPoint slides]. Presented at the CCSSO National Conference on Student Assessment, Detroit, MI.

Easton, J. Q. (2009, July). *Using data systems to drive school improvement.* Keynote address at Decisions Begin with Good Data: STATS-DC 2009, Bethesda, MD.

Feldman, J., & Tung, R. (2001). Using data-based inquiry and decision making to improve instruction. *ERS Spectrum, 19* (Summer), 10–19.

Firestone, W. A., & Gonzalez, R. A. (2007). Culture and processes affecting data use in school districts. In P. A. Moss (Ed.), *Evidence and decision making: 106th yearbook of the National Society for the Study of Education: Part I* (pp. 132–154). Malden, MA: Blackwell Publishing.

Gage, N. L. (1978). *The scientific basis of the art of teaching.* New York, NY: Teachers College Press.

Garet, M. S., Porter, A., C., Desimone, L., Birman, B. F., & Yoon, K. S. (2001). What makes professional development effective? Results from a national sample of teachers. *American Educational Research Journal, 38,* 915–945.

Gewertz, C., & Robelen, E. W. (2010, September 15). U.S. tests awaiting big shifts: Most states part of groups winning federal grants. *Education Week, 30*(3), 1, 18–19.

Goertz, M. E., Nabors Olah, L., & Riggan, M. (2009a, December). Can interim assessments be used for instructional change? *CPRE Policy Briefs* (RB-51). Philadelphia: University of Pennsylvania, Graduate School of Education.

Goertz, M. E., Nabors Olah, L, & Riggan, M. (2009b, December). *From testing to teaching: The use of interim assessments in classroom instruction* (CPRE Research Report #RR-65). Philadelphia: University of Pennsylvania, Graduate School of Education.

Hakel, M. D., Koenig, J. A., & Elliott, S. W. (Eds.). (2008). *Assessing accomplished teaching: Advanced-level certification programs.* Washington, DC: National Academies Press.

Halverson, R., Grigg, J., Prichett, R. B., & Thomas, C. (2005, July). *The new instructional leadership: Creating data-driven instructional systems in schools.* Paper presented at the annual meeting of the National Council of Professors of Education Administration, Washington, DC.

Halverson, R., Prichett, R. B., & Watson, J. G. (2007). *Formative feedback systems and the new instructional leadership.* Madison: University of Wisconsin.

Halverson, R., & Thomas, C. N. (2007). The roles and practices of student services staff as data-driven instructional leaders. In M. Mangin & S. Stoelinga (Eds.), *Instructional teachers leadership roles: Using research to inform and reform* (pp. 163–200). New York, NY: Teachers College Press.

Hamilton, L., Halverson, R., Jackson, S., Mandinach, E., Supovitz, J., & Wayman, J. (2009). *Using student achievement data to support instructional decision making* (NCEE 2009-4067). Washington, DC: National Center for Education Evaluation and Regional Assistance, Institute of Education Sciences, U.S. Department of Education. Retrieved from http://ies.ed.gov/ncee/wwc/publications/practice guides/

Hamilton, L. S., Stecher, B. M., & Klein, S. P. (2002). *Making sense of test-based accountability in education*. Santa Monica, CA: RAND Education.

Hammerman, J. K., & Rubin, A. (2002). Visualizing a statistical world. *Hands On!, 25*(2), 1, 4–7.

Hammerman, J. K., & Rubin, A. (2003). *Reasoning in the presence of variability*. Paper presented at The Third International Research Forum on Statistical Reasoning, Thinking, and Literacy (SRTL-3), Lincoln, NE.

Hawley, W. D., & Valli, L. (1999). The essentials of professional development: A new consensus. In L. Darling-Hammond & G. S. Sykes (Eds.), *Teaching as the learning profession: Handbook of policy and practice* (pp. 127–150). San Francisco, CA: Jossey-Bass.

Heritage, M. (2007, June). *Formative assessment in the classroom*. Presentation to the EED Winter Conference, Informing Instruction, Improving Achievement, Anchorage, AK.

Heritage, M. (2010a). *Formative assessment and next-generation assessment systems: Are we losing an opportunity?* Washington, DC: Council of Chief State School Officers.

Heritage, M. (2010b). *Formative assessment: Making it happen in the classroom*. Thousand Oaks, CA: Corwin.

Heritage, M., & Niemi, D. (2006). Toward a framework for using student mathematical representations as formative assessments. *Educational Assessment, 11*, 265–282.

Heritage, M., & Yeagley, R. (2005). Data use and school improvement: Challenges and prospects. In J. L. Herman & E. Haertel (Eds.), *Uses and misuses of data for educational accountability and improvement: 104th yearbook of the National Society for the Study of Education, Part II* (pp. 320–339). Malden, MA: Blackwell.

Herman, J., & Gribbons, B. (2001). *Lessons learned in using data to support school inquiry and continuous improvement: Final report to the Stuart Foundation* (CSE Technical Report 535). Los Angeles, CA: UCLA Center for the Study of Evaluation.

Herman, J. L., & Haertel, E. H. (Eds.). (2005). *Uses and misuses of data for educational accountability and improvement: The 104th yearbook of the National Society for the Study of Education: Part II*. Malden, MA: Blackwell Publishing.

Huffman, D., & Kalnin, J. (2003). Collaborative inquiry to make data-based decisions in schools. *Teaching and Teacher Education, 19*(6), 569–580.

Hupert, N. (2005, March). *Supporting teachers' use of DIBELS data with handheld computers*. Paper presented at the DIBELS Summit 2005, Albuquerque, NM.

Hupert, N., Heinze, J., Gunn, G., & Stewart, J. (2008). Using technology-assisted progress monitoring to drive improved student outcomes.

In E. B. Mandinach & M. Honey (Eds.), *Data-driven school improvement: Linking data and learning* (pp. 130–150). New York, NY: Teachers College Press.

Hupert, N., Martin, W., Heinze, C., Kanaya, T., & Perez, H. (2004, June). *Trends in the use of handheld technology to support student reading assessment.* Paper presented at the National Educational Computing Conference, New Orleans, LA.

Ikemoto, G. S., & Marsh, J. A. (2007). Cutting through the "data-driven" mantra: Different conceptions of data-driven decision making. In P. A. Moss (Ed.), *Evidence and decision making: 106th yearbook of the National Society for the Study of Education: Part I* (pp. 104–131). Malden, MA: Blackwell Publishing.

Ingram, D., Louis, K. S., & Schroeder, R. G. (2004). Accountability policies and teacher decision making: Barriers to the use of data to improve practice. *Teachers College Record, 106*(6), 1258–1287.

Jamentz, K. (2001). Beyond data mania. *Leadership Magazine, 31*(2). Retrieved from http://www.acsa.org/publications/pub_detail.cfn?leadershipPubID-1023

Jimerson, J. B., & Wayman, J. C. (2011, April). *Approaches to data-related professional learning in three Texas school districts.* Paper presented at the annual meeting of the American Educational Research Association, New Orleans, LA.

Kearns, D. T., & Harvey, J. (2000). *A legacy of learning.* Washington, DC: Brookings Institution Press.

Kerr, K. A., Marsh, J. A., Ikemoto, G. S., Darilek, H., & Barney, H. (2006). Strategies to promote data use for instructional improvement: Actions, outcomes, and lessons from three urban districts. *American Journal of Education, 112*, 496–520.

Knapp, M. S., Copland, M. A, & Swinnerton, J. A. (2007). Understanding the promise and dynamics of data-informed leadership. In P. A. Moss (Ed.), *Evidence and decision making: 106th yearbook of the National Society for the Study of Education: Part I* (pp. 74–104). Malden, MA: Blackwell Publishing.

Knapp, M. S., Swinnerton, J. A., Copland, M. A., & Monpas-Huber, J. (2006). *Data-informed leadership in education.* Seattle, WA: University of Washington, Center for the Study of Teaching and Policy.

Koretz, D. (2003). Using multiple measures to address perverse incentives and score inflation. *Educational Measurement: Issues and Practice, 22*(2), 18–26.

Lachat, M. A., & Smith, S. (2005). Practices that support data use in urban high schools. *Journal of Education for Students Placed at Risk, 10*(3), 333–349.

Laurillard, D. (2007). Pedagogic forms of mobile learning: Framing research questions. In N. Pachler (Ed.), *Mobile learning: Towards a research agenda* (pp. 153–177). London, England: University of London, Institute of Education.

Leithwood, K., Louis, K. S., Anderson, S., & Wahlstrom, K. (2007). *Review of research: How leadership influences student learning.* Minneapolis, MN: University of Minnesota, Center for Applied Research and Educational Improvement.

Long, L., Rivas, L., Light, D., & Mandinach, E. B. (2008). The evolution of a homegrown data warehouse: TUSDStats. In E. B. Mandinach & M. Honey (Eds.), *Data-driven school improvement: Linking data and learning* (pp. 209–232). New York, NY: Teachers College Press.

Love, N. (2002). *Using data/getting results: A practical guide for school improvement in mathematics and science.* Norwood, MA: Christopher-Gordon Publishers.

Love, N. (Ed.). (2009). *Collaborative inquiry: Bridging data and results.* Thousand Oaks, CA: Corwin.

Love N., Stiles, K. E., Mundry, S., & DiRanna, K. (2008). *A data coach's guide to improving learning for all students: Unleashing the power of collaborative inquiry.* Thousand Oaks, CA: Corwin.

Mandinach, E. B. (2009a, October). *Data use: What we know about school-level use.* Presentation at the Special Education Data Accountability Center Retreat, 2009, Rockville, MD.

Mandinach, E. B. (2009b, October). *How LEAs use data to inform practice: The opportunities for and challenges to use in schools and districts.* Presentation at the National Evaluation Institute Research and Evaluation that Inform Leadership for Results Conference, Louisville, KY.

Mandinach, E. B. (2010, August). *Using data-driven decision making to inform practice: From research to practice.* Presidential speech for Division 15, American Psychological Association, San Diego, CA.

Mandinach, E. B. (2012). A perfect time for data use: Using data-driven decision making to inform practice. *Educational Psychologist, 47*(2).

Mandinach, E. B., & Cline, H. F. (1994). *Classroom dynamics: Implementing a technology based learning environment.* Hillsdale, NJ: Lawrence Erlbaum Associates.

Mandinach, E. B., & Gummer, E. (2010). *An examination of what schools of education are doing to improve human capacity regarding data.* Proposal to the Spencer Foundation Data Initiative. Washington, DC, and Portland, OR: WestEd and Education Northwest.

Mandinach, E. B., & Gummer, E. S. (2011). *The complexities of integrating data-driven decision making into professional preparation in schools of education: It's harder than you think.* Alexandria, VA, Portland, OR, and Washington, DC: CNA Education, Education Northwest, and WestEd.

Mandinach, E. B., & Honey, M. (Eds.). (2008). *Data-driven school improvement: Linking data and learning.* New York, NY: Teachers College Press.

Mandinach, E. B., Honey, M., & Light, D. (2006, April). *A theoretical framework for data-driven decision making.* Paper presented at the annual meeting of the American Educational Research Association, San Francisco, CA.

Mandinach, E. B., Honey, M., Light, D., & Brunner, C. (2008). A conceptual framework for data-driven decision making. In E. B. Mandinach & M. Honey (Eds.), *Data-driven school improvement: Linking data and learning* (pp. 13–31). New York, NY: Teachers College Press.

Mandinach, E. B., Honey, M., Light, D., Heinze, C., & Nudell, H. (2005, March). *Creating an evaluation framework for data-driven instructional decision-making.* Paper presented at the SITES conference, Phoenix, AZ.

Mandinach, E. B., Honey, M., Light, D., Heinze, J., & Rivas, L. (2005, November–December). *Technology-based tools that facilitate data-driven instructional decision making.* Paper presented at the ICCE Conference, Singapore.

Mandinach, E. B., Lash, A., & Nunnaley, D. (2009). *Using data to inform decisions: How teachers use data to inform practice and improve student performance in mathematics.* Proposal submitted to and funded by the Institute of Education Sciences. Alexandria, VA: CNA.

Mandinach, E. B., Rivas, L., Light, D., & Heinze, C. (2006, April). *The impact of data-driven decision making tools on educational practice: A systems analysis of six school districts.* Paper presented at the meeting of the American Educational Research Association, San Francisco, CA.

Mandinach, E. B., & Snow, R. E. (1999). *Integrating instruction and assessment for classrooms and courses: Programs and prospects for research* (Special Monograph). Princeton, NJ: Educational Testing Service.

Mann, B., & Simon, T. (2010, July). *Teaching teachers to use data.* Presentation at the Educate with Data STATS-DC 2010 Conference, Bethesda, MD.

Marsh, J. A., Pane, J. F., & Hamilton, L. S. (2006). *Making sense of data-driven decision making in education.* Santa Monica, CA: RAND Education.

Mason, S. (2002, April). *Turning data into knowledge: Lessons from six Milwaukee public schools.* Paper presented at the annual meeting of the American Educational Research Association, New Orleans, LA.

Mason, S. (2003, April). *Learning from data: The role of professional learning communities.* Paper presented at the annual meeting of the American Educational Research Association, Chicago, IL.

May, H., & Robinson, M. A. (2007). *A randomized evaluation of Ohio's personalized assessment reporting system (PARS).* Philadelphia, PA: Consortium for Policy Research in Education.

Means, B., Chen, E., DeBarger, A., & Padilla, C. (2011). *Teachers' ability to use data to inform instruction: Challenges and supports.* Washington, DC: U.S. Department of Education, Office of Planning, Evaluation, and Policy Development.

Means, B., Padilla, C., & Gallagher, L. (2010). *Use of education data at the local level: From accountability to instructional improvement.* Washington, DC: U.S. Department of Education, Office of Planning, Evaluation, and Policy Development.

Mieles, T., & Foley, E. (2005). *Data warehousing: Preliminary findings from a study of implementing districts.* Providence, RI: Annenberg Institute for School Reform.

Miller, M. (2009). *Achieving a wealth of riches: Delivering on the promise of data to transform teaching and learning* (Policy Brief). Washington, DC: Alliance for Excellent Education.

Militello, M. (2005, April). *Too much information: A case study of assessment and accountability in an urban school district.* Paper presented at the annual meeting for the American Educational Research Association, Montreal, Canada.

Mitchell, D., Lee, J., & Herman, J. (2000, October). *Computer software systems and using data to support school reform.* Paper prepared for Wingspread Meeting, Technology's Role in Urban School Reform: Achieving Equity and Quality. Sponsored by the Joyce and Johnston Foundations. New York: EDC Center for Children and Technology.

Moss, P. A. (Ed.). (2007). *Evidence and decision making.* Malden, MA: Blackwell Publishing.

Murnane, R., Boudett, K., & City, E. (2009). *Usable knowledge: The heart of data wise.* Retrieved from http//www.uknow.gse.harvard.edu/decisions/DD6-1-207.html.

National Board for Professional Teaching Standards. (2002). *What teachers should know and be able to do.* Arlington, VA: Author.

National Board for Professional Teaching Standards. (2007). *A research guide on National Board certification of teachers.* Arlington, VA: Author.

National Center for Education Statistics. (2010a). *The condition of education 2010*. Washington, DC: U.S. Department of Education, Institute of Education Sciences. Retrieved from http://nces.ed.gov/pubsearch/pubsinfo.asp?pubid=2010028

National Center for Education Statistics. (2010b). *Statewide longitudinal data systems grant program*. Retrieved from http://nces.ed.gov/programs/slds/

National Center for Education Statistics. (2010c). *Statewide longitudinal data systems grant program: Grantee states*. Retrieved from http://nces.ed.gov/programs/slds/stateinfo.asp

Nichols, S. L., & Berliner, D. C. (2007). *Collateral damage: How high-stakes testing corrupts America's schools.* Cambridge, MA: Harvard Education Press.

No Child Left Behind Act of 2001. (2001). Retrieved from http://www.nclb.gov

Obama, B. (2009, March). *Remarks by the President to the Hispanic Chamber of Commerce on a complete and competitive American education.* Washington, DC. Retrieved from http://www.whitehouse.gov/the_press_office/Remarks-of-the-President-to-the-United-States-Hispanic-Chamber-of-Commerce/

Olsen, L. (2003, May 21). Study relates cautionary tale of missing data. *Education Week, 22*(37), 12.

Penuel, W. R., & Yarnall, L. (2005). Designing handheld software to support classroom assessment: An analysis of conditions for teacher adoption. *The Journal of Technology, Learning, and Assessment, 3*(5), 50–70.

Perie, M., Marion, S., & Gong, B. (2007). *Moving towards a comprehensive assessment system: A framework for considering interim assessments.* Dover, NH: National Center for the Improvement of Educational Assessment.

Petrides, L. A. (2006, April). Using data to improve instruction. *THE Journal.* Retrieved from http://thejournal.com/articles/18239

Popham, W. J. (1999). Why standardized tests don't measure educational quality. *Educational Leadership, 56*(6), 8–15.

Porter, A. C. (2002). Measuring the content of instruction: Uses in research and practice. *Educational Researcher, 31*(7), 3–14.

Prensky, M. (2005, September/October). "Engage me or enrage me": What today's learners demand. *Educause Review,* 60–64.

Rodosky, R. J. (2009, October). *Millman award presentation.* Presentation made at the National Evaluation Institute Research and Evaluation that Inform Leadership for Results, Louisville, KY.

Rose, D. H., & Meyer, A. (2002). *Teaching every student in the digital age: Universal design for learning.* Alexandria, VA: Association for Supervision and Curriculum Development.

Rubin, A., & Hammerman, J. (2006). Understanding data through new software representations. In G. Burill (Ed.), *Thinking and reasoning with data and chance: Sixty-eighth yearbook* (pp. 241–256). Reston, VA: National Council of Teachers of Mathematics.

Samuels, C. A. (2011, July 13). Report details 'culture of cheating' in Atlanta schools. *Education Week.* Retrieved from http://www .edweek.org/ew/articles/2011/07/13/36atlanta.h30.html?qs= Atlanta+cheating+scandal

Schafer, W. D., & Lissitz, R. W. (1987). Measurement training for school personnel: Recommendations and reality. *Journal of Teacher Education, 38*(3), 57–63.

Schmoker, M. J. (1999). *Results: The key to continuous school improvement.* Alexandria, VA: Association for Supervision and Curriculum Development.

Schmoker, M. J., & Wilson, R. B. (1995). Results: The key to renewal. *Educational Leadership, 51*(1), 64–65.

Schneider, M. (2009, April 23). Imagining IES's future. *The Education Gadfly, 9*(14). Retrieved from http://www.edexcellencemedia .net/gadfly/2009/Gadfly042309.html

Senge, P. M. (1990). *The fifth discipline: The art & practice of the learning organization.* New York, NY: Doubleday.

Senge, P., Cambron-McCabe, N., Lucas, T., Smith, B., Dutton, J., & Kleiner, A. (2000). *Schools that learn.* New York, NY: Doubleday.

Severson, K. (2011, July 6). Systematic cheating is found in Atlanta's school system. *New York Times.* Retrieved from http://www .nytimes.com/2011/07/06/education/06atlanta.html?scp= 2&sq=Atlanta%20cheating&st=cse

Sharp, D. (2004). *Supporting teachers' data-driven instructional conversations: An environmental scan of Reading First and STEP literacy assessments, data visualizations, and assumptions about conversations that matter* (Report to the Information Infrastructure Project). Chicago, IL: John D. and Catherine T. MacArthur Foundation.

Sharp, D., & Risko, V. (2003). *All in the palm of your hand: Lessons from one school's first steps with handheld technology for literacy assessments* (Report to the Information Infrastructure Project, Network on Teaching and Learning). Chicago, IL: John D. and Catherine T. MacArthur Foundation.

Shulman, L. S. (1986). Those who understand: Knowledge growth in teaching. *Educational Researcher, 15*(2), 4–14.

Smith, N. (2009, October). *Data accuracy in longitudinal data systems.* Presentation given to the Special Education Data Accountability Center Retreat, Rockville, MD.

Snow, R. E. (1980). Aptitude, learner control, and adaptive instruction. *Educational Psychologist, 15,* 151–158.

Spellings, M. (2005, June 14). *Seeing the data, meeting the challenge.* Speech given at the Indiana High School Summit: Redesigning Indiana's High Schools, Indianapolis, IN. Retrieved from http://www.ed.gov/news/speeches/2005/06/06142005.html

Stecher, B. M., & Hamilton, L. S. (2006). *Using test-score data in the classroom.* Santa Monica, CA: RAND Education.

Stiggins, R. J. (2002). Assessment crisis: The absence of assessment FOR learning. *Phi Delta Kappan, 83*(10), 758–765.

Stiggins, R. (2005). From formative assessment to assessment FOR learning: A path to success on standards-based skills, *Phi Delta Kappan, 85*(4), 324–328.

Stringfield, S., Wayman, J. C., & Yakimowski-Srebnick, M. E. (2005). Scaling up data use in classrooms, schools, and districts. In C. Dede, J. P. Honan, & L. C. Peters (Eds.), *Scaling up success: Lessons learned from technology-based educational improvement* (pp. 133–152). San Francisco, CA: Jossey-Bass.

Supovitz, J. (2006). *The case for district-based reform: Leading, building, and sustaining school improvement.* Cambridge, MA: Harvard Education Press.

Supovitz, J. A., & Klein, V. (2003). *Mapping a course for improved student learning: How innovative schools systematically use data to guide improvement.* Philadelphia, PA: University of Pennsylvania, Consortium for Policy Research in Education.

Symonds, K. W. (2004). *After the test: Closing the achievement gap with data.* Naperville, IL: Learning Point Associates.

Thorn, C. A. (2001). Knowledge management for educational information systems: What is the state of the field? *Education Policy Analysis Archives, 9*(47), 17–36.

Thorn, C. (2002). *Data use in the classroom: The challenges of implementing data-based decision making at the school level.* Madison: University of Wisconsin, Wisconsin Center for Education Research.

Tufte, E. R. (1990). *Envisioning information.* Cheshire, CT: Graphics Press.

Tufte, E. R. (2001). *The visual display of quantitative information* (2nd ed.). Cheshire, CT: Graphics Press.

Tufte, E. R. (2006). *Beautiful evidence.* Cheshire, CT: Graphics Press.

U.S. Department of Education. (2009). *Race to the Top program: Executive summary.* Washington, DC: Author.

U.S. Department of Education. (2010a). *Race to the Top Assessment Program.* Retrieved from http://www2.ed.gov/programs/racetothetop-assessment/index.html

U.S. Department of Education. (2010b). *Transforming American education: Learning powered by technology: National education technology plan 2010.* Washington, DC: Office of Educational Technology.

Wayman, J. C. (2005a). Involving teachers in data-driven decision-making: Using computer data systems to support teacher inquiry and reflection. *Journal of Education for Student Placed at Risk, 112*(4), 521–548.

Wayman, J. C. (Ed.). (2005b). [Special Issue]. *Journal of Education for Students Placed at Risk, 10*(3).

Wayman, J. C. (Ed.). (2006). Data use for school improvement [Special Issue]. *American Journal of Education, 112*(4).

Wayman, J. C. (2007). Student data systems for school improvement: The state of the field. *TCEA* In *Educational Technology Research Symposium: Vol. 1* (pp. 156–162). Lancaster, PA: ProActive Publications.

Wayman, J. C., & Cho, V. (2009). Preparing educators to effectively use student data systems. In T. J. Kowalski & T. J. Lasley II (Eds.), *Handbook on data-based decision-making in education* (pp. 89–104). New York, NY: Routledge.

Wayman, J. C., Cho, V., Jimerson, J. B., & Snodgrass Rangel, V. W. (2010, May). *The data-informed district: A systemic approach to educational data use.* Paper presented at the annual meeting of the American Educational Research Association, Denver.

Wayman, J. C., Cho, V., & Johnston, M. T. (2007). *The data-informed district: A district-wide evaluation of data use in the Natrona County School District.* Austin, TX: The University of Texas.

Wayman, J. C., Jimerson, J. B., & Cho, V. (in press). Organizational considerations in establishing the data-informed district. *School Effectiveness and School Improvement.*

Wayman, J. C., Midgley, S., & Stringfield, S. (2006). Leadership for data-based decision-making: Collaborative educator teams. In A. B. Danzig, K. M. Borman, B. A. Jones, & W. F. Wright (Eds.), *Learner-centered leadership: Research, policy, and practice* (pp. 189–206). Mahwah, NJ: Lawrence Erlbaum Associates.

Wayman, J. C., Snodgrass Rangel, V. W., Jimerson, J. B., & Cho, V. (2010). *Improving data use in NISD: Becoming a data-informed district.* Austin, TX: University of Texas.

Wayman, J. C., & Stringfield, S. (2006). Technology-supported involvement of entire faculties in examination of student data for instructional improvement. *American Journal of Education, 112*, 549–571.

Wayman, J. C., Stringfield, S., & Yakimowski, M (2004). *Software enabling school improvement through analysis of student data* (CRESPAR Tech. Rep. No. 67). Baltimore, MD: Johns Hopkins University, Center for Research on the Education of Students Placed at Risk. Retrieved from www.csos.jhu.edu/crespar/techReports/Report67.pdf

Webb, N. (2002, April). *Assessment literacy in a standards-based urban education setting*. Paper presented at the annual meeting of the American Educational Research Association, New Orleans, LA.

Wellman, B., & Lipton, L. (2004). *Data-driven dialogue: A facilitator's guide to collaborative inquiry*. Sherman, CT: MiraVia.

Whitaker, A., & Young, V. M. (2002). Tensions in assessment design: Professional development under high-stakes accountability. *Teacher Education Quarterly, 29*(3), 43–60.

Whitehurst, G. J. (March, 2006). *State and national activities: Current status and future directions*. Speech given at the meeting, Improving Educational Outcomes: Why Longitudinal Data Systems Are Necessary, Washington, DC.

Williams Rose, L. (2006). *Middle Start schools striving for excellence: Steadily improving high-poverty schools in the Mid South Delta*. New York, NY: Academy for Educational Development.

Wise, S. L., Lukin, L. E., & Roos, L. L. (1991). Teacher beliefs about training in testing and measurement. *Journal of Teacher Education, 42*(1), 37–42.

Wohlstetter, P., Datnow, A., & Park, V. (2008). Creating a system for data-driven decision making: Applying a principal-agent framework. *School Effectiveness and School Improvement, 19*(3), 239–259.

Woolfolk Hoy, A., Hoy, W. K., & Davis, H. (2009). Teachers' self-efficacy beliefs. In K. Wentzel & A. Wigfield (Eds.), *Handbook of motivation at school* (pp. 627–654). New York, NY: Routledge.

Index

CORWIN

A SAGE Company

The Corwin logo—a raven striding across an open book—represents the union of courage and learning. Corwin is committed to improving education for all learners by publishing books and other professional development resources for those serving the field of PreK–12 education. By providing practical, hands-on materials, Corwin continues to carry out the promise of its motto: **"Helping Educators Do Their Work Better."**